THE
DEATH
OF
PUBLIC
SCHOOL

THE
DEATH
OF
PUBLIC
SCHOOL

How Conservatives Won the War
Over Education in America

CARA FITZPATRICK

BASIC BOOKS
New York

Basic Books
Hachette Book Group
1290 Avenue of the Americas, New York, NY 10104
www.basicbooks.com

Printed in the United States of America

First Edition: August 2023

Published by Basic Books, an imprint of Hachette Book Group, Inc. The Basic Books name and logo is a trademark of the Hachette Book Group.

The Hachette Speakers Bureau provides a wide range of authors for speaking events. To find out more, go to www.hachettespeakersbureau.com or email HachetteSpeakers @hbgusa.com.

Basic Books copies may be purchased in bulk for business, educational, or promotional use. For more information, please contact your local bookseller or the Hachette Book Group Special Markets Department at special.markets@hbgusa.com.

The publisher is not responsible for websites (or their content) that are not owned by the publisher.

Print book interior design by Linda Mark.

Library of Congress Cataloging-in-Publication Data
Names: Fitzpatrick, Cara, author.
Title: The death of public school : how conservatives won the war over education in America / Cara Fitzpatrick.
Description: First edition. | New York : Basic Books, [2023] | Includes bibliographical references and index.
Identifiers: LCCN 2022050482 | ISBN 9781541646773 (hardcover) | ISBN 9781541646780 (ebook)
Subjects: LCSH: Public schools—Political aspects—United States. | Conservatism—United States—21st century. | Education and state—Social aspects—United States.
Classification: LCC LA217.2 .F574 2023 | DDC 379.73—dc23/eng/20230329
LC record available at https://lccn.loc.gov/2022050482

ISBNs: 9781541646773 (hardcover), 9781541646780 (ebook)

LSC-C

Printing 1, 2023

For Michael and our children

Contents

Introduction
A New Definition of Public Education

Public education in America is in jeopardy. Since the coronavirus pandemic began, enrollment has declined—dramatically in some places—and some students have moved to private schools, charter schools, and homeschooling. Other students seem to have dropped out altogether. At the same time, the public schools have been under attack in many states by conservatives who see them as fertile ground for the latest round of culture wars. Republican lawmakers across the country have passed laws to restrict how teachers in public schools talk about race, racism, and LGBTQ issues. It's difficult to predict how these efforts will play out in the years to come, but some polling in the summer of 2022 indicated that Republicans' messaging was working. The Republican Party had gained an edge over Democrats on education, reversing a decades-long trend in which voters typically put more faith in the Democratic Party on that issue. Overall trust in public schools had also declined.[1]

Conservatives aren't just looking to win elections, however salient education is as a political issue. Their aim is to radically redefine public education in America, to use public dollars to pay for just about any educational option a family might envision. Prominent Republican governors have made this clear in recent years. In the summer of 2022, Arizona's Republican governor, Doug Ducey, stood in the gymnasium of a private Christian school in Phoenix and proclaimed, "Public education means educating the public." The scene was strikingly similar to one just three years earlier, when Florida's Republican governor, Ron DeSantis, attended an event at a small Christian school in Orlando and declared, "If the taxpayer is paying for education, it's public education."[2]

Needless to say, this definition of public education is not the traditional one. For more than a hundred years, Americans have typically defined a public school as one that is operated by the government, paid for with tax dollars, accountable to voters, and free of religious instruction.[3] In Florida, one of the state's major newspapers called DeSantis's attempt to redefine public education "absurd."

Is it though? For decades, conservatives have pushed to redefine public education in the United States in precisely this way, and with key legal victories in both state and federal courts, they have largely succeeded. The line between public and private education has become increasingly blurred. The result is that far more public dollars are flowing to private schools than ever before, a trend that seems likely to continue, if not increase, for decades to come. Many of those private schools are sectarian institutions, where instruction is often imbued with religious values. It is now possible for some K–12 students in this country to have their entire education paid for by the government without ever stepping into a traditional public school.

For decades, conservatives have advocated this view of public education under the umbrella of "school choice." The concept has evolved over time, but right now it means tax dollars follow a student to their preferred educational option, whether that's a traditional public school, a private school, or even homeschooling. In recent years, conservatives also have referred to school choice as "educational freedom," with the accompanying rallying cry of "Fund students, not systems."[4] So far, no state truly operates under such a model. Instead, state lawmakers have passed laws to create various mechanisms that push the boundaries of publicly funded education. School vouchers subsidize tuition at private schools. Tax-credit scholarships function similarly, though the money comes from donations made in exchange for a state tax credit. With education savings accounts, parents can remove their children from public schools, putting a deposit of tax money into a restricted-use savings account, which can then be used to pay for private school, educational therapies, or tutoring. Charter schools are publicly funded but privately run. (Considered by law to be a type of public school, charters exist in a sort of gray zone as some legal cases turn on the question of whether charters are, in fact, public.)

This book tells the story of how the country reached this place, where Americans are debating the very definition of public education. It charts a strange and circuitous journey that began in the 1950s on what was then the far-right fringes of conservative intellectual thought. It is a story of how white Republicans embraced unlikely political alliances with Black Democrats to win crucial legislative victories, how they tested the boundaries of state and federal law to win landmark court cases, how they built an influential movement funded by conservative philanthropists and backed by powerful think tanks, and how they test-drove different rationales for school choice with the American public, gradually shifting public opinion to be more favorable to their cause.

Ultimately, it is a story of how conservatives successfully advocated for an expansive vision of publicly funded education—driven by the values of the free market—by adopting the language of civil rights while simultaneously attacking public schools. Betsy DeVos, who served as President Donald Trump's secretary of education and is a long-standing advocate of school choice, encapsulated this strategy in her 2022 book when she wrote, "America is *not* a racist nation. But in one important area—education—we *do* have a system that is institutionally racist against blacks and other minorities; a system that traps them in failing schools and with no possibility of escape."[5] (Italics are hers.) It's a revealing comment at a time when Republican lawmakers have been restricting how teachers in public schools can teach about the nation's history. It seems conservatives can find systemic racism in at least one public institution: the school system.

What DeSantis said in 2019, and Ducey echoed in 2022, struck some people as a new take on public education. It is not. Conservatives have been using similar language for years. Three decades ago, President George H. W. Bush said, "Whether a school is organized by privately financed educators or town councils or religious orders or denominations, any school that serves the public and is held accountable by the public authority provides public education." Similarly, in 1995, Tommy Thompson, Wisconsin's governor at the time, described public education as "education serving the public." Even further back, in the late 1960s, James J. Kilpatrick, a segregationist and conservative columnist, wrote, "A state's valid interest in a child lies in the child's education—not necessarily in his 'public education,' but simply in his education, period."[6]

The US Supreme Court also gave some credence to conservatives' definition in 2002 when it upheld Cleveland's school voucher program in *Zelman vs. Simmons-Harris*, even though 96 percent of students used the vouchers at religious schools. That stunning 5–4 court victory happened in part because some conservative justices chose to evaluate the voucher program within the broader context of the city's educational landscape, which they held as including traditional public schools, charter schools, and private schools participating in the program. All were educational options supported by tax dollars. At the court hearing for the *Zelman* case, Justice Sandra Day O'Connor said she wasn't sure it made sense to draw a firm line between public and private education. In the opinion for the majority, Chief Justice William Rehnquist also blurred those once hard-and-fast lines, writing that the school voucher program was part of a "broader undertaking by the State to enhance the educational options of Cleveland's schoolchildren." It didn't matter to him that those efforts included private religious schools. (The dissenting liberal justices strongly disagreed with this view.)[7]

In recent years, the US Supreme Court, leaning further right than it has in decades, has decided several cases that build on *Zelman*. In one from 2022, *Carson vs. Makin*, the court ruled 6–3 that a state cannot bar private religious schools from participating in any state program that includes secular private schools. The difference between *Zelman* and this case, as some pundits have observed, is that the court shifted from saying that a state *may* fund religious schools—through the independent choices of parents—to saying that it *must* fund religious schools, if it chooses to pay for private education at all. In an opinion for the majority, Chief Justice John Roberts reiterated a point he had made in a previous case: "A State need not subsidize private education. But once a State decides to do so, it cannot disqualify some private schools solely because they are religious."[8] Roberts framed the issue as a straightforward matter of religious discrimination, though as Justice Sonia Sotomayor noted in her dissent, the ruling raises a number of lingering questions about whether the state could fund other types of discrimination by paying tuition at private schools. Some religious schools don't hire gay teachers or admit gay students. Some Catholic schools will expel a student who has an abortion. Such policies reflect religious beliefs but perhaps not the values that all Americans want supported by tax dollars.

The war over school choice has been the fiercest of this country's education battles because it is the most important: it is a struggle over the definition of public education. Today's Democrats draw that line firmly between public and private education, while Republicans see no line at all. Consider the granular arguments among pundits in recent years about the language we use to describe a public school. Charter schools, a publicly financed option available in many states since the 1990s, are often derided by Democratic opponents as private schools masquerading as public.[9] Some conservatives have pushed back against even using the term "public school," saying "government school" is more accurate. (The latter term often is used as a pejorative, however.) These seemingly inconsequential debates over language are, at the core, about the larger battle.

These thorny questions—about what type of education the government should pay for, whose values are reflected in schooling, and what these issues mean for society and democracy—have been waged since the country's birth. The American public school system is the nation's best attempt to educate all its children. That system formed over time. Early American leaders debated how children should be educated, who should pay for it, and how much education the public required. Thomas Jefferson, president and enslaver, argued in the eighteenth century for publicly supported elementary schools to foster a common cultural identity in a new and uncertain nation. Benjamin Rush, another framer, made a similar argument and also said a system of tax-supported schools would pay for itself by preventing crime. Thomas Paine, a prominent American writer and political theorist, proposed giving money directly to poor families to pay for education.[10]

However great the country's founding ideals were—and the US Constitution doesn't list education as a right—discrimination has always been a feature of American public education. Historian Carl F. Kaestle, in his classic book *Pillars of the Republic: Common Schools and American Society, 1780–1860*, wrote, "Even the most ringing statements about the equality of all men were not taken to include women or black people, and non-English immigrants faced various forms of discrimination."[11]

Debates over how to educate American children grew more intense in the nineteenth century, as Protestant school reformers pushed for "common schools" to promote social equality and patriotism. Their cause was helped by anti-Catholic bigotry, which grew with a massive influx of Catholic immigrants into the country. Catholics were, in some ways, among the nation's earliest advocates of school choice. In response to the overtly Protestant nature of public schools at the time, they built their own schools and lobbied for public funds to support them. Some towns also experimented with public-private school systems. Ultimately, Catholics didn't receive the public funding they desired, and they built a parallel, private, and highly regarded school system. Public education grew to resemble what Jefferson and Rush envisioned, though some regions of the country were faster than others to provide public schools.[12]

DeSantis and Ducey may not have been thinking of the broader intellectual implications of their statements about public education. However unwittingly, though, they touched on one of the biggest debates running through American education today. Government-funded school-choice programs have spread rapidly across the country since 1990—after many years of choice being mostly theoretical—and that spread has emboldened conservative supporters who want to see a revolution within America's system of public education. A wave of school-choice bills passed in 2021 amid the disruption of the pandemic; more than a dozen states created new programs or expanded existing ones. Since then, more than half the states in the country now have publicly funded private school options.[13] Some of the programs, which were originally intended for low-income students, have expanded to include more affluent ones. Some families who were already paying for private school now have their children's tuition paid by the state. What once would have seemed unimaginable—the government paying for the educational preference of each student instead of a system of public schools for all—now feels not that far off. In some places, it's already here. At least a half-dozen states have made most or all students eligible for an education savings account.

Americans haven't yet fully considered as a nation what the spread of government-funded school-choice options means for the future of public education. Does public funding necessitate public accountability? What type and how much? How do we measure success, and how central a measuring stick should racial equality be? What obligation does any parent have to the other children in their surrounding community? If we value the individual right to choose education above all other considerations, what does that mean for the common purpose of public education? If public education is any education paid for with public dollars, what does that mean for the future of the public school? For the future of democracy?

The battle over school choice has, at key times, defied traditional political lines. The leadership of the Democratic Party and one of its historical allies, the teachers' unions, often have lined up against a core constituency: Black and Latino parents. Republicans have secured critical victories by forming alliances with Democrats who were willing to cross the aisle. Those alliances have sometimes fractured in the aftermath over questions about accountability, regulations, and who is really being served by the programs. Many of the Democrats who favored charter schools as a bipartisan reform were reluctant to join hands with Republicans pushing for options outside the public sphere; in many cases, Democrats deliberately pushed charter schools as a policy alternative to school vouchers. With the wildfire spread of charter schools, however, some Democrats have come to regret their support, causing tension with some families of color who support charters as an alternative to traditional public schools, particularly in urban areas.[14]

These fault lines explain why the history of school choice is, in many ways, complex and fragmented. The school-choice movement has often been defined as a coordinated effort to provide parents with more educational options and improve public schools through competition—but the movement has included supporters with different goals. Some wanted more options only for children from marginalized groups. Some wanted greater choice only within school districts. Others wanted to completely dismantle the present public school system. Supporters of charter schools have also formed their own separate movement; some charter advocates, in fact, oppose choice policies that send public dollars to private schools.

Once obscure, school choice is now a potent, deeply polarizing, partisan issue. Opposition to school choice was a major feature in a wave of teacher strikes in 2018 and 2019, from California to West Virginia, and played prominently alongside pleas for better compensation and classroom conditions.[15] In 2022, President Joseph Biden found himself in political crosswinds after the US Department of Education proposed tighter regulations for a federal program that provides money to charter schools. The recommended rules reflected long-standing concerns about charter schools and their effects on the traditional public system, but the responses from supporters and opponents alike underscored how polarizing the debate has become.

School choice also has become a political purity test for Republicans. In some parts of the country, particularly in rural areas, conservative legislators have sometimes voted against private school choice options, largely because the policies don't make as much sense in communities with only a few schools. Texas has seen more than fifty failed attempts to pass private school choice legislation. But Republican legislators have experienced far more backlash in recent years for opposing such legislation. The *Texas Tribune* reported that two prominent Republicans in Texas, Senator Ted Cruz and Governor Greg Abbott, endorsed different candidates in the Republican primary runoff races for the state house in 2022, with Cruz backing only those who said they support school choice. Cruz called school choice "the most important domestic issue in the country."[16] (Considering how divisive other domestic issues are, that's quite a statement.) Since then, Abbott has made a far greater show of supporting school choice.

How did we get to this place? Florida's former governor Jeb Bush, who is largely responsible for turning that state into a laboratory for school choice, put it succinctly: "One reform creates the possibility for the next one."[17] In a single sentence, Bush effectively explained the broader strategy of longtime advocates of school choice nationwide: start a small program, and then expand while testing the boundaries of state and federal law. The strategy has played out in Wisconsin, Ohio, Arizona, and Florida, all battlegrounds for school choice in the last three decades. Many attempts have failed, but enough have succeeded to transform some states' education systems.

Many of the arguments for school choice are compelling—and have gained traction legislatively—because of long-standing inequities in public education. Affluent families often buy access to the so-called best schools by purchasing a home in wealthier neighborhoods with better-resourced schools. That's unlikely to change as long as the system is funded, in part, by property taxes and organized through school districts. In cities like New York, Boston, and Philadelphia, elite public schools with gatekeeping admissions policies often enroll a disproportionate number of affluent white and Asian American students. Well-connected families fight any boundary change or admissions plan that might alter the status quo. Questions of exclusion often loom as large within the public school system as outside of it. As Henry Levin, an economist, wrote, "The problem is that schooling takes place at the intersection of two sets of rights, those of the family and those of society."[18] In that sense, it is both a public and a private good, he argued. For parents, the politics of school choice are inherently personal. That is why some advocates for public education send their own children to private school. That is why it is the most vulnerable children, the ones with the fewest choices, who are often asked to sacrifice their needs for the good of the whole. Often, those families have been the ones to seek out school-choice options.

In 1955, Milton Friedman, a Nobel Prize–winning economist, made an extreme argument: he wanted the government to fund education but not to run the schools. He envisioned parents using school vouchers to pay for education on the free market. He was not coy about the fact that such a system would lead to fewer public schools; he wanted fewer public schools. The title to one of his later pieces made that clear—"Public Schools: Make Them Private." Friedman never wavered from his position, but the idea was tainted by southern segregationists who were considering privatizing the public schools to circumvent 1954's *Brown vs. Board of Education of Topeka*, the Supreme Court decision that found state-mandated racial segregation in public schools unconstitutional. After the ruling, southern lawmakers employed a number of tricks to keep Black and white children separate. They gerrymandered school boundaries. They created admissions criteria for public schools. They offered school vouchers. They even closed down some public schools, depriving many children of an education. It wasn't the best time for an economist in Chicago to propose that the entire country's school system be converted to a marketplace, but Friedman did it anyway. He believed that such a system was better.

Many Americans aren't comfortable with Friedman's vision for education. Universal vouchers weren't his entire aim. He considered it a "partial solution"—and, in fact, believed that vouchers could move the country gradually toward "greater direct parental financing." In other words, he believed many parents, particularly wealthier ones, should pay for their children's schooling. He also grew to believe that compulsory schooling laws weren't necessary. (He acknowledged, too, that most people would consider his views "extreme.")[19] As a nation, Americans have valued public schools, relying on them as a safety net for families. Beyond education, public schools often provide childcare for families and healthy meals and medical care for students. School closures, remote learning, and quarantines during the COVID pandemic wreaked havoc on many families as thousands of women were forced to quit their jobs or reduce their work hours to care for children who usually would have been in school.

School choice also hasn't proven to be the panacea that some early advocates suggested. With several decades of research now available, the picture that emerges is complicated but certainly not a solid win for advocates. By one of the most common benchmarks of school performance—test scores—neither private school choice programs nor charter schools consistently outperform traditional public schools. The effect of private school choice programs on test scores is mixed, and research in recent years has shown that scores in math have actually declined.[20] Similarly, charter schools don't outperform traditional public schools on average.[21] Some charter schools in major cities have produced sizable gains in test scores.[22] But questions have been raised about whether struggling students are encouraged to leave and whether such schools "select" students with some of their requirements. Charter schools also have had numerous high-profile cases of fraud and grift, an issue even some supporters have acknowledged.[23] (Accountability requirements vary widely with charter schools and private school choice programs; some choice programs have strengthened their regulations over time to address concerns.)

School choice hasn't been a failure either. Some private school choice programs have been found to have positive effects on life outcomes: students were more likely to graduate high school and attend college, and they were less likely to engage in criminal behaviors.[24] Family satisfaction also tends to be high. And contrary to what some critics claim, traditional public schools have seen some positive effects from competition.[25] One recent study found that the presence of charter schools resulted in improvements for students in district-run schools. (Part of the overall improvement came from low-performing district-run schools closing.)[26]

In some ways, however, what the research shows no longer matters. This has become a debate about values, with most Democrats lining up behind traditional public education and most Republicans arguing for greater "freedom" for families. The movement that has grown around school choice has never been monolithic, but it is clear that Friedman's vision has triumphed. Most advocates now support universal school choice—tax dollars following the child regardless of their family's income—rather than a progressive view that focuses on empowerment for low-income families. Such a universal system would inevitably lead to the decline of the traditional public school, as Friedman intended.

School-choice supporters often include public schools in the array of options available to families in a system of universal choice. Indeed, some people push back against the idea that universal choice would dismantle public education. But in the last few years, that posture has come to seem increasingly disingenuous. As the Republican Party has moved further right, some conservatives have made their intentions known. In a speech in the spring of 2022, Christopher Rufo, a conservative activist, outlined his strategy for winning on choice: "To get universal school choice you really need to operate from a premise of universal public school distrust," he said. Rufo has done his part to sow distrust: he took critical race theory, an academic framework about systemic racism, and turned it into a catchphrase for all diversity and inclusion efforts in public schools. He also has attacked public schools for teaching children "gender ideology," which largely means using inclusive language for transgender Americans and teaching about LGBTQ people and history. Similarly, Jay Greene and James Paul wrote a piece in the same year for the Heritage Foundation, a conservative think tank, in which they suggested that the school-choice movement should embrace the culture wars to rack up more legislative wins.[27] Republican politicians' attacks on public schools have grown increasingly ugly, with accusations about "woke indoctrination." (Some Republicans have struggled to define that phrase.) Such strategies risk

alienating the broader coalition around school choice, including its progressive supporters. It also suggests that at least a few advocates are
comfortable with the public school system—where most American
children still are educated—becoming collateral damage in the battle
for school choice. Support for traditional public education has become
another partisan divide in our already divided country.

With political rhetoric growing ever more extreme, this is a dangerous moment for public schools in America. To understand this
moment, when it feels as if there is no middle ground to be found
in education, it's critical to look at the long journey of school choice.
It begins in the 1950s, when Friedman first argued for a revolution
in public education; when a Jesuit priest, the Reverend Virgil Blum,
called for public money to support religious schools; and when some
white segregationists declared that they would rather abandon public
schools than allow Black families to share in them equally. It begins
when Earl Warren, then the new chief justice of the US Supreme
Court, drew a line in the sand with *Brown vs. Board* and proclaimed
that "separate but equal" had "no place" in public schools. In that historic case, Warren declared public education to be "perhaps the most
important function of state and local governments" and the "very foundation of good citizenship."[28]

1

Private in Name Only

PUBLIC EDUCATION WAS IN DANGER.

Faced with the prospect of white and Black students one day going to school together, lawmakers across the South began to consider the unthinkable: abandoning the public schools altogether. It started in Georgia. After trying to force southern states to spend more on schools for Black children, the NAACP, the country's foremost civil rights organization, switched tactics. In the fall of 1950, the group filed a federal lawsuit challenging Atlanta's racially segregated and unequal public school system. Roy V. Harris, a former speaker of the state's House and a campaign manager for Democratic governor Herman Talmadge, had been a strong supporter of public education, but he vehemently opposed integration. In the newspaper he owned, the *Augusta Courier*, he declared that it would be better to abolish the public schools than to desegregate them. He wrote, "If the public school system is to mean the destruction of the pattern of segregation, then we ought to do away with the public school system and devise another to take its place."[1] An influential political figure in the South who was considered Georgia's "kingmaker," Harris made national news with his comments. A headline in the *New York Times* on October 3 of that year read, "Private School System Urged in Georgia to 'Foil' Negro Anti-Segregation Plan." A headline in the *Baltimore Sun* appearing on the same day read, "Georgia May Scrap Public School System."

Segregationists in the South knew it was only a matter of time before the US Supreme Court struck down legal segregation in the public schools. Earlier that summer, the court had ruled that the University of Texas had to admit a Black student to its law school, ending a four-year legal battle by Heman Marion Sweatt, who said he would enroll "without malice" toward those who had kept him out. In a separate case, the court ruled that the University of Oklahoma could not force George McLaurin, a graduate student, to sit, study, and eat separately from his white classmates. School integration threatened the iron-clad racial caste system that governed life in the South. After the Supreme Court rulings against the University of Texas and the University of Oklahoma, Talmadge, the first southern governor to respond publicly, declared, "As long as I am governor, Negroes will not be admitted to white schools." For many Black southerners, who attended underfunded public schools and were constrained from pursuing higher education, the rulings were a hopeful sign. An editor at a Black newspaper in Atlanta said the court's decisions could be a "means by which the South will join the parade of democracy."[2]

At first, southern governors didn't pursue Harris's idea to abandon public education. It was a shocking proposal but unnecessary as long as segregated schools had the full force of the law behind them. Some elected officials instead rushed to improve their states' long-neglected Black schools, an acknowledgement that they had fallen far short of the "separate but equal" legal doctrine upheld by the US Supreme Court in 1896's *Plessy vs. Ferguson*. There was nothing equal about the schools Black children attended. In South Carolina, it wasn't uncommon for a county to have only one high school for its Black students; some had none at all. In Louisiana, Black students in New Orleans attended school in shifts because of the crowded conditions. In Virginia, Black students at Moton High School in Prince Edward County walked out in protest due to their overcrowded school conditions in 1951. A building meant to hold 180 students enrolled more than 400. Classes met in hallways and on buses. There were just two bathrooms. Rather than replace the high school, white officials added three tar paper buildings. Even with those conditions, Moton High was considered one of the best all-Black high schools in Virginia.[3] Some counties had no high school at all.

Barbara Johns, who organized the students' strike at Moton High, said she had prayed for better school conditions: "God, please grant us a new school. Please let us have a warm place to stay where we won't have to keep our coats on all day to stay warm. God, please help us. We are your children, too." After the strike, the NAACP filed a lawsuit on the students' behalf. The brief in *Davis vs. County School Board of Prince Edward County* read, in part, "Virginia's separation of the Negro youth from his white contemporary stigmatizes the former as an unwanted, that the impress is alike on the minds of the colored and the white, the parents as well as the children, and indeed of the public generally, and that the stamp is deeper and the more indelible because imposed by law."[4]

As the NAACP began to directly challenge segregated schooling, some governors returned to Harris's idea and threatened to abandon the public schools. Talmadge's administration proposed a three-pronged solution in the winter of 1951: the state would stop funding any university or public school that admitted Black students, give grants to individuals to use for tuition at private schools or universities, and turn over public school properties to private individuals. In effect, it was a plan to privatize the state's public school system. To do it, voters would have to change Georgia's constitution, which required the state to provide citizens with an education. That would take time. Instead, legislators moved forward with one piece of the plan, which they made more severe: if any single all-white public school or university enrolled a Black student, all the state's schools would lose state funding.[5] Without state funds, the schools would shut down.

In South Carolina, Governor James Byrnes's administration prepared a constitutional amendment to remove public education from among the state's responsibilities. In a speech to white teachers in March 1951, Byrnes said the state would attempt to "preserve the public school system and at the same time maintain segregation. . . . If that is not possible, reluctantly we will abandon the public school system." His comments made headlines. The *New York Herald Tribune* called the fight over school segregation in the South the "biggest issue since secession."[6]

By the fall of 1952, the US Supreme Court sent waves of panic through the white South when it agreed to consider five separate school-segregation cases brought by the NAACP, folding them into one case. Before the justices had even heard arguments in *Brown vs. Board of Education of Topeka*, the voters of South Carolina, urged on by their governor, passed a referendum to strike public education from the constitution.[7] It passed by a more than two-to-one margin.

The next month, Thurgood Marshall, the NAACP's head of litigation, argued in front of the Supreme Court that Black children would never forget the humiliation of state-sanctioned segregation. He said the harm to their sense of self was greater even than the damage done by their inferior school facilities. He declared, "Slavery is perpetuated in these statutes." Virginia's attorney general, J. Lindsay Almond Jr., made the position of segregationists clear: he warned the court that desegregation would "destroy the public school system of Virginia as we know it today. That is not an idle threat."[8]

Even as parts of the historic case were argued again in 1953, Alabama legislators weighed their own "private school plan," which failed to pass. In Georgia, the Talmadge administration drafted a constitutional amendment similar to the one that had passed in South Carolina. In his State of the State speech, Talmadge warned that white Georgians needed to prepare for an adverse ruling. He said they were in "grave danger."[9]

Six months later, the Supreme Court ruling came down: on May 17, 1954, a unanimous court struck down legal segregation in the public schools. The decision affected twenty-one states and the District of Columbia, all of which either mandated or permitted segregation. The New York Times estimated that 40 percent of students in the country, or nearly eleven million schoolchildren, were affected by state-mandated segregation.[10]

In an opinion for the court, Chief Justice Earl Warren praised public education as "perhaps the most important function of state and local governments" and the "very foundation of good citizenship." He wrote,

> In these days, it is doubtful that any child may reasonably be expected to succeed in life if he is denied the opportunity of an education. Such an opportunity, where the state has undertaken to provide it, is a right which must be made available to all on equal terms. . . . We conclude that, in the field of public education, the doctrine of "separate but equal" has no place. Separate educational facilities are inherently unequal.[11]

A month later, James J. Kilpatrick, editor of the Richmond News Leader in Virginia and an ardent segregationist, wrote in a private letter to another newspaper editor that a "satisfactory solution for the South lies in some combination of public and private schools, by which parents could be granted some sort of tax rebate for the cost of educating their children privately." There were a few potential downsides to the plan, he acknowledged, suggesting that states "might see a rash of fly-by-night 'private schools' established by mountebanks and quacks."[12]

In Georgia that fall, 54 percent of voters approved an amendment to the state constitution, relieving the state of its duty to provide citizens with an "adequate education." But Harris, who had first proposed abandoning the public schools four years earlier, had reconsidered. He worried the plan wouldn't withstand a future legal challenge because the state's private schools would be private in "name only."[13]

＋

LESS THAN A year after the historic court ruling, Milton Friedman, a forty-two-year-old economist at the University of Chicago, argued in an essay that the government shouldn't be in the business of running the public school system. He proposed that the government instead give parents a voucher redeemable for a "specified maximum sum per child per year if spent on 'approved' educational services."[14] The government's role would be to supply money for tuition and ensure that the participating schools met "minimum standards." The type of school, whether for profit or not, made no difference to him. An "excellent example" of his proposal already existed in the country: to help veterans of World War II, President Franklin D. Roosevelt had signed the Servicemen's Readjustment Act of 1944, or the GI Bill, which allowed veterans to get their college tuition paid for up to $500. Friedman's plan would function similarly.

The economics professor, a father of two young children, wasn't an education reformer and had shown no great interest in education policy. The only son and youngest child of Jewish immigrants from Eastern Europe, Friedman had attended public schools in his hometown of Rahway, New Jersey. He had been a precocious child, loud and good-humored, and he enrolled in Rutgers University at age sixteen on a merit scholarship. He planned to study mathematics and also toyed briefly with the idea of becoming a journalist. Early in his college career, Friedman read the book that would shape his political identity for years to come: *On Liberty*, by the prominent nineteenth-century English philosopher John Stuart Mill. In it, Mill had written, "That the only purpose for which power can be rightfully exercised over any member of a civilized community, against his will, is to prevent harm to others." Friedman would say later that it was a clear explanation of libertarian principles.[15]

As it happened, economic disaster dictated Friedman's career. The Great Depression started while he was in college. At the height of the crisis, nearly a quarter of the nation's workers had no job. Wages fell, factories closed, and farmers lost their land. Families split up or moved to find work; people went hungry. Observing the shocking downturn as an undergraduate student at Rutgers, Friedman decided to become an economist. In an interview later in life he said, "Put yourself in 1932 with a quarter of the population unemployed. What was the important urgent problem? It was obviously economics and so there was never any hesitation on my part to study economics."[16]

By his forties, Friedman had become a man out of step with the politics of his time: an "extremist libertarian" economist when Keynesian economics ruled the day. British economist John Maynard Keynes was a capitalist who believed the government should intervene in the economy when necessary. (Keynes wrote, "The important thing for government is not to do things which individuals are doing already, and to do them a little better or a little worse; but to do those things which at present are not done at all.")[17] But as a professor Friedman enjoyed and encouraged debate. Despite standing barely over five feet tall and with a naturally cheerful disposition, he was known as a formidable debater.

In his 1955 essay "The Role of Government in Education," Friedman turned his attention to what he considered to be the monopoly of American public education. He described school vouchers as "public financing but private operation of education." It was a bold idea, though not without precedent in American education. Aside from the GI Bill, two New England states had long-standing programs to pay tuition costs for students living in rural areas without public schools. Vermont's program began in 1869, Maine's in 1873. In both states, students could attend either a public or a secular private school, and the tax dollars would go to the school of their choice. Friedman's proposal was similar.

But southern segregationists got to the concept first, something Friedman said he wasn't aware of initially. Friedman had spent the 1953–1954 academic year at the University of Cambridge in England, and he traveled with his family in Europe during academic breaks before returning to Chicago. He claimed he didn't learn of the connection between his ideas and those of the segregationists until he had largely completed his essay. Rather than abandon the idea, he attached a lengthy footnote in which he acknowledged that his initial reaction, and likely that of "most readers," would be that segregationists' interest in vouchers was a strike against the idea. But he strongly believed that "principles can be tested most clearly by extreme cases."

> Willingness to permit free speech to people with whom one agrees is hardly evidence of devotion to the principle of free speech; the relevant test is willingness to permit free speech to people with whom one thoroughly disagrees. Similarly, the relevant test of the belief in individual freedom is the willingness to oppose state intervention even when it is designed to prevent individual activity of a kind one thoroughly dislikes. I deplore segregation and racial prejudice.... It is clearly an appropriate function of the state to prevent the use of violence and physical coercion by one group on another; equally clearly, it is not an appropriate function of the state to try to force individuals to act in accordance with my—or anyone else's—views, whether about racial prejudice or the party to vote for, so long as the action of any one individual affects mostly himself.

Committed to limited government, Friedman said he opposed both "forced segregation" and "forced non-segregation." He preferred a private system in which "exclusively white schools, exclusively colored schools, and mixed schools" could develop, giving parents a choice. Friedman said the "appropriate activity for those who oppose segregation and racial prejudice is to try to persuade others of their views; if and as they succeed, the mixed schools will grow at the expense of the non-mixed, and a gradual transition will take place."[18]

Friedman's view, however, seemed either naive or willfully ignorant of the racial oppression in the South, where poll taxes severely curtailed the voting rights of Black citizens, and the Democratic Party, then the party of the segregationists, controlled the vast majority of legislative seats. There was so little political opposition in the South that V. O. Key Jr., a political scientist, said the Republican Party "scarcely deserves the name of party."[19] Black southerners who challenged the entrenched white-power structure faced threats, intimidation, and violence. They risked their jobs and their lives.

Before the book containing Friedman's essay was published, Friedman's editor, Robert A. Solo, pressed him to think more deeply about the nature of state-sanctioned segregation. He sent Friedman a lengthy and impassioned letter in the fall of 1954—about five months after the *Brown vs. Board* ruling—suggesting that "individual action" within the market was not enough to effect change. School vouchers in the South would not allow Black families to have a "free choice of segregated or non-segregated schools," he wrote. And any effort by Black children to attend school with white children could "mark the parent and his child for persecution later." Solo's letter did not change Friedman's mind.[20]

Friedman's view was consistent with his own long-held principles, though it didn't reflect the reality of life in the segregated South. Years earlier, as a graduate student, he had written that he saw "little point" in any history that "aims to solely explain a theory in terms of the conditions existing at the time of its ascendancy." What mattered, he said, was the truth. "If there be such a thing as truth, how a theory arose has little to do with the truth of it. And to me the primary interest of the economist is to find out the truth."[21]

>‹

WITHIN FOUR YEARS of the *Brown* ruling, at least seven southern states had taken steps to abandon public schools if necessary. Some white lawmakers held out hope that *Brown* could be overturned or finagled in some way. If not, the laws had been rewritten to prevent desegregation and to privatize school systems. Some states amended their laws to allow public schools to be privately rented, to make private school teachers eligible for state retirement systems, and to put special boards in charge of assigning students to schools. Five states created grants that students could use to pay tuition at private schools—the first steps toward creating a school voucher system similar to what Friedman envisioned. Walter F. Murphy, a constitutional scholar at Princeton, wrote in 1958 that threats to abolish public education were "at once the most deft and the most crude of the efforts to maintain racial separation in the schools."[22]

For many southern lawmakers after *Brown*, the guiding principle was delay, delay, delay. With its second ruling on the issue in May 1955, an enforcement decree known as *Brown II*, the Supreme Court did little to discourage this approach. Rather than impose a deadline for states to comply, the court said desegregation should occur "with all deliberate speed." Two months later, a judge's ruling in *Briggs vs. Elliott*, the South Carolina case remanded to the district court after *Brown*, interpreted the Supreme Court's decision to mean that school districts didn't have to desegregate at all. District Court judge John B. Parker wrote:

> Nothing in the Constitution or in the decision of the Supreme Court takes away from the people freedom to choose the schools they attend. The Constitution, in other words, does not require integration. It merely forbids discrimination. It does not forbid such segrega-

tion as occurs as the result of voluntary action. It merely forbids the use of governmental power to enforce segregation. The Fourteenth Amendment is a limitation upon the exercise of power by the state or state agencies, not a limitation upon the freedom of individuals.[23]

Freedom to choose. Freedom of individuals. In *Briggs*, the court had perhaps inadvertently given segregationists the language and strategies to oppose *Brown*. Alabama lawmakers used that language in 1956 when they asked voters to approve a constitutional amendment to give parents the "freedom of choice" to decide if their children should attend segregated schools. The racist intent of the law was still abundantly clear. The chief economist at the US Chamber of Commerce, Emerson Schmidt, also tried to draw attention to Friedman's essay, which used the expression "freedom of choice" in a footnote. Schmidt wrote a letter to Senator Garland Gray of Virginia in January 1956—Gray had just chaired a commission that recommended grants to pay for private education—and informed him that a "noted scholar of the University of Chicago" had already developed a plan for "public financing of education without necessarily having public administration of education." Friedman's plan was "entirely apart from any question of segregation," he wrote.[24]

Much of the political rhetoric after *Brown*, however, was consumed by notions of states' rights as lawmakers considered whether they could invoke an old (and invalid) legal doctrine called interposition that allowed states to assert their authority against the federal government to protect their citizens. Kilpatrick, the racist editor, dusted off the idea in November 1955 in the *Richmond News Leader*. "We resist now, or we resist never," he wrote in an editorial. For three months, Kilpatrick wrote editorial after editorial about the idea, even printing speeches from Thomas Jefferson, James Madison, and other American framers to give it legitimacy in the eyes of readers. The newspaper packaged his pieces in a pamphlet, which sold more than thirteen thousand copies by the end of the year. Kilpatrick mailed it to governors in at least four south-ern states; even a senator in Connecticut received a copy in the mail.[25]

"After six weeks and fifty-thousand words in the *News Leader*, the strange new word, 'interposition' had entered the vocabulary of most adult Virginians and of politicians all across the South," journalist Ben-jamin Muse wrote later.[26] Interposition resolutions passed in states across the South. The idea was immensely popular but unlikely to ac-complish anything, a fact that even some of its supporters realized. But it was a compelling rallying cry for white southerners, far more so than the rather dense economic language in Friedman's voucher essay.

In February 1956, Virginia senator Harry Byrd Sr. urged the South to unite against *Brown* in a show of power he called "massive resistance." A month later, nearly all the senators and representatives from the South—about one-fifth of the United States Congress—signed the so-called Southern Manifesto, which admonished the US Supreme Court for judicial overreach and called for white southerners to resist by exhausting all "lawful means." The manifesto claimed that desegre-gating the public schools would cause "chaos and confusion." Marshall, the NAACP's indefatigable litigator, said the signers were "encouraging lawlessness and mob violence by their action."[27]

The South wasn't quite as unified as Byrd might have wished, how-ever. In Arkansas, where Governor Francis Cherry said state officials would follow the law, several school districts began to desegregate as soon as the fall of 1954. (The state board of education in Arkansas, however, called on school districts to wait for *Brown II*; after the rul-ing, it seemed clear that most large districts in that state, including Lit-tle Rock, would delay. In the 1956–1957 school year, only one more school district in Arkansas desegregated—and it was in a single class, auto mechanics, which was held in a garage.) In some of the border states, such as Missouri, Delaware, Maryland, and West Virginia, resis-tance to the ruling wasn't as fierce, and some efforts were made quickly to desegregate the schools. Major cities such as Washington, DC, and

Baltimore also desegregated, though the superintendent in Baltimore took a passive approach. John Fischer said, "Our purpose was to open the doors of all of our schools . . . but not to push or pull anybody through a door."[28]

In much of the South, however, many lawmakers were in lockstep with Byrd, and they took steps to give school segregation the imprint of the law. In Louisiana, state officials made it a crime to operate an integrated school. In North Carolina, an education advisory committee recommended eight separate bills in the summer of 1956. A pamphlet for voters said the proposals were "so that no child in North Carolina will be forced to attend a school with a child of another race." The constitutional amendment would allow for "education expense grants to any child for whom no public school is available, or who is assigned against his parent's wishes to a mixed public school, and to provide by a vote of the people for suspending the operation of a school or schools in a community where conditions become intolerable." Every white voter knew *what* conditions were intolerable—if this was "freedom of choice" in action, the choices were only for white families. Oddly, the plan was promoted as "an effort to preserve North Carolina's public school system." The referendum passed by an overwhelming margin.[29]

Similarly, legislators in Virginia passed a package of laws in the summer of 1956 that created a three-person student assignment board, stripped funds from schools that desegregated, gave the governor the ability to close schools, and authorized tuition grants for students whose schools were closed. A federal judge ruled Virginia's law unconstitutional in 1957, writing that it was "directly in the teeth of the language of the Supreme Court." State officials promised to appeal, but the ruling gave other states an idea of what might get struck down.[30]

In Prince Edward County, Virginia, where Black students had walked out in 1951 to protest their deplorable school conditions, white officials quickly took steps to circumvent the *Brown* ruling. They voted

in 1955 to withhold funds from public education. In 1957 they announced that they had formed a private organization, Prince Edward
Educational Corporation, and raised "more than $10,000 in cash and
renewal of $190,000 in pledges" to finance and run all-white private
schools, if necessary. All but one of the principals and teachers in the
white public schools agreed to work in the new private schools. White
officials recommended that Black families make similar arrangements
for all-Black private schools. The Reverend Francis Griffin, president
of the county's NAACP branch, refused. Black families would not
compromise on desegregation. A headline in the *New York Times* read,
"Virginia Schools for Whites Ready: Prince Edward County Has Organized System to Thwart Integration."[31]

THE LEADERSHIP OF the NAACP soon realized the fight was far
from over to dismantle school segregation in the South. After the initial elation following the *Brown* ruling faded, it became clear that the
organization would have to sue school districts one at a time to get
even minimal compliance. Within a year of *Brown II*, the civil rights
organization had filed more than fifty lawsuits across the South.[32] The
strategy was slow going but fairly effective. North Carolina, despite
passing a series of anti-integration laws the previous year, began ad-
mitting small numbers of Black students to all-white schools in the fall
of 1957 in Greensboro, Charlotte, and Winston-Salem. The efforts to
desegregate, however slight, were a victory for the NAACP and were
viewed with alarm by segregationists in other states.

It wasn't clear whether President Dwight D. Eisenhower, a Republican, would intervene if the South simply stayed the course of
"massive resistance." He seemed to take a cautious approach in the
immediate aftermath of *Brown vs. Board*. In response to a reporter's
question after the ruling, he said only this: "The Supreme Court has
spoken, and I am sworn to uphold the constitutional process in the

country. And I will obey." It wasn't exactly an endorsement.[33] But Eisenhower soon took a stand.

In Little Rock, after twenty-seven Black students were turned away from four all-white schools, the NAACP sued. The courts upheld Little Rock's plan for gradual desegregation, even though it stretched out over more than a decade. Under the plan, just nine Black students would start at Central High School on September 4, 1957. But Arkansas's new governor, Orval Faubus, had taken a harder stance on desegregation than his predecessor and championed laws that helped school districts maintain segregation. He tried to prevent the students from attending Central High, calling in the National Guard to stop them. To justify the move, he made the dubious claim that gun and knife sales had skyrocketed and that he feared widespread violence would erupt if the students entered the school.[34]

A judge ordered Faubus to let the students in on September 20. He did—after removing the National Guard and leaving crowd control to the police department, a move designed to create chaos. The nine students slipped inside during the commotion, but the mob grew more threatening, repeatedly charging police lines. Some white students left the building in protest, including one girl who ran out, crying and shouting, "They're in, they're in." The crowd loved her hysterics. At one point the white mob attacked Black journalists after mistaking them for the students. Within hours the students were evacuated out a side door. Two days later, Eisenhower flew in federal troops from Kentucky and federalized the Arkansas National Guard to contain the mob and escort the nine students to school every day. Newspapers across the country ran photos of the troop convoys. A headline in one Chicago paper blasted in all caps, "U.S. TROOPS IN LITTLE ROCK."[35]

In an address to the nation, Eisenhower described the city's leaders as "demagogic extremists" and said, "Disorderly mobs have deliberately prevented the carrying-out of proper orders from a federal court." The situation in Little Rock had international repercussions, he warned, as the actions of the mob were being used by the country's enemies to "misrepresent our whole nation." The sight of a white mob threatening Black students on their way to school could undermine the United States' stand against communism overseas. "At a time when we face grave situations abroad because of the hatred that communism bears toward a system of government based on human rights, it would be difficult to exaggerate the harm that is being done to the prestige and influence, and indeed to the safety, of our nation and the world," he said.[36] The *New York Times* devoted an entire page to a reprint of the speech.

With the eyes of the nation now fixed on Little Rock, public education in the South hung in the balance. Already it seemed clear that Friedman's seemingly simple theory could be twisted to create enclaves of race and privilege for some students while weakening public schools for others—a problem that would reverberate through battles over school choice for decades to come.

2

"New Weapons and New Tactics"

I N THE LATE SUMMER OF 1958, GOVERNOR ORVAL FAUBUS WAS in a race against time and the US Supreme Court. A lower court had agreed to delay desegregation in Little Rock after the events of the previous school year. But an appellate court had overruled the decision, and now it was in the hands of the Supreme Court. With little time before a ruling, Faubus asked the Arkansas legislature in a special session to give him emergency powers to close any school under federal orders to integrate.

In a nationally televised address on August 26, he accused the courts of risking the lives of students in Little Rock, exaggerating the situation in the city and ignoring his own role the year before in allowing a mob to threaten students. He declared, "It matters not how bad the conditions that may exist; it matters not if a hundred people are slain in the streets or the corridors of a school; it matters not how great the destruction of property; it matters not whether the parents know that their children may return home grievously wounded because of disorders, or whether they may return at all. Integration is paramount to these considerations."[1]

His hyperbole did not sway the Supreme Court. Justices ruled on September 12 that desegregation of the high schools in Little Rock should proceed as planned. Within hours of the ruling, Faubus signed the anti-integration legislation sitting on his desk. The bills empowered the governor to close the public schools and create a grant program to help students pay for private school. It also authorized a special election to be held to ask voters whether to open desegregated schools. After he signed the bills, Faubus held a press conference, where he informed reporters that he would read a statement and take no questions. "Acting under the powers and responsibilities imposed upon me by these laws, I have ordered closed the senior high schools of Little Rock."[2] Battle lines had been drawn.

At the same time, in Virginia, Democratic governor J. Lindsay Almond Jr. took control of a single high school in Front Royal that had been ordered by a federal court to admit twenty-two Black students at the start of the school year. Warren County High School was about seventy miles east of the nation's capital but a world apart. Washington, DC's, public schools already had started desegregating. Almond announced that the school would be closed and "removed from the public school system." Almond, who ran for governor in 1957 on a pledge to support Senator Harry Byrd's campaign of massive resistance, had made it clear over the summer that he was prepared to close the public schools that fall. If President Eisenhower sent federal troops into Virginia, they would "patrol empty school houses," he warned.[3] Now he had made good on his promise—with the one school in Front Royal. Charlottesville and Norfolk also were under federal orders to desegregate, and the school year would start soon. Would he close those schools too, leaving thousands of white students without a school? It was a political gamble.

A few state lawmakers had expressed uneasiness earlier about giving the governor so much control over the fate of Virginia's public schools. In a speech in the state senate, where legislators were voting on new anti-integration bills, Senator Armistead Boothe asked, "Is there a man on this floor today who believes this would be constitutional?" Senator Edward Haddock warned his colleagues who were aligned with Byrd—and the Byrd Organization, which ruled state politics— that they were heading in a dangerous direction. "You've got the votes, the power, but you've got tremendous responsibilities with that power. When tyranny comes in, I make the prediction you will lose that power." The bill passed, as did one intended to make it harder for the NAACP to operate. After Almond closed the high school in Warren County in September, a headline in the *Afro-American*, a Black-owned newspaper in Baltimore, read, "'Massive Resistance' Reaches Point of No Return."[4]

EVEN AS SOME states in the South mounted a resistance to federally mandated desegregation, a priest in the Midwest had emerged as a vocal advocate for school vouchers for families interested in religious education. The Reverend Virgil Blum, a forty-five-year-old priest and political science professor at Marquette University in Milwaukee, proposed that the government subsidize the cost of tuition with either a tax credit or a voucher. To his mind it was a question of freedom in a pluralistic society. In his 1958 book, *Freedom of Choice in Education*, he wrote, "If the state demands the surrender of the right to freedom of choice in education, then it violates freedom of mind and freedom of religion. If, on the other hand, the state denies educational benefits to children and students who choose to attend independent schools, it imposes a penalty on the exercise of a constitutional right."[5]

He had made similar arguments in another piece published the year before and republished in *U.S. News & World Report*. His support for state aid to religious schools, which he rested on the First Amendment's guarantee of religious liberty, caught the attention of other Catholics. The Reverend Vernon Gallagher, president of Duquesne University, a Catholic college in Pittsburgh, told an alumni group that Blum's article "represents the first shot in a long battle."[6]

Blum's advocacy, though drawing new attention to the issue, was actually another shot in one of the oldest battles in American education. The country's Catholic school system had grown, in large part, in response to the development of a public school system in the nineteenth century that was Protestant in character. Horace Mann, considered the father of the common schools, argued against public funding of religious schools. Initially he wasn't fighting against Catholic education so much as pushing back against evangelical Protestants who thought the new public schools weren't religious enough.

Many Catholics were troubled by a school system that claimed to be religiously neutral yet used a Protestant Bible, among other items, for instruction. Reactions to Catholic requests for state funding or even for Catholic students to use a Catholic Bible in public school were often met with derision—and sometimes violence. In Philadelphia, some Catholic homes and at least two churches were burned in a riot after Catholic students were given permission to use their own Bible in public school. A Protestant newspaper in New York warned that Catholics wanted state funding to "worship a ghostly monarch of vicars, bishops, archbishops, cardinals and popes." By 1852, the Plenary Council of Catholic Bishops began calling on Catholics to "make every sacrifice" to support a separate system of Catholic education.[7]

Hostilities only increased amid a wave of Catholic immigration in the latter half of the nineteenth century. Catholics accounted for about 15 percent of the country's population by 1900; fifty years earlier that figure had been 5 percent. By the turn of the century, Catholic schools enrolled about 854,000 students. Tuition was low or free, relying both on donations and the low-cost labor of nuns and priests. In some cities,

Catholic school enrollment rivaled that of the public schools. Advocates of public education and many like-minded politicians viewed this growing alternative school system as a threat to public schools. In a sermon, a Methodist pastor said in 1889 that parochial schools would "destroy the most splendid system of public education that the world has seen." Anti-Catholic sentiment and a desire to protect the nation's public schools resulted in a wave of amendments to state constitutions to prohibit public financing of private religious education. Twenty-nine states had adopted such measures by 1890.[8]

Some of those battles continued well into the twentieth century. Blum was a young boy when Oregon passed a law that required children to attend public school, making it a misdemeanor offense if their parents didn't send them. The Society of Sisters, a Catholic organization that ran private schools, challenged the law. The US Supreme Court ruled unanimously in *Pierce vs. Society of Sisters* in 1925 that the law was unconstitutional, upholding the right of private schools to operate. Justice James C. McReynolds wrote for the court, "The fundamental theory of liberty upon which all governments of this Union repose excludes any general power of the State to standardize its children by forcing them to accept instruction from public teachers only."[9]

Blum's writing later echoed that sentiment. In 1957 he penned a piece calling for "educational benefits without enforced conformity." If education was a "welfare benefit," and he believed it was, then no American child should be denied access to it, regardless of their choice of public or private school.[10]

The US Supreme Court did not agree. More than twenty years after *Pierce*, the court issued a ruling that seemed to make it clear justices would not support direct state aid to religious schools. In *Everson vs. Board of Education of the Township of Ewing*, issued in 1947, the court ruled 5–4 that a state could pay the transportation costs for students at public and private schools, some of which were Catholic, but only because the program didn't directly support the religious schools; it just helped students get to school. The court said the First Amendment had "erected a wall between church and state" that "must be kept high and impregnable."[11] The "simplest solution" to this constitutional problem, Blum argued, was to give financial support to the family rather than to the religious school. He also read Milton Friedman's 1955 essay, which he acknowledged in his book, noting approvingly that such a program could serve as an important check on government power.

A fierce and sometimes irascible defender of Catholic education, Blum despaired that Catholics weren't taking advantage of their potential power as a voting bloc, and he warned Catholic parents not to allow their children "to be discriminated against as second-class citizens." During a speech he gave in Iowa in 1955, Blum mentioned both the Supreme Court cases, saying that *Pierce* had been a great victory not only for private religious schools but also for parents. The court had "ruled in favor of liberty" by asserting that parents had the right to direct their children's education. But "the child who attends such a school has been forced to pay a high price," he said, adding that their parents pay for two school systems, through taxes for the public school system and tuition for the private school.[12]

Blum wanted government subsidies for all religious schools, however, not just parochial ones. He felt that America's guarantee of religious freedom protected the country from the growing threat of communism and the Soviet Union. The first sentence in his book reads, "The USSR challenge to world freedom is a challenge to America to solve its educational problems."[13]

Blum sought government aid for religious schools, but others quickly saw that his ideas, like Friedman's, could be applied to the school-segregation battle being waged in some southern states. In the fall of 1957, David Lawrence, a conservative syndicated columnist and founder of *U.S. News & World Report*, wrote that although Blum had not said anything about school segregation, his proposal was "plainly applicable to such disputes." With a tax credit or school voucher, Lawrence suggested, public schools could become the "mixed schools, while the private schools would become the institutions in which the color line or the religious line is drawn." He noted that "any discriminating done would be by the parents and the schools they chose to support" rather than the public school system.[14] Apparently this was an advantage in Lawrence's mind.

Those weren't views Blum endorsed. Some Catholic schools in the South, including in parts of Tennessee, North Carolina, and Virginia, had started to integrate their schools both before and after the *Brown* ruling. In the speech he gave in 1955, Blum also had called upon Catholics to form their own organization to defend their rights as a religious minority. He told his audience that recent civil rights victories in the South, including *Brown*, could be "credited, in large measure, to the constant work of the National Association for the Advancement of Colored People." Catholics, he argued, needed their own NAACP.[15]

As MASSIVE RESISTANCE continued in the South, James J. Kilpatrick, the influential editor of the *Richmond News Leader*, had identified a major problem with the strategy employed against school desegregation: white southerners were largely the only ones defending it. In a letter in 1957 he wrote, "We need to win friends and influence people in New England, the upper midwest, the Southwest, and the Pacific Coast states. We need to sell our position to them . . . but we have yet to find any method of merchandising that seems to get the story across."[16]

Kilpatrick thought the concept of states' rights could win favor with conservatives nationally who didn't like the direction of the US Supreme Court under Chief Justice Earl Warren and were distressed by the New Deal's enlargement of government programs, which hadn't diminished since the Great Depression. With the encouragement of a conservative publisher, Kilpatrick wrote a book titled *The Sovereign*

States, which reiterated many of the positions he had taken in the newspaper's editorial section. Historian William P. Hustwit observes that the publisher "believed Kilpatrick's thesis addressed the essence of postwar American conservatism—the defense of local communities against big government."

Despite Kilpatrick's desire to win the support of Americans outside the South, he devoted more than a dozen pages of the book's original manuscript to trying to prove the inferiority of Black southerners. His editor removed most of it, but the book still ended with Kilpatrick arguing that Black people were inferior to white people, according to Hustwit. Some critics saw the book for what it was: a cherry-picked defense of the indefensible. The *Harvard Law Review* called it "ill-intentioned nonsense." Some conservatives, however, appreciated Kilpatrick's work, including Lawrence, of *U.S. News & World Report*, and William F. Buckley Jr., founder of the *National Review*, a conservative magazine. Both asked him to contribute pieces to their publications. Buckley also echoed Kilpatrick's racist sentiments in an editorial titled "Why the South Must Prevail." Their support elevated Kilpatrick's status nationally as a conservative writer, but it did little to help the segregationist cause at home, where Virginia's Governor Almond was in a tense standoff with the federal courts.[17]

After closing Warren County High School in the fall of 1958, Almond held firm and closed two schools in Charlottesville and then six in Norfolk. He couldn't say how long the public schools would remain closed—whether it was "days, weeks, or months," the *New York Times* reported. More than twelve thousand students were out of school, but it didn't seem as though Almond had thought through what would happen next. After shuttering the first three schools, he asked parents for their patience. State officials also moved forward with a "test lawsuit" in the Supreme Court of Virginia to explore whether the massive resistance laws were constitutional, including the provision of tuition grants for students shut out of the public schools. (The grants couldn't be paid out while the lawsuit proceeded.)[18]

In Arkansas, where Faubus had closed Little Rock's high schools, the school board started emergency classes on television. But some students, both Black and white, had enrolled in other public schools or left the state, the school superintendent said. Faubus quickly started a campaign to raise money to operate private schools for displaced students in Little Rock—the white ones. Two new all-white private schools opened in October.[19]

The spectacle of the school closures captured the nation's attention. Under the headline "Virginia Children Hungry for School," a columnist in the *Boston Sunday Globe* wrote in early October, "If ideas of white supremacy are dying in the Old Dominion they sure are dying hard." He called students "pawns in a long, grim deadlock between Virginia and the federal courts."[20]

In Virginia, public support for school closures waned as some white families learned what it was like to have their children denied an education. Some mothers held makeshift classes in basements. In Warren County, a private school was thrown together for displaced white students. Seventy-eight Protestant ministers signed a letter urging the governor to reopen the schools, while white students at a Norfolk high school held a rally to protest being kept out. The state's roughly seven thousand teachers, at their annual conference, passed a resolution calling for the schools to open. It read, in part, "This is no time for closed schools in Virginia, in the South or in the nation." In November, white parents in Norfolk sued the state; unlike in Front Royal and Charlottesville, too many children were out of school in Norfolk for makeshift private academies to be a viable alternative to public schools. Some groups advocating for the public schools to reopen were careful not to take a position on whether the public schools should desegregate. By December, a headline in a Black newspaper in Norfolk proclaimed, "Change of Heart by Many White Southerners: Closed Schools of 1958 Jar 'The Solid South.'"[21]

In January 1959, about four months after the first school closed in Virginia, two courts ruled that the school closures were unconstitutional. A federal court found that closing some public schools but not others violated the equal protection clause of the Fourteenth Amendment. The Supreme Court of Virginia struck down some of the state's massive resistance laws, ruling 5–2 that the governor did not have the power to close individual schools and the state did not have the right to offer grants to displaced students to pay for private schools at the expense of the public system. The justices also rejected the argument by state leaders that *Brown* voided not only the state statute requiring segregated schools but also the state's obligation to offer public education.[22]

After the rulings, Almond gave a statewide television address in which he pleaded with white Virginians to continue to defy the courts and spewed racist lies about what had occurred after Washington, DC, started to integrate its public schools, saying that "sadism, sex, and pregnancy [were] infesting the mixed schools of the District of Columbia and elsewhere." The school superintendent in Washington, DC, said Almond's comments were "unfounded in fact, with no justification, and in poor taste." Norfolk's Black newspaper called Almond's remarks "fanatical."[23] Despite Almond's militant speech, the strategy of massive resistance had failed.

A month later, a small number of Black students started attending some all-white public schools in Virginia. But twenty-one Black students were attending school by themselves. At Warren County High School, the first school Almond had closed, about a thousand white students chose to finish the disrupted school year elsewhere. The imagery of Black students attending a formerly white school with no white students delighted segregationists. Still, Virginia's stand against the courts was mostly over. Even Kilpatrick, one of the biggest supporters of massive resistance, had conceded a couple months earlier that it was time for "new weapons and new tactics."[24]

><

WHEN THE US Supreme Court ruled in the fall of 1958 that Little Rock must continue desegregating its public schools, the justices were clear: lawmakers could not skirt *Brown* through "evasive schemes for segregation."[25] Southern segregationists had been scheming for years, however, and already had found effective strategies to thwart desegregation. If they couldn't keep all Black students out of all-white schools, they would try to keep out most.

One of the most successful work-arounds was the pupil placement law. By 1959, at least eight states had passed legislation in which assignment of students to schools was approved by a local board, or in Virginia's case, a statewide commission. Most of the laws didn't explicitly mention race, but they kept Black students from enrolling in all-white schools by weighing other, seemingly race-neutral criteria. Five states, including Alabama, Louisiana, and Texas, considered "the possibility of threat of friction or disorder," the "psychological effect upon the pupil of attendance at a particular school," and "the morals, conduct, health and personal standards of the pupil," according to the US Commission on Civil Rights.[26]

The subjectivity of the pupil assignment criteria meant any child could be denied for just about any reason. But for many segregationists, the criteria weren't as race neutral as they appeared on paper. Like Kilpatrick, they argued that Black citizens had higher rates of disease and lower moral standards than white citizens, making it impossible to integrate the schools without harming white children. Some of Virginia's elected officials submitted documents to the US Supreme Court in 1955 in which they said Black Virginians had higher rates of illegitimate pregnancies—proof, they said, of lower morals—and lower IQs. They also argued that Black people had higher rates of syphilis and gonorrhea. For these reasons, elected officials argued, the issue wasn't about "racial dislike." It just wasn't "practical" to proceed with school desegregation. "No white parent will welcome Negro students into the white schools when to do so would increase his child's exposure to such contagious diseases," read a memo submitted to the court.[27]

In Virginia, where a statewide commission handled pupil placement, it was clear that board members knew their purpose was to halt desegregation. In 1959, a lawsuit found that out of 450,000 student assignments, the board had never assigned a Black child to an all-white school. One of the three board members testified in court that he couldn't think of a reason to ever approve the transfer of a Black student to a white school.[28]

With the collapse of massive resistance in Virginia, two things seemed clear: many citizens would not tolerate abandoning the public school system, and with less aggressive strategies desegregation could be kept to a minimum. After the court rulings in January 1959, Governor Almond formed a commission to come up with recommendations for the legislature to consider in a special session. It was the second education commission and at least the third time Virginia had amended its laws to account for the *Brown* ruling.

One of the ideas that found favor with commission members was to repackage pupil placement laws and tuition grants under the banner of "freedom of choice." Leon Sebring Dure Jr., a retired editor at the *Richmond Times-Dispatch* and a former White House correspondent for the *Washington Post*, had been advocating for the concept for at least a year in newspaper op-eds, letters to the editor, and even a published pamphlet. In a letter to the *New York Times*, Dure suggested that segregation by "free individual choice is a natural human right" that "can be maintained in schools without violating the court decision." Looking for solutions, he had written to a constitutional lawyer about the idea of school assignments based on racial preferences—an all-white school for the parents who wanted it, for instance, as well as an all-Black school and an integrated school. Just a few days before his letter to the editor ran, Dure received a response. The lawyer, Ralph T. Catterall, wrote, "You want everybody to have the right to go to a school of his choice. If he prefers to mingle with his own race only, you want him to have that right. He cannot have that right unless one school excludes all blacks. Then if a black wants to attend that school he is denied freedom of choice. If that school is supported by public funds, it is a publicly supported school. That is the unhappy merry-go-round."[29] School vouchers appeared to sidestep that problem by allowing students to attend segregated private schools. Dure had read both Milton Friedman's 1955 essay and Virgil Blum's 1958 book and saw that their reasoning could be used to advance his cause.

Historian James H. Hershman Jr. wrote that some Virginia lawmakers liked the sound of freedom of choice. One legislator told Dure that "freedom of choice, which is the main idea, is first rate." Kilpatrick, too, suggested that Dure was "on the right track." Others were concerned about Dure's support for tuition grants and worried about the effect such a program could have on the public school system. Businessmen had been arguing that school closures and threats against public education were harming the state's economy. One prominent group told business leaders that the school crisis had to be "resolved in a manner which preserves public education." Two economists at the University of Virginia, James Buchanan and G. Warren Nutter, suggested that the public school system could be privatized, but the idea appealed largely to those still committed to massive resistance. Hershman wrote that Buchanan and Nutter's argument "rang hollow" to "urban and suburban parents who had been forced by the school crisis to consider the private alternative." In that sense, Dure's push for freedom of choice was a "handy concept available at the right time."[30]

In a special session in the spring of 1959, Virginia lawmakers narrowly repealed the massive resistance laws and voted for a package of compromise measures recommended by the governor's education

commission. Legislators amended the pupil placement plan, restored local control over school closures, and enacted a tuition grant program for
the 1959–1960 school year. After a close vote, lawmakers also agreed
not to hold a referendum to ask voters whether to strike public education from the constitution. The changes weren't what the extremists
aligned with Senator Harry Byrd wanted—Byrd believed massive resistance should continue—but neither did it satisfy Black Virginians
who wanted the state to comply with *Brown*.

Oliver Hill, a lawyer from the NAACP who had been overseeing
lawsuits against Virginia's various schemes, saw freedom of choice
as a cover for discrimination. At a public hearing, he testified that "no
one in a democratic society has the right to have his private prejudices
financed at public expense."[31]

IN THE SPRING of 1959, the high schools in Little Rock remained
closed. The Arkansas Supreme Court in late April upheld the package of anti-integration bills that gave Governor Faubus the authority
to close the public schools. A federal court ruling still was pending. But
months after voters had backed closing the public schools, Faubus was
losing his support in Little Rock. High school students had been out of
their regular schools all year, leaving them in limbo. Some were attending hastily arranged private schools or taking correspondence courses.
Some had moved away. Others weren't in school at all.

Faubus had signed a law to require public school teachers to dis-
close any organization to which they donated money or belonged, an
obvious intimidation tactic. He also tried unsuccessfully to intervene in
Little Rock's school board election in an attempt to keep segregationists
in power. He backed three segregationists in December 1958 who lost
to candidates who favored some desegregation, a sign of the public's
growing frustration. The board now was divided evenly between moderates and pro-Faubus segregationists.

In early May, tensions spilled over in the city after the three moderate board members left a meeting and the remaining members fired more than forty teachers and principals without charges or a hearing. One of the board members acknowledged later that it was because they believed the school employees supported the *Brown* ruling. The Chamber of Commerce and the parent-teacher association condemned the terminations. More than 150 people organized a committee, Stop This Outrageous Purge, or STOP, to back a recall effort against the segregationist board members. Segregationists created their own group, Committee to Retain Our Segregated Schools, or CROSS, and petitioned to recall the moderate board members. Faubus promised to stay out of the special election, only to back the segregationists in a televised address the day before voters went to the polls. He told voters the real issue at stake in the election was school segregation.[32]

When it was over, the three moderate candidates kept their seats. The segregationists were removed from office. A day later, Faubus told a reporter that the election results weren't a reflection of voters' views on school segregation after all. "In fact," he said, "the issue was not integration or segregation but only the dismissal of the [school employees]." Little Rock's former school superintendent, who left his job two months after Faubus closed the public schools, saw it rather differently. He called the results the "first major blow" against the governor's actions—and an indication that the people of Arkansas would not accept abandoning public education to preserve segregation. He said, "I think it was a very strong reaction on the part of the people in favor of public education, and it comes as a result of their having been denied public education for an entire school year."[33]

In June, a federal court struck down the state's anti-integration laws, returning local control to the school board in Little Rock. Like Governor Almond in Virginia, Faubus had lost his battle with the courts. After new members joined the Little Rock school board, it voted to reopen the city's high schools for the 1959–1960 school year and to resume the gradual desegregation plan. Operators of the all-white private schools announced they would close their doors in the fall. Donations had already dried up, and the court struck down state laws to lease out public school buildings and provide public funding to private schools.

The public school shutdown had exacted a heavy toll on Black students: about half the city's Black high school pupils received no education that year. Some students called it "the lost year."

3

The Test Case for School Vouchers

S EVEN YEARS AFTER *BROWN VS. BOARD*, THE US CIVIL RIGHTS Commission examined how much progress the South had made in desegregating its public schools and concluded: not much. The year was 1961. Four states—Alabama, Georgia, Mississippi, and South Carolina—still had completely separate schools for Black and white children. Other states, including Arkansas and Virginia, had undergone token desegregation after state leaders tried and failed to defy the courts. Only about 7 percent of Black children attended public school with white children in the region during the 1960–1961 school year, the commission estimated.

The "evasive schemes for segregation" the US Supreme Court had warned against were everywhere. The report, using sometimes blunt and contemptuous language, noted the most egregious examples of defiance. In New Orleans, four first-grade girls who had enrolled in two all-white schools in November 1960 faced a mob of angry white women, rioting teenagers, and a last-minute effort by lawmakers to prevent their entry. Most white students in the city had abandoned the public schools; those who remained faced a coordinated campaign of harassment from segregationists. Louisiana's own attorney general described the state's resistance effort as "legislate and litigate." The commission noted in its report that lawmakers in Louisiana were rapidly passing new laws to circumvent *Brown*, and just as quickly the courts were striking them down. In Virginia, where several school districts had started desegregating, commission members concluded that the campaign of massive resistance was "legally dead in Virginia, but its spirit lingers on." The commission derided Arkansas governor Orval Faubus's efforts to keep the high schools in Little Rock closed as "a national and international embarrassment."[1]

Commission members also were alarmed by southern lawmakers' seeming lack of commitment to public education after *Brown*. Compulsory attendance laws, which had been enacted "in all states except Alaska since 1918," were being repealed, and some students were dropping out of high school. Some public schools had been closed. States were turning to "tuition grants and other devices allowing substitution of private (and segregated) schools for public (and possibly desegregated) schools." They wrote, "These measures appear to threaten a fundamental concept of American society—that of free, universal, and compulsory education."

Virginia had become the South's test case for school vouchers.

By the winter of 1961, at least five states had grant laws on the books, but only Virginia had started giving students public dollars to pay for private school. Leon Dure, a retired newspaper editor, had devoted himself to advocating for "freedom of choice" plans, crisscrossing the South to convince lawmakers that vouchers, often called tuition grants, were the solution to the failures of massive resistance. He noted with satisfaction that both Louisiana and Georgia turned to vouchers after failed efforts to resist federal court orders to desegregate New

Orleans's public schools and the University of Georgia. In Georgia, Governor Ernest Vandiver backed an "open schools" plan that repealed many of the earlier resistance measures and included a new voucher program. Vandiver might have been willing to close some public schools in Atlanta, but he didn't want the political nightmare that would come from closing the state's premier university. A headline in the *Christian Science Monitor* declared, "Georgia Drops Massive Segregation," while the *Washington Post and Times Herald* asserted, "Solid South's Segregation Armor Begins to Crack."[2]

Tuition grants were the solution, Dure said, to the "spitting, cursing, screaming mothers" who had been threatening six-year-old Black girls outside elementary schools in New Orleans. (In an editorial, Dure excused the women's hateful behavior, saying they were "obeying an old law of nature" and asking, "Can anyone doubt that they would treat them with the greatest sympathy, even affection, in other circumstances?") The *Daily Progress*, in Charlottesville, described Dure as "spreading his gospel" across the South. The opinion piece was titled, "Leon Dure Finds the Whole South Turning to Freedom of Choice as Schools Solution."[3]

Dure claimed that Virginia was pioneering two new First Amendment freedoms: "freedom of education" and "freedom of association." He suggested that the US Supreme Court would ultimately need to decide if an "individual receiving public help can retain his freedom to associate, or congregate, as he pleases—in education as in welfare, in labor, and in a host of other things."[4] Dure believed white people had the right not to associate with Black people in publicly financed settings, such as public schools.

Dure was an effective mouthpiece for these ideas, but he wasn't the sole originator of them; they had been percolating in some form for years. Donald R. Richberg, a prominent lawyer who served in the Roosevelt administration before defending segregation, had invoked freedom of association in the 1940s when he argued against the reauthorization of

the Fair Employment Practices Committee, which was created by Roosevelt in 1941 to prevent racial discrimination in government employment. In a law review article Richberg asked, "Have minorities a 'civil
right' to force other minorities, or majorities, to associate with them?"
and "Does freedom to associate include freedom not to associate?"[5]

With the freedom of choice plan, Dure said, Virginia "abandons
compulsory congregation in education. Thus whatever congregation
takes place is individually agreeable." Arkansas's Governor Faubus echoed
Dure's reasoning in a pitch for tuition grants in his state when he described it as "just carrying a little bit further the rights of an individual."[6]

In the first year of Virginia's voucher program, about forty-seven
hundred students participated; the vast majority of the vouchers were
used by white students to attend private schools, though a small number
of Black students used grants, and some students used them to attend
public schools. Numbers for the second year vary from about sixty-one
hundred to eighty-one hundred.[7] Dure believed the program could grow
to ten thousand students in its third year as parents and private school
operators became familiar with it. Most of the state's private schools
were religious and ineligible. To support a growing program it seemed
likely that new secular private schools would have to open.

In 1961, the state spent $1.7 million on grants. Some Virgin-
ians complained that the new program bled resources from the public schools. A parent-teacher association in Norfolk wrote a letter to
Governor J. Lindsay Almond Jr. to request "prompt remedial action"
because the grants posed a "threat to the very existence of the public
school system." In a letter he wrote in response, Almond defended the
tuition grants as "complementary to public education."[8]

In a piece Dure wrote in 1961 for the *Georgia Review*, a literary
journal, he said, "Clearly, we are dealing here with something new. That
it could have far-reaching and profound consequences is obvious."[9]

✄

ONE COUNTY IN Virginia hadn't gotten the message that the era of massive resistance had ended. Facing a federal order to desegregate in the fall of 1959, white officials in Prince Edward County shut down the public school system. For the first year, white students went to school in churches and people's homes. Makeshift classes were funded with donations and furnished with items stripped from the shuttered public schools. With donations and some volunteer labor, Prince Edward Academy's brand-new "upper school" opened in the fall of 1961. The *New York Herald Tribune* described it as a "monument to the concept of white supremacy." The newspaper ran a picture of Moton High School—the all-Black school students had walked out of on strike ten years earlier—with a sign out front that read "No Trespassing." A caption said the school was "closed to avoid integration."[10]

In its first year, the fledgling all-white private school system didn't charge families tuition. The next year, white families paid with tuition grants and local tax credits. Families could get credits if they donated to the county's private secular schools; Prince Edward Academy's schools were the only ones in the county.

Black families in the county largely refused to use tuition grants and rebuffed efforts by white officials to set up a similar all-Black private school. They knew—and white officials knew—that Black participation could give the privately segregated school system legitimacy. A headline in a Black newspaper in Pittsburgh read, "Va. Whites Beg Negroes to Establish [Private] Schools." The Reverend Francis Griffin, head of the local NAACP, avowed that Black families would not quit the fight for public education. He said, "Every reactionary force in the South is concentrating its efforts and attention on aiding the segregationists to make a noble stand here. If they win, the cause of justice will be set back 100 years."[11]

Many Black families made painful sacrifices rather than give up on desegregated public schools. Some sent their children away to live with relatives. Volunteer efforts also sprang up to help displaced students.

Families in the Midwest and the Northeast took in children. The Virginia Teachers Association, a professional organization for Black teachers, helped send some students to other public schools in Virginia, and the American Federation of Teachers, a national teachers' union, created summer programs for students. Still, more than fifteen hundred Black students in the county were going without a formal education. Speaking about the county's school closures at a rally in Richmond, the Reverend Dr. Martin Luther King Jr. warned white Virginians that the struggle for civil rights was an "unstoppable movement" that was far from over. "We will wear you down by our capacity to suffer," he said.[12]

White officials in the county thought they were setting an example for the rest of the South to follow, and they hosted a number of visitors to tour the private school. James J. Kilpatrick, editor of the *Richmond News Leader*, donated thousands of books to Prince Edward Academy's library and gave money to support the school. Some officials with the Prince Edward School Foundation, the organization running the new private schools, predicted that public education would end up being a "brief interlude in the history of southern education."[13]

If Prince Edward County had become a symbol for white southern resistance, it also was a national scandal. US Attorney General Robert F. Kennedy filed a motion in federal court in the spring of 1961 asking for the United States to officially intervene in the case. He said it was necessary to "protect the integrity of the judicial process of the United States." (The request was denied.) The NAACP amended its original 1951 complaint against segregated schooling to charge that Prince Edward County was now using tuition grants and tax credits to circumvent court-ordered desegregation.

Arguing the case in court in May 1961, a lawyer for Prince Edward County's school board called the actions taken by white officials "color-blind" and compared the tuition grants to the GI Bill, echoing an argument that Milton Friedman had made in his 1955 voucher essay. "We gave to the colored people and all the people of Prince Edward the same freedom we gave to ourselves. They can educate their children in any school they please," he said.[14]

On August 25, 1961, a district court ruled that closing the public schools had "effectively deprived the citizens of Prince Edward County with a freedom of choice between public and private education." The judge agreed that tuition grants and tax credits had been used to uphold school segregation, but he didn't invalidate the state's tuition grant program. Instead he said that state lawmakers had clearly intended it to operate alongside public education.[15] To use the grants, Prince Edward County had to open the public schools, which would allow for some desegregation.

It was a victory for Dure but not for the hard-line segregationists of Prince Edward County. Without tax dollars to support their cause, white officials once again relied on donations to support their private schools. Later that year, when a district court asked for a desegregation plan, they didn't submit one. Rather, they gave the court a report on the willingness of Black and white parents to send their children to desegregated public schools. According to a survey conducted by county officials, more than one thousand Black parents would send their children to integrated public schools. Only thirteen white families were willing.[16]

One Black student who couldn't go to school was drafted into the US Army and served in Vietnam. He recalled later, "I could go to war for my country, but I could not go to school in Prince Edward County."[17]

THE LAST STAND in Prince Edward County was a thorn for anyone trying to argue that Virginia's school vouchers were color-blind. Dure acknowledged that it was a "trouble spot" but believed that once Prince Edward County reopened its public schools and used tuition grants as designed, the "Virginia school plan may be recognizable as one of the most fascinating educational experiments of all time."[18]

Dure sought support for his experiment from both the Reverend Virgil Blum and Milton Friedman, known voucher supporters. Neither made natural allies. Blum wanted financial support for religious schools, while the South limited its programs to secular schools. Lawmakers in Louisiana, for instance, excluded parochial schools from its voucher program *because* they were desegregated, despite the long-standing popularity of Catholic education in the state. Friedman proposed a radically different structure for America's system of public education, and he said he despised "segregation and racial prejudice." Friedman also wasn't an obvious ally for Blum. He warned Blum candidly in a private letter that if school vouchers became widespread, the Catholic schools might suffer from the increased competition.[19] All three men had settled on the same idea—school vouchers—but with different motivations.

In an effort to find common ground with Blum, Dure told him he had advocated for the inclusion of religious schools, and he mentioned that some students in Virginia were using grants to leave segregated schools for integrated ones. He tried to persuade the priest that their fight was the same: Dure sought freedom of association, while Blum wanted freedom of religion. "All our First Amendment freedoms are just facets of the same jewel," he wrote in a letter to Blum. Still, he had to concede that "many clergymen condemn the Virginia plan because of its genesis." He wrote himself into a corner trying to dismiss those concerns. "People like and dislike one another for thousands of reasons, many of them simply esthetic and beyond any logic. To require people to associate is the wrong way to go about it. We don't need laws on this subject. We need no law at all."[20] But, as Blum surely knew, it wasn't for "thousands of reasons" that white Virginians didn't want to associate with Black Virginians. Nor were Black families the ones trying to escape the public schools or threatening to dismantle public education.

For his part, Blum observed what was happening in the South with both interest and dismay. Historian Jim Carl wrote that Blum "neither supported nor condemned southern tuition grants publicly," but he "lamented the actions" of Attorney General Kennedy, who viewed the programs as circumventing *Brown*. He hoped the courts wouldn't invalidate the programs before they could be shown to work. Blum and a married couple, Mae and Martin Duggan, had started an advocacy organization in 1959 called Citizens for Educational Freedom to lobby for parochial schools to get their "fair share" of federal grants. The group's members held rallies with students wearing private school uniforms and holding signs that read, "Why don't we count?"[21]

In his advocacy for Virginia's program, Dure invoked the economic arguments in Friedman's work as well as the opinions of James Buchanan and G. Warren Nutter, two economists at the University of Virginia who had written a paper years before in which they suggested it was possible, even preferable, to privatize public education. In some of his writing, Dure said tuition grants were less expensive than public education and referred to the "advantages of individual liberty in education over the old state monopoly of education." But Dure's primary interest wasn't economic; it was to circumvent desegregation. In a 1959 letter to James J. Kilpatrick, a segregationist editor, Dure had written, "The only way to get rid of compulsory integration was to erect the old marketplace right of free choice."[22]

In his 1962 book, *Capitalism and Freedom*, Friedman acknowledged that Virginia's tuition grant program had "many features in common" with his proposal. But he predicted that the outcome of the program, if it was allowed to continue, would not be what was intended by legislators in Virginia. "Though adopted for the purpose of avoiding compulsory integration, I predict that the ultimate effects of the law will be very different. . . . We should see a flowering of the schools available in Virginia, with an increase in their diversity, a substantial if not spectacular rise in the quality of the leading schools, and a later rise in quality of the rest under the impetus of the leaders."[23]

⋗⋖

ALABAMA, MISSISSIPPI, AND South Carolina were among the last
to give up outright resistance in the years after *Brown vs. Board of Education.* With federal desegregation orders looming, lawmakers turned
to tuition grants as a last resort, a means for white students to flee any
school that desegregated. Some of the governors advocated for tuition
grants even as they insisted that the battle against the courts wasn't
over. South Carolina's Governor Donald Russell vowed to keep up the
fight, "as we are confident in the ultimate rightness of our stand." In
Alabama, Governor George Wallace lost a standoff at the University
of Alabama in 1963 when he tried to stop two Black students, Viv-
ian Malone and James Hood, from entering by blocking the doorway.
Federal troops ended his "stand at the schoolhouse door." Two years
later Wallace pushed to amend the existing tuition grant law, just weeks
before Black students were to start attending all-white public schools.[24]

Many lawmakers in the South had been clear about their original
intentions for tuition grant programs: they were a mechanism for white
families to avoid school desegregation. Many families used them for
exactly that purpose. But others used them in unexpected ways. Some
parents sought grants for private school even in communities where
the public schools remained segregated. In the 1962–1963 school year,
the second year of Louisiana's program, the state's Financial Assistance
Commission received "thousands of requests" for grants, including from
"parishes where segregated education had not even been challenged and
from pupils who wished to attend expensive private schools in the New
Orleans Metropolitan area." Virginia's amended law allowed students
to use tuition grants out of state, and some students did. In Fairfax,
which hadn't desegregated its public schools, students used grants to
attend private schools in other southern states as well as in Connecticut, Massachusetts, and New Jersey. Families also used grants to move
from segregated public schools to desegregated ones and to attend
schools closer to their homes. A headline in the *Washington Post and
Times Herald* said, "Virginia Tuition Grants Go Astray."[25]

Some southerners viewed the growing tuition grant programs with alarm. Some feared the grants were pulling money and support away from the public schools. The result could be another separate and un-equal system of education—a private and well-resourced one for white students and a public and underresourced one for Black students. In Atlanta, school board members refused to approve grant requests in the fall of 1961 because the requests were coming from families whose children already attended private school. They called the amended law an "unworkable monstrosity." Robert F. Williams, executive secretary of the Virginia Education Association, a state teachers' union, wrote in 1964 that the tuition grants were being "abused" by students who were using them to attend integrated private schools. "Certainly the intent was not to subsidize private education generally," he opined in an ed-ucation journal. The Reverend Fred L. Shuttlesworth, who had been beaten, along with his wife, by Klansmen after trying to enroll their children in an all-white school in Birmingham in 1957, called tuition grants "one of the South's trump cards" that segregationists hoped to use "to leave Negroes holding the bag."

Hardy Cross Dillard, dean of the law school at the University of Virginia, wrote in the *Virginia Quarterly Review* that the "freedom of choice" concept "deserves to be resisted rather than encouraged." He doubted that it was constitutional, but he also warned that such a pro-gram could either impair the public school system or cause its "demise." If all the white students fled to private schools with state support, the white community would be unlikely to support taxes for predomi-nantly Black public schools. In that case, tuition grants could "spell the doom of the public school system."[26]

>‹

In the spring of 1964, the US Supreme Court ruled that Prince Edward County must open its public schools for both Black and white students. In an opinion for the majority, Justice Hugo Black wrote,

"There has been entirely too much deliberation and not enough speed in enforcing the constitutional rights which we held in *Brown vs. Board of Education*." The Supreme Court ruled that the district judge could force white officials in Prince Edward County to levy taxes to operate public schools, and it upheld the lower court's injunction against using tuition grants and tax credits while the public schools remained closed.[27]

The ruling did not end the matter. Within a month, the all-white board of supervisors voted 4–2 to open the public schools. They adopted a budget to support sixteen hundred students in the fall—roughly the number of Black students in Prince Edward County. They voted to levy $189,000 for public schools and $375,000 for tuition grants. It seemed clear the board expected the majority of the white students to remain in the private school system, which they could now support with tuition grants while underfunding the public schools. (The county's school board had requested $339,000 for a system of sixteen hundred.)[28]

Black students had been locked out of the public schools for five years. Now, with the public schools set to reopen, they could once again face an underresourced and segregated public school system. It had been thirteen long years since the student strike at Moton High School, and Black families were still fighting for an equal public education.

The plaintiffs in *Griffin vs. County School Board of Prince Edward County* asked the district judge to stop payments of tuition grants and order the county's board of supervisors to levy enough money to reopen desegregated schools. The judge agreed to an injunction on the grants and a hearing about the school budget. The state board of education then took a unanimous vote to pay the grants with state funds.[29] The court intervened again, ordering an injunction against back payments. But the judge didn't forbid future payouts, a loophole Prince Edward County's white officials immediately noticed.

Officials moved quickly. The board of supervisors increased the amount of the tuition grants and authorized an immediate half payout to families. The board held a meeting at two a.m. on August 5 to process more than twelve hundred grant applications from white families. By nine a.m. most of the checks had been cashed at a local bank. The NAACP called it a "midnight raid on the county treasury."[30]

White officials were later held in contempt of court and ordered to repay the funds. A federal court ruling in 1965 then further restricted the use of tuition grants. Judge Albert V. Bryan ruled that grants could be used at a segregated private school if the grants didn't constitute the bulk of the school's funding. They could not be used if governmental agencies knew the public money would provide "the whole or greater part of the cost of operation of a segregated school."[31]

Once again, Prince Edward County was limited in its use of tuition grants to support its segregated private school system.

4

The "New Left" and the "Old Right" Concur

"**I**S THE PUBLIC SCHOOL OBSOLETE?"
Christopher Jencks, a twenty-nine-year-old sociologist, posed the question in a piece he wrote for the *Public Interest*, a right-leaning public policy journal, in the winter of 1966. Not long after, he published an article in *Dissent*, a small but influential left-wing magazine, titled, "Who Should Control Education?"[1]

Jencks argued that public education didn't work well for "slum children," and it shouldn't be expected to solve problems of "racism or poverty, illness or crime." He attacked large urban school systems— "Were it not for their monopoly on educational opportunities for the poor, most big city school systems would probably go out of business"—and called neighborhood schools an "increasingly irrelevant tradition." He proposed several solutions: provide low-income children with tuition grants to pay for private school, get rid of neighborhood schools and create "real choice" in a citywide open-enrollment system with different types of schools, and contract the running of a public school to an outside organization. He also thought groups of teachers could "manage a school on contract" with "ultimate control" over "hiring and firing teachers, budget-making, programming and so forth." If such a school failed in its mission, and he thought many would, the "contract could be terminated." (This notion drew little attention at the time but includes many of the principles of charter schools.) All his ideas shared a common goal: "radical decentralization of both power and responsibility."

Jencks's writing attracted attention, not only for the radicalism of his views but because of his pedigree. A liberal Harvard graduate who had studied sociology at the London School of Economics and served as an editor at the *New Republic*, Jencks seemed an unlikely advocate for school vouchers, an idea that had been championed by Milton Friedman, a libertarian economist, and embraced by some southern segregationists to evade school desegregation. Like Friedman, Jencks also seemed to place little value in public education. In *Dissent*, he acknowledged that a free-market system would likely increase enrollment in private schools at the expense of public ones, but said there is "no inherent virtue in public administration of the schools any more than in public administration of universities, post offices or the telephone system." In his article in the *Public Interest*, he took it a step further. "And if, as some fear, the public schools could not survive in open competition with private ones, then perhaps they *should* not survive." (Italics are his.)

Although the civil rights movement dominated the national news, Jencks didn't directly mention in either of his pieces that some states in the South already were providing students with tuition grants, or that at least one state had halted its program under a court-ordered injunction. In his article in *Dissent* he briefly noted, without any other context, that some parents' "educational preferences do not deserve to be indulged." He wrote, "Parents who want their children to attend all-white schools should not be allowed to use public funds to pursue this preference."

Friedman, whose national stature had grown since the publication of his best-selling book, *Capitalism and Freedom*, declared in the spring issue of *Public Interest* that he was "delighted to welcome Christopher Jencks to the company of those who favor the voucher system." He wrote, "The welcome is all the warmer because Mr. Jencks is of the still smaller company of those who recognize that market competition would be far more effective than governmental operation in fostering diversity, experimentation, and improvement in the quality of schooling. As he points out, one great merit of the system of tuition grants is that it would very likely lead to the large scale replacement of governmentally operated schools by non-governmental schools."[2]

Henry Levin, an assistant professor at Stanford University, observed the unusual alliance on school vouchers between Jencks and Friedman and later wrote, "The fact that the 'new left' (Jencks) and the 'old right' (Friedman) can concur on the same educational palliative is reason enough to consider the market approach to education."[3]

IN THE SOUTH, white students had been fleeing to all-white private schools in increasing numbers despite largely successful efforts by white officials to keep desegregation to a minimum through gerrymandered school zones, gradual integration plans, and "freedom of choice" policies that put the onus on Black families to switch schools. If those formal efforts to keep out Black families didn't work, threats and violence often followed. In one Mississippi town, the Ku Klux Klan fired thirty-two times into the house of a Black family whose child had enrolled in an all-white school. In another case in the state, white men attacked and beat a Black father and shot him in both legs. Schools that admitted Black students also were targeted by hate groups. In Elba, Alabama, where two Black students had enrolled in a high school, two explosives rocked the school a half hour after two hundred people left a banquet. It was perhaps no surprise that the US Civil Rights Commission in 1966 estimated that fewer than 3 percent of Black children had attended school with white children in the Deep South as of 1964; the figure rose to a modest 10.9 percent if the border states were included.[4]

In four states—Virginia, Louisiana, Mississippi, and Alabama—government dollars were helping white students flee. Tuition grants were now race neutral on paper but widely understood and used as a mechanism for white families to avoid school desegregation. Most of the grants, which ranged from $185 to $250 a year, went to white students. But it wasn't clear how long the programs would last. Nearly all were being challenged in the courts. In South Carolina, a legal challenge had already curtailed the program; a judge agreed in 1965 to put it on hold during litigation. Few grants had been used. In Georgia, lawmakers added regulations in the second year that diminished the program. By 1964, grants were no longer distributed.[5]

Louisiana and Virginia had the largest and most successful grant programs, giving thousands of students each year public dollars for private education. As Leon Dure had predicted, Virginia's program grew rapidly after the first two years, with more than twelve thousand grants distributed in 1966. Louisiana gave out more than fifteen thousand grants the same year. Mississippi's and Alabama's programs were smaller, in part because efforts to avoid desegregating the public schools had initially been so successful. In Alabama some private schools also declined the funds because they feared future federal intrusion—still, the state had made nearly every student at private schools eligible for the financial assistance. Mississippi, which created its program in 1964, gave out 600 grants at sixteen private schools the first year, followed by 1,736 at twenty-six schools the next year, according to the *Southern Education Report*.[6]

Both public and private support fueled the "private school movement," as some southerners called the region's shift toward private education. At least two hundred new segregated private schools were opened in the South by 1967. The Virginia Education Fund, an "organization of businessmen and citizens interested in private schooling," announced in 1966 that it would hold a $3 million donation drive to support private education through 1971. Some newly formed private schools also received under-the-table support from white officials at public school districts, benefiting from deeply discounted sales of books and furniture, even buses and buildings. Some of the new private schools were near replicas of the public schools white families fled, adopting the same mascots and school colors, only "leaving behind the shell of the building." In Lowndesboro, Alabama, the entire football team— all the players and the coach—moved from the public high school to a new, all-white private school, leaving the old school with no team. Ray D. Bass, head of the Lowndes County Private School Foundation, said tuition grants would "help out," but the school didn't want to run the risk of being forced to integrate. "We're not counting on the tuition grant law," he said.[7]

National and regional newspapers covered the shift to private education in the South—and it was clear who was leaving the public schools and why. In the summer of 1966, the *Wall Street Journal* wrote, "More Southern Whites Open Private Schools That Exclude Negroes." A headline in the *Austin Statesman* read, "Selma Starts Private School 'Whites Only,'" while the *Hartford Courant* said, "State Helps Segregation in Alabama."[8]

Two landmark bills signed by President Lyndon B. Johnson—the Civil Rights Act of 1964 and the Elementary and Secondary Education Act of 1965—seemed poised to alter the educational landscape in the South with a carrot-and-stick approach to school desegregation. The Civil Rights Act allowed the federal government to withhold funds from segregated school districts, while the ESEA greatly increased the federal dollars available to school districts. Poor states, such as Mississippi, stood to gain from the legislation, but only if they desegregated their public schools. Southern and border states received about $176 million in federal education dollars in 1964. With the passage of the

ESEA, nearly $590 million was added in 1966. Even before Johnson signed the ESEA, the *New York Times* reported public school officials in the South feared the loss of federal money. One southern educator told the newspaper somewhat bitterly that school districts would reluctantly welcome some Black students to all-white public schools for "that great equalizer—the Yankee dollar."[9]

As historian Matthew F. Delmont has written, some southern congressmen were irritated by the "blatant hypocrisy" of the Civil Rights Act, which targeted school desegregation in the South but not in the North. Northern lawmakers often framed school segregation in their own communities as the natural result of where people chose to live, ignoring the city, state, and federal actions that had created segregated neighborhoods in the first place. (Integrated neighborhoods in some cities were destroyed by the federal government during the Great Depression to make way for segregated public housing, for instance. A number of cities also had racist zoning ordinances, which restricted Black residents from moving to majority-white areas.) Northern lawmakers preferred the term "racial imbalance" to "segregation." Yet some white families in the North fiercely opposed even minor efforts to desegregate schools. In New York City, a couple of months before the floor debate on the Civil Rights Act, between ten thousand and fifteen thousand parents, most of them white mothers, staged a huge protest in the streets over a plan that would have done very little to create meaningful integration.[10]

To pass the landmark legislation, senators defined desegregation as "the assignment of students to public schools and within such schools without regard to their race, color, religion, or national origin." But, the act continued, it "shall not mean the assignment of students to public schools in order to overcome racial imbalance." In the floor debate, some southern senators raised the recent protest in New York City and asked why northern senators were so interested in school desegregation in the South while ignoring it in the North, Delmont wrote. Senator

James Eastland of Mississippi wryly described two New York senators as "pretty good segregationists." Eastland couldn't argue, however, that Mississippi wasn't directly aiding all-white private schools. In Jackson, some of the new academies were opened by the Citizens' Councils, a network of dangerous white supremacist organizations whose principles were "states' rights and racial integrity." In 1966, a newspaper advertisement for a new council school claimed that "teaching [in public schools] was fast being subordinated to social experimentation." W. J. Simmons, a national administrator of the Citizens' Councils, bluntly explained the move to private education: "As integration moves in, white people move out."

Students who attended the Citizens' Councils schools received tuition grants.[11]

>‹

IN THE SPRING of 1967, a federal court struck down Alabama's tuition grant program and ordered state officials to force its remaining segregated school systems to submit plans for Black students to enroll in all-white schools in the fall. It was a sign of things to come.

Over the next three years, the courts dismantled tuition grant policies in Louisiana, Mississippi, South Carolina, and Virginia one by one. The rulings were clear: tuition grants were primarily used to assist white students who were fleeing public school desegregation. In Alabama, the court found that "every dollar paid" during the 1965–1966 school year went to all-white private schools opened after public schools began to enroll Black students. In Mississippi, the court found that all but one of the forty-nine private schools accepting tuition grants during the 1967–1968 school year were all-white. A state agency said Mississippi distributed more than six thousand grants in 1969. A federal court ruled that Virginia's grants "have been a principal means of evading public school integration."[12]

In Louisiana, a federal appeals court noted the nearly ten-year evolution of the tuition grant law from the first racist version in 1958. "In each succeeding act the scheme became more subtle, the language more sophisticated." But the motive hadn't changed, the court ruled. "The purpose . . . is to give state aid to private discrimination." The judges concluded Louisiana "nourished segregated schools which could not have come into existence or have continued without the nourishment provided under the early discriminatory schemes."[13]

Newspapers, particularly Black news outlets, blasted the rulings across their pages. "ALABAMA SCHOOLS TOLD TO END BIAS," the *New York Times* announced in all caps. "Federal Judges Knock Down Mississippi's Tuition Grants," the *Afro-American* wrote. "S.C. Tuition Grants Junked by Top Court" and "La. Tuition Grants Out, U.S. Court Judges Rule," stated the *New Journal and Guide*. The *Washington Post and Times Herald* wrote about Virginia, "Tuition Grants Are Outlawed."

Virginia had been the epicenter for Leon Dure's broader concept of "freedom of choice." He believed the US Supreme Court would eventually agree that people had a constitutional right not to associate with one another, and a series of lower court rulings offered some hope. Judges across the South had reached different conclusions about such plans, depending on whether they were found to be discriminatory. But in 1968, the US Supreme Court rendered its judgment, ruling that a "freedom of choice" plan in New Kent County, Virginia, didn't go far enough to desegregate schools because it placed the burden for change on families and not on the school board. Providing a choice between an all-white school and an all-Black school, as New Kent County had done, wasn't acceptable. The ruling on tuition grants came the next year. Afterward, Virginia's governor decided against an appeal on grants because the mounting number of adversarial court rulings gave "little ground for encouragement" that it would be successful.[14] The state had spent more than $20 million on grants since the program had started a decade earlier.

James J. Kilpatrick, who had begun writing a nationally syndicated column from a conservative perspective, noted that the justices essentially rejected the entire principle of "freedom of choice." After the US Supreme Court affirmed a lower court's ruling striking down Louisiana's grants, he complained the justices were too focused on the program's racist origins. He acknowledged that the grants were conceived in an effort to "maintain segregated education," but insisted lawmakers also had stumbled on a new idea, "an educational concept of great utility, novelty and promise." Grants, if administered without discrimination, could rest on the notion "that a state's valid interest in a child lies in the child's education—not necessarily in his 'public education,' but simply in his education, period."[15] His description was not unlike Friedman's. But the era of southern tuition grants was over.

Dure had devoted a decade of his life to promoting tuition grants and "freedom of choice" in numerous private letters, newspaper op-eds, and other publications. He had traveled all over the South to get laws passed. With the final judgment of the courts, his ideas were at an end. He made one last effort in 1968 to get his notion of "freedom of assembly" added to the state constitution but was rebuffed. He returned to retirement.[16]

Even as the courts began to unravel the South's grant programs, new voices were joining Milton Friedman, Virgil Blum, and Christopher Jencks to call for radical changes to America's system of public education.

In the winter of 1968, Kenneth Clark, a psychologist who was involved in the *Brown* cases, wrote in the *Harvard Educational Review* that the public schools needed "realistic, aggressive, and viable competitors." He also made a case for a broader definition of public education: "I would argue further that public education need not be identified with the present system of organization of public schools. Public education can be more broadly and pragmatically defined in terms of that form of organization and functioning of an educational system which is in the public interest."[17]

In his article, titled "Alternative Public School Systems," Clark took aim at urban schools—identifying himself as a "severe" critic of them—and said they were suffocating from "dank stagnation." The concept of neighborhood schools, too, was a "fetish." Clark, a Black man, had not lost his belief in integrated public schools as a force for good for both Black and white children. His frustration was triggered by the resistance in both the North and the South to creating meaningful school desegregation. He argued that public schools had become "captives of a middle class who have failed to use them to aid others to move into the middle class."

Clark suggested creating new types of schools outside the power of school districts, including "regional state schools" to cut across urban and suburban lines, schools run by colleges or universities that weren't restricted to the children of the faculty, and schools sponsored and paid for by the US Department of Defense, labor unions, and businesses. "With strong, efficient, and demonstrably excellent parallel systems of public schools, organized and operated on a quasi-private level . . . it would be possible to bring back into public education a vitality and dynamism which are now clearly missing," he wrote.

Unlike Friedman, Jencks, or Blum, Clark connected the goal of public education directly to eradicating racism: "Specifically, in America the goal of democratic education must be to free Americans of the blinding and atrophying shackles of racism." He also dismissed the suggestion by some within the growing Black Power movement that Black children should attend all-Black schools organized and run by Black teachers, school boards, and superintendents. (Part of this idea was to get back what had been lost in the Black community after *Brown*, when Black teachers were fired and Black students began to face increasing discipline and lowered expectations by white teachers in integrated school settings.)

Jencks, however, agreed with the idea of Black-run private schools in a lengthy piece for the *New York Times* in 1968, saying it might make sense for Black families to follow the precedent set by Catholics in the nineteenth century and create all-Black private schools outside of and parallel to the public school system.[18] Clark dismissed Black-run private schools as a "return to the pursuit of the myth of an efficient 'separate but equal'—or the pathetic wish for a separate and superior—racially organized system of education."

A few months later, Theodore Sizer, dean of Harvard University's Graduate School of Education, and Phillip Whitten, head of the education school's student association, published "A Proposal for a Poor Children's Bill of Rights," which called for tuition grants for low-income children. "What all this boils down to is that *we must discriminate in education in favor of the poor*," they wrote. (Italics are theirs.) The mechanism they proposed was not unlike Friedman's idea—a "coupon to a poor child who would carry the coupon to the school of his choice"—but in their view the grant was supplementary, a sum that had to be "large enough to motivate the school to compete for it." A sliding scale of grants could also work, they said. Like both Friedman and Jencks, they believed that competition, even between public schools, would force schools to improve and be more responsive to communities, "particularly in black urban areas."[19]

Sizer and Whitten noted that the origins for vouchers could be found over the last "two centuries" in ideas from "Adam Smith, Thomas Paine, John Stuart Mill and more recently from Milton Friedman." But much like Jencks, they largely ignored the tuition grant programs in the South, going so far as to say that a school vouchers program "has never been tried." As others had done, Sizer and Whitten dismissed concerns about the effects of such a plan on the public school system.

Unlike other advocates, Sizer and Whitten pitched their idea as part of a much broader package of policies targeting poverty, which should include "some form of guaranteed annual income and the provision for health and welfare services at a level of accommodation far higher than at present." Far from offering a savings, they said their plan would have significant costs and would expand the role of the federal government in education. It was a voucher proposal but one that was far removed from what Friedman had been championing.

IN WISCONSIN, THE Reverend Virgil Blum had watched closely the ups and downs of the Johnson administration's efforts to pass the Elementary and Secondary Education Act, as did other groups advocating for state aid to religious schools. When the legislation passed with some funds included for religious schools, his group, the Citizens for Educational Freedom, or CEF, hailed it as a victory.

At his Marquette University office in Milwaukee, Blum clipped and saved news stories about the ESEA and set aside a brochure about the Johnson administration's "war on poverty." He also watched over the next few years as more than a dozen states passed laws providing private schools, including religious ones, with textbooks, transportation, and remedial instruction.

Then, in 1968, the US Supreme Court ruled 6–3 to uphold a New York program in which all schools, including religious ones, received secular textbooks. The church-state ruling in *Board of Education vs. Allen* gave hope to advocates like Blum that other types of aid might pass constitutional muster.[20]

Blum suggested that to receive more financial support from the government, parochial schools would have to become more accountable to the public. In one letter he opined that Catholic schools would need elected school boards. In another he wrote that teacher qualifications would have to match those of the public school system and that parochial schools would need to be open to government auditing. These weren't ideas that all Catholics supported, as they would have opened their private schools to unprecedented government intrusion.[21]

Even as the tuition grant programs were being struck down in the South, Blum wrote enthusiastically about the CEF's efforts to get school voucher bills passed in Rhode Island and Michigan. He hoped Wisconsin would be next. He also mentioned in a letter that the CEF had launched a "program of information and education" in Louisiana, without pointing out that the state's tuition grant program had just been ruled unconstitutional by the US Supreme Court. Blum's interest was in aid to religious families—and Louisiana's program had been only for secular schools—but it was an odd omission. The CEF also had gone on record against voucher policies used for racial segregation. The organization filed an amicus brief in the US Supreme Court case involving Prince Edward County, Virginia, to advocate against Virginia's tuition grant program. The brief said the organization was "vitally concerned that no discrimination restrictions be placed on the use of tuition grants or tax credits."[22]

Still, some opponents of the CEF's efforts in the North worried that the grants would exacerbate segregation, and many of those opponents were from religious communities. A Methodist minister, the Reverend Dr. John M. Swomley, acted as a spokesperson for the Citizens to Advance Public Education at a meeting of the Michigan State Board of Education in the spring of 1968, saying such vouchers would create "racial and religious segregation." One of the lessons of racially segregated schools in the South was that it wasn't possible to pay equally well for two separate systems of education, he said. "The one that suffers is the one with the least political pressure. If you once adopt this legislation in Michigan, the combination of powerful church pressure plus middle-class parents who will get the tuition grants will cause the public school appropriation to suffer drastically."[23]

Despite opposition, the idea of tax support for private schools, through tax credits or tuition grants, was spreading quickly nationwide. The *Wall Street Journal* counted at least seventeen states in March 1969 with campaigns to expand state aid to private schools.

By summer, United Press International was reporting campaigns in twenty-six states. In many of those states, Catholic schools would benefit the most at a time when enrollment in those schools was declining and costs were rising. For the 1967–1968 school year, Catholic schools enrolled about 4.5 million students nationwide, a drop of about 500,000 students from the prior year, according to the *Wall Street Journal*. An assistant superintendent in the Diocese of Providence called 1968 "the most disastrous year in the history of Catholic education in the diocese." Monsignor James Donohue, a spokesperson for the United States Conference of Catholic Bishops, said the country should help Catholic schools stay in business; otherwise the public schools would be overrun by an influx of private school students. "The public has a large stake in the survival of the private education system," he said.[24]

Advocates from CEF, however, were careful not to emphasize their Catholic connections, fearing those connections would limit widespread support for tuition grants. Blum told the *Journal* the word "Catholic" wasn't on any of the literature promoting the bills. He said, perhaps a little too candidly, "Part of our job is to convince people we're not just Catholics." Their opponents weren't at all convinced. Protestants and Other Americans United for the Separation of Church and State referred to CEF as a "militant Roman Catholic Action Group." In Rhode Island, opposition emerged from other religious groups, including Protestant and Jewish ones. One Baptist minister told his congregation that the state should not consider tuition grants until it met its financial obligation to public schools.[25]

Still, much of the public support for the legislation in Rhode Island and Michigan came from Catholics. A bill for tuition grants in Michigan had failed the previous year, after Catholics wrote more than two hundred thousand letters to lawmakers, inadvertently irritating many of them. Nuns at parochial schools even instructed their students to write letters. The result was a mail jam that crippled the legislature midsession. One legislator said the "whole legislative process broke down" because staff members were sorting through the massive influx of correspondence.[26]

It was as Blum had been saying for years: Catholics could be a powerful political bloc if they wanted to be.

5

A (Failed) Federal Experiment

CHRISTOPHER JENCKS, THE PROGRESSIVE SOCIOLOGIST WHO had come out in favor of school vouchers, soon got a chance to consider how his ideas about transforming public education would work in practice. In late 1969, the US Office of Economic Opportunity requested a study on vouchers from the Massachusetts think tank where Jencks worked. The following year, Jencks and his colleagues turned in *Education Vouchers: A Report on Financing Elementary Education by Grants to Parents*. The 353-page report concluded that "some proposed voucher systems were unworkable, that some were unconstitutional, and that many would work against the interests of disadvantaged children." But some voucher models could help children from low-income families, Jencks and his colleagues argued. The report said:

> In order to deserve support from the Office of Economic Opportunity, a voucher plan should have two objectives:

—To improve the education of children, particularly disadvantaged children;

—To give parents, and particularly disadvantaged parents, more control over the kind of education their children get.[1]

This wasn't Milton Friedman's pitch for universal vouchers. This was a pitch for highly regulated vouchers for children living in poverty. The authors, who worked at the Center for the Study of Public Policy, in Cambridge, wrote that closing the gap between the advantaged and the disadvantaged was "of paramount importance"—at least in education—and suggested the country "reallocate educational resources" to help children from low-income families. They underlined the words "reallocate educational resources." They proposed a five- to eight-year trial period to test the idea. To prevent racial and economic segregation, Jencks and his colleagues concluded that the system would have to be tightly controlled. Such an idea was anathema to Friedman, who believed in the power of the free market.

By the spring of 1971, the OEO had begun to shop around for communities willing to conduct a voucher experiment. About half a dozen expressed interest, including Seattle; Gary, Indiana; New Rochelle, New York; Alum Rock, California; and San Francisco.

The *Los Angeles Times* forecast dramatic changes for the future of the American public school. "The neighborhood schoolhouse—symbol of free American public education for over 100 years—may have to make room in the 1970s for the private academy, the parochial school, and perhaps even some new form of schooling not yet invented," the story said. The newspaper conjectured that all these different types of schools, including "profit-making schools," could one day be included in a "new definition of 'public schools.'"[2]

><

AFTER MORE THAN a decade of advocating for state aid to religious schools, the Reverend Virgil Blum enjoyed a brief period in which it seemed that there was a growing political will to help America's Catholic school system. President Richard Nixon, on the campaign trail in the summer of 1971, praised Catholic schools and promised to support them. Although tuition grant legislation had failed in Wisconsin a year earlier, at least five other states, including Rhode Island, Connecticut, Pennsylvania, and New York, passed a variety of laws to support private religious schools. Legislators in New York took a three-pronged approach in 1972: tuition reimbursement for low-income families, a tax credit for more affluent families, and money for repairs and building maintenance for schools. Rhode Island and Pennsylvania agreed to use state dollars to pay a portion of teachers' salaries at private schools. All those programs could lift Catholic education at a time when one parochial school was closing per day, on average, across the country.

Whatever political momentum existed, however, ran headlong into the courts. Within a few years, the US Supreme Court issued two rulings that seemed to spell the end for state aid to religious schools. In 1971's *Lemon vs. Kurtzman*, the court ruled 8–1 against the statute in Rhode Island and 8–0 against the one in Pennsylvania. A lower court found that a quarter of elementary-age students in Rhode Island attended private schools, and the vast majority were enrolled in Catholic schools. About 250 teachers were paid through the law; all were teaching in Catholic schools. In Pennsylvania, most of the private schools benefiting from the new law also were Catholic. In an opinion for the majority, Chief Justice Warren Burger acknowledged that the contribution of church-related schools "has been and is enormous," but said the laws violated the separation of church and state established in the First Amendment because they created "excessive entanglement" between government and religion. Two years later, in *Committee for Public Education vs. Nyquist*, the court struck down New York's program in a 6–3 ruling. New York lawmakers had argued the legislation helped both the public schools and the private schools because the demise of private schools would "massively increase public school enrollment and costs, seriously jeopardizing quality education for all children." The assistance offered was "clearly secular, neutral and nonideological." The court disagreed. Whatever the intention, the effect was to help religious institutions. Justice Lewis Powell wrote, "It is precisely the function of New York's law to provide assistance to private schools, the great majority of which are sectarian."[3]

The Supreme Court also declined to review a case in Ohio in which the state court found tuition grants unconstitutional, letting the ruling stand. In Michigan, the state supreme court upheld a constitutional amendment barring state aid to religious schools, a ruling that invalidated new legislation with support for sectarian schools. The rulings were a gut punch for Blum. Newspapers ran the bad news in bold print again and again:

Parochial System Hurt by a Ruling

Parochaid Loses Again

Parochaid Ruled Illegal by High Court[4]

A month before the *Nyquist* decision came down, Blum founded the Catholic League for Religious and Civil Rights, an organization to defend Catholics against discrimination in public life. He had long believed Catholics needed to exert themselves as a united force in American politics. He had argued as early as 1955 that Catholics needed their own NAACP. Finally, he decided to found the organization himself; he felt he was witnessing anti-Catholic bias at the highest levels of government. The US Supreme Court had struck down several key forms of state aid for religious schools and earlier that year had guaranteed a woman's right to abortion in *Roe vs. Wade*. Blum felt the *Roe* ruling unfairly singled out "Catholics as virtually the only people who opposed abortion."

In a piece for the *Homiletic and Pastoral Review* in 1974, Blum unleashed his anger and indignation about the recent court rulings. He called the *Lemon* decision a "degrading insult" to Catholics that relegated them to "second-class" citizenship. He referred to the "*Lemon-Nyquist* Anti-Catholic gag rule," and he compared the court's treatment of Catholics to that of Black Americans in 1896's *Plessy vs. Ferguson*, which had codified the doctrine of "separate but equal" and was overturned by 1954's *Brown vs. Board of Education*. The only member of the court to escape Blum's wrath was Justice William Rehnquist, who had joined the court in 1972 and dissented in part of *Nyquist*. Rehnquist didn't find New York's tuition reimbursement or tax credits to be a church-state violation. Blum called his dissent "brilliant." The rulings, however, were "undemocratic, oppressive and tyrannical." The headline of Blum's piece asked, "Is the Supreme Court Anti-Catholic?"[5]

Within a couple of years, Blum would step down from the Citizens for Educational Freedom and focus his efforts on the Catholic League, hoping to convince his fellow Catholics to press harder for their rights.

Of the communities that expressed interest in the government's voucher experiment, just one committed to it. In Northern California, Alum Rock, a small town on the east side of San Jose, agreed to a limited trial run with six public schools. With a $2 million grant from the Office of Economic Opportunity, the six schools developed twenty-two "mini schools" from which parents could shop with their voucher, worth $680 per elementary child and $970 per middle school student. Children who qualified for subsidized lunch, a federal measure of poverty, received about a third more, called a "compensatory voucher," to encourage schools to compete for disadvantaged children. Mini schools ranged from those espousing a structured "back-to-basics" approach to multiage classrooms to a fine arts school. After the first year, the superintendent and the teachers' union praised the model.

There was just one problem: Alum Rock's experiment wasn't really a voucher system. No private or parochial schools were included. All the new programs were created and controlled by the school district. "The experiment here is a far cry from the Friedman model—so much so that both supporters and critics of the voucher principle contend that it is not a true test of voucher education. They say it may be seriously misleading as an example of the concept in practice at a time when districts around the country are considering voucher experiments," said a story in the *New York Times*. Alum Rock couldn't even be considered a true test of Jencks's ideas. Still, the headline in the *Times* read, "A School Voucher Experiment Rates an 'A' in Coast District."[6]

For conservatives in the Nixon administration's OEO, the Alum Rock experiment was a disappointment. They were determined to test a true Friedman-style voucher model with public, private, and religious schools. As historian Jim Carl wrote, the administration had trouble finding a suitable place for such a test: "With northern cities reluctant to adopt vouchers, southern states and school districts under desegregation orders that prohibited vouchers, and most suburbanites satisfied with their public schools, there were few options available for conservative free marketeers."[7]

They soon zeroed in on New Hampshire, a state with a conservative governor and a new dual-enrollment program that allowed students to attend both public and parochial schools at the same time. The arrangement, created several years earlier, saved the Catholic schools money and gave families flexibility to attend classes in each system. Similarly, the state allowed students in some towns to attend school in nearby Vermont, if they chose. Although Friedman preferred urban areas—reasoning that rural areas had too few schools for robust competition—New Hampshire's conservative politics and voucher-like programs seemed promising.

Friedman, still a professor at the University of Chicago, had become a conservative star. He wrote a regular column in *Newsweek*. He had been an advisor to Barry Goldwater, the far-right Republican nominee for president in 1964 who had lost in a landslide to Lyndon B. Johnson, but that didn't tarnish his image. He now was an advisor to President Nixon. In the winter of 1973, he did a lengthy and lively interview in *Playboy*. The magazine described the sixty-year-old economist as something of a paradox: some of his ideas might appeal to liberals but with a far-right twist. "Friedman's own reputation, for example, as the most original economic thinker since John Maynard Keynes is due in large part to his exhaustive criticism of the theories first set forth by Keynes." What tied all of Friedman's ideas together was his "deep and abiding belief in free enterprise."[8]

It was largely Friedman who had kept the idea of market-driven vouchers alive despite the stain of their use by segregationists in the South and the complication of recent court rulings. Other prominent voucher supporters, including Jencks, expressed serious reservations about Friedman's concept of universal vouchers. Friedman was not deterred. Six months after his interview in *Playboy*, Friedman published a lengthy article about school vouchers in the *New York Times Magazine* with a headline that read, "The Voucher Idea: Selling Schooling like Groceries." He wrote that he had "great sympathy" for the compensatory voucher, which Jencks and his colleagues supported, but he couldn't recommend it. Friedman also held out hope that the US Supreme Court might find a voucher plan favorable if it applied to all students, rather than some, and gave each student the same amount. He noted some justices viewed state aid to religious schools differently if vouchers "go to parents not to schools." If religious schools couldn't be used, he still believed a voucher system with other private schools would be superior to the public school system.[9] He was a man committed to his beliefs.

In New Hampshire, where the OEO hoped to persuade school districts to try a Friedman-style voucher experiment, the recent court rulings posed a problem. After *Nyquist*, a lower court ruled the state's dual-enrollment plan unconstitutional. The OEO couldn't include religious schools in its own experiment without running afoul of the law. But without them, the supply of private schools was far more limited.[10] Still, government officials pressed on in New Hampshire.

Many conservatives around the country eagerly backed the idea. Alum Rock was dismissed as an example of how too much regulation could ruin a good thing, but New Hampshire seemed promising to those who wanted to see a Friedman plan tried. William F. Buckley Jr., publisher of the *National Review*, wrote in his syndicated column that New Hampshire was testing "perhaps the most exciting educational experiment of the century." Referring to Alum Rock, Buckley called Jencks a "resourceful socialist" whose plan was "so heavy with qualifications as to be, in the end, not very interesting." James J. Kilpatrick, who had successfully repackaged himself as a conservative with regrets about his past segregationist views, wrote in his syndicated column that the New Hampshire plan made "great good sense." Still irritated that the US Supreme Court struck down Virginia's tuition grants, Kilpatrick wrote, "Contrary to the apprehensions of many public school superintendents, the plan did not wreck the public schools or significantly diminish their funds. Contrary to the hopes of many libertarians, relatively few parents chose to participate. But until the Supreme Court killed the plan . . . the program offered a choice." If it moved forward, New Hampshire's plan would do the same, he said. Russell Kirk, a writer whose 1953 book, *The Conservative Mind: From Burke to Eliot*, had helped revive conservatism after World War II, observed some of the opposition to the voucher pilots, even within the federal government, and asked, "Is there something wicked about competition for educational improvement?"[11]

✦

NEITHER ALUM ROCK nor New Hampshire turned out to be much of a test of what the *New York Times* called "one of the most provocative notions raised in American schooling."[12] New Hampshire didn't happen at all.

Governor Meldrim Thomson Jr., a far-right conservative, supported a voucher experiment in New Hampshire, as did the state's largest newspaper, the *Union Leader*, a right-leaning publication in Manchester. Friedman, who often spent summers in New England, promoted it. Liberal academics from the Center for the Study of Public Policy in Cambridge—Jencks's group—agreed to consult on the project. By 1976, seven school districts had agreed to participate. But the voters, who had to approve any voucher field test in their communities, balked. School vouchers were shot down in every town that put it to a vote.

Friedman and other supporters blamed strong opposition from the National Education Association and other groups. But as Carl, the historian, has noted, some voters might not have seen the use for vouchers in rural communities, especially once Catholic schools were restricted from participation.[13]

In Alum Rock, after four years and $8 million, the voucher experiment was "basically dead," a federal official said. The project had grown to include fourteen public schools and about fifty-four mini schools. But the driving forces that federal officials had expected to see—consumer choice and competition—didn't occur in any meaningful way. Teachers in the district didn't want to compete with each other, nor did they want programs to fail and close if they proved unpopular with parents. Families took advantage of many of the choices, with nearly 30 percent of children enrolling in schools outside their neighborhood, but the test had been limited from the outset. "What it brought instead, nearly everyone agrees, were some innovations in teaching, some new ways to run a school district, a little more parent interest in the schools, and a lot of paperwork," one newspaper reported.[14] The program lasted one more year before ending in 1977.

Afterward, the *Los Angeles Times* concluded the field run had showed that many parents enjoyed having choices for their children, but no revolution had occurred. The headline proclaimed, "Voucher Experiment Is Mostly Ballyhoo."[15]

※

DESPITE THE COURT rulings and setbacks in Alum Rock and New Hampshire, the idea of tax support for private education proved surprisingly resilient, and several more failed efforts kept vouchers and tax credits in the news. The *Christian Science Monitor* called it the "push that just won't quit."[16]

In New York, a small group of Black and Latino parents boycotted the 1975–1976 school year and demanded the public school system give them the per-pupil funding for private schooling. E. Babette Edwards, a spokesperson for the group, had fought for integrated schools and community control before turning to the idea of school vouchers. In a speech before state officials, Edwards said no one wanted to destroy the public school system, but Black and Latino children were not receiving an "effective public education" in New York City. "Certainly, we have the right to reject that which harms us and our children; we certainly have the right to petition our government to cease funding these failing schools and start funding our children's right to an effective education," she said. Friedman later spoke to Edwards's group. He told them that the solution to educational problems was to "give parents more power, more control over their own children's schooling"—through school vouchers.[17]

Edwards's view of school vouchers was more in line with the opinion of progressive voucher supporter Jencks. She, too, saw that vouchers could be used to empower low-income parents in large urban school districts. As historian Brittney Lewer wrote, "Edwards focused on vouchers not as past instruments of racial discrimination, but as liberatory tools for marginalized students." At the same time that Edwards pitched vouchers for Black and Latino parents in Harlem, a well-known conservative in New York City was promoting Friedman-style vouchers. Rosemary Gunning, who had led a fight against integrated schools in 1964, envisioned a program in which parents could supplement the voucher with their own funds. The result would likely be that low-income parents would still be unable to afford top private schools, Lewer noted. Two bills arose out of the women's efforts, but neither passed. Though Edwards's and Gunning's interest in vouchers didn't go anywhere, it showed how the concept could appeal to people with radically different intentions.[18]

In 1978, Senator Daniel Patrick Moynihan, a Democrat from New York, crafted a bill with Senator Bob Packwood, a Republican from Oregon, to provide tax credits up to $500 per student in private schools and universities. The bill received strong bipartisan support, with twenty-six Republicans and twenty-four Democrats as cosponsors. Moynihan said it was an idea "whose time has come." He wrote in *Harper's*, "A generation ago this was a Catholic issue. It is nothing of the sort any longer. It is an issue that reflects a broad revival of interest in religious education, an upheaval in constitutional scholarship, and a pervasive sense in American society that government has got to stop choking the life out of institutions that could be seen to compete with it." The piece was titled, "Government and the Ruin of Private Education." President Jimmy Carter, elected in 1976, had supported the idea on the campaign trail but opposed it once in office. He instead proposed a $1.2 billion program to assist college students, prompting Moynihan to wryly observe, "You have got to not want something pretty badly to be willing to spend $1.2 billion to keep from getting it."[19] Despite the bipartisan support, the legislation failed. Moynihan vowed to try again.

In 1978, two progressive law professors at the University of California, Berkeley, John E. Coons and Stephen D. Sugarman, published *Education by Choice: The Case for Family Control*, building on work they had done previously. Much like Jencks, Coons and Sugarman viewed vouchers as a mechanism for low-income families to have more control in education. The pair was known for their role in three landmark court cases—the Serrano decisions of 1971, 1976, and 1977—in which the California Supreme Court found that funding school districts primarily through local property taxes discriminated against children from property-poor communities.[20] Coons and Sugarman believed that a monopoly in public education hurt those families with the least ability to choose.

Coons and Sugarman tried to put a measure on the 1980 ballot in California that would restructure public education with a voucher model. It was a bit of a Hail Mary; they needed nearly six hundred thousand signatures to even bring it to voters. The effort drew attention to the idea, though some conservatives viewed their plan as too complicated—too much Jencks, not enough Friedman—and the teachers' unions predicted it would siphon wealthy white students from the public schools. The head of the teachers' union in Los Angeles called the idea a "cruel and vicious attempt at apartheid." The Coons-Sugarman plan ultimately went nowhere: the professors failed to get enough signatures.[21]

Before the signature drive failed, the *New York Times* asked Coons if the plan would weaken public education, as union officials said. "That suggests that the public schools are so bad that anybody with brains would get out of them. That's a funny argument by which to defend the public system," he said.[22]

Coon's argument would be echoed by other supporters of school choice for decades to come.

6

A New Type of Public School

FOR YEARS, ALBERT SHANKER VIEWED PROPOSALS FOR TAX
credits and school vouchers with concern, but so far the bills had
stalled or had been struck down by the courts. The Coons-Sugarman
effort failed in California. New York senator Daniel Patrick Moynihan's efforts to pass tax credit legislation had been held back in large
part by President Carter's opposition. But in 1981, Shanker, president
of the American Federation of Teachers, a national teachers' union, had
reason to be truly alarmed: Ronald Reagan, a conservative who supported tax credits, had been elected president. With Reagan in office,
there was no longer a veto waiting for Moynihan's bill or another like it.

Shanker believed public education upheld American democracy
by producing "an educated citizenry capable of exercising the rights of
liberty and being productive members of society." The son of Jewish
immigrants from Eastern Europe, he had learned English as a child in
New York City's public school system, as did many other immigrants
in public schools across the country. In his view, tax support for private education threatened the future of public schools. Affluent parents

could use a tax credit or school voucher to abandon public schools, allowing students to segregate in private schools based on religion, race, and class. When the *New York Times* asked Shanker in 1979 if school vouchers were a serious threat to the public school system, he had been unequivocal: "It poses the question of whether there will *be* public education in America."[1]

><

SHANKER HAD OTHER problems to worry about under a Reagan administration. Once in office, the new president didn't move on the tuition tax credit legislation waiting for him. Instead, he focused on cuts in taxes and domestic spending, including spending on elementary and secondary education. Reagan called for a 25 percent reduction in the $3 billion going to low-income students and a similar decrease in the $1 billion going to students with disabilities. Congress didn't approve nearly that much, but Reagan came back in the fall of 1981 with requests for more cuts. Newspapers ran ominous headlines. "More Cuts Slated for Education," the *Chicago Tribune* said. "Deeper Education Cuts Planned," read the *Boston Globe*. Administration officials insisted they still supported tuition tax credits, but they wanted to focus first on tax and budget cuts. John E. Chapoton, assistant treasury secretary, told a Senate subcommittee that the tax credits would be "at the top of our agenda at the appropriate time." But Moynihan predicted Reagan's domestic cuts would make it that much harder to muster support for his bill because advocates of public education would fight even harder at a time when their budgets were being slashed. The *Boston Globe* summed up where tax credits stood in 1981: "Reagan Wants Tuition Tax Credits—Later."[2]

Reagan made good on his promise, though, and a year later returned to the issue. But he did it in a way that seemed almost designed to kill the effort. First, in January 1982, he said the Internal Revenue Service couldn't deny tax exemptions to segregated private schools, a regulation that dated to the Nixon era. After a furious backlash, Reagan asked Congress to correct his mistake. Then, in the spring, he brought forward a proposal for a tuition tax credit—without a provision for the IRS to monitor private schools for racial discrimination. It seemed like Reagan was deliberately sending a message. Moynihan said he was "shaken" by Reagan's initial move in January. He and the bill's cosponsor, Republican senator Bob Packwood, called for stricter civil rights enforcement to be added to the bill. James J. Kilpatrick, the conservative columnist and voucher proponent, deemed tuition tax credits a "dead horse" and wrote wearily in his column, "Let us beat it anyhow." The episode was a bad look for the administration on a deeply controversial issue, and it generated embarrassing press coverage. In an editorial in August, the *Washington Post* said the Reagan administration needed "to choose which it wants more: a tuition tax credit bill or an endorsement of segregated private schools."[3]

During the summer, the country's other national teachers' union, the National Education Association, organized a massive protest against the tax credit proposal. When Reagan visited Los Angeles, about seven thousand teachers and their families marched through the downtown area. They chanted, "America's strength: public education." Their protest made headlines. The *Boston Globe* ran "Teachers March Against Reagan."

By the fall, Reagan's tax credit proposal had stalled. It seemed to some as if he had sabotaged it himself, a fact that couldn't have bothered Shanker.[4]

>‹

IN THE SPRING of 1983, the federal government released *A Nation at Risk: The Imperative for Educational Reform*, a report that portrayed the American school system as in crisis, its students falling behind their peers around the world. The report, commissioned by US Secretary of Education Terrel Bell, used the language of the Cold War to equate the "rising tide of mediocrity" in American schools with "an act of unthinking, unilateral educational disarmament." As political scientist Patrick J. McGuinn wrote later, Reagan had hoped the report would support his vision for education, which was to put God in the classroom, support private education with public dollars, abolish the federal education department, and leave the responsibility for children's education primarily to parents.[5]

A Nation at Risk focused its reforms on the public education system, however, with such recommendations as merit pay for teachers, raised academic expectations for students, a longer school day and year, and a guiding role for the federal government. But in a ceremony in the Rose Garden at the White House, Reagan "praised the report for its call to eliminate the education department and for its support of vouchers, tuition tax credits, and school prayer, none of which the report actually endorsed," McGuinn wrote in his book No Child Left Behind and the Transformation of Federal Education Policy, 1965–2005. The chairman of the commission said later that Reagan hadn't read the report before making his remarks. Still, tax credits and school vouchers didn't seem to be going anywhere—at least not yet. In the same year, Reagan floated a modest proposal for school vouchers for low-income children. The vouchers would be paid for with federal dollars and would be worth about $500 per student. Advocates for public education attacked the proposal, and Reagan retreated. Then, in the fall of 1983, a tuition tax credit proposal failed.[6]

As Reagan approached reelection, he used A Nation at Risk to his advantage, calling for merit pay for teachers and taking credit for a flurry of state-level reforms that both preceded and followed the report. One official in the administration said, "What this president has done is to place education at its highest level on the national agenda of any president in the last quarter of a century." The messaging proved effective and distracted from his budget cuts, which Democrats had planned to use against him. An official with the National Education

Association complained that Reagan had "pulled the political rabbit out of his hat."[7]

The US Supreme Court had offered some measure of hope to supporters of tuition tax credits with a 5–4 ruling in *Mueller vs. Allen* in 1983. The court upheld Minnesota's long-standing tax credit, which had passed in 1955 and then faced a lawsuit after lawmakers revised the statute in 1978. In an opinion for the majority, Justice William Rehnquist called the case "vitally different" from *Nyquist*, which had struck down New York's tuition reimbursement and tax credits a decade earlier. Unlike in that case, Minnesota offered benefits to parents with children in private or public schools. If any religious schools benefited, Rehnquist wrote, it was "only as a result of numerous private choices of individual parents of school-age children."[8]

The court ruling and Reagan's landslide victory in the fall of 1984 kept alive the hopes of proponents of tuition tax credits and school vouchers, as well as the fears of opponents like Shanker who saw the potential for an attack on public education.

IN MINNESOTA, DEMOCRATIC governor Rudy Perpich took seriously the message in *A Nation at Risk*. In 1985, he proposed a plan for public education called Access to Excellence, which would allow high school juniors and seniors to enroll in public and private colleges, earning both high school and college credit. He also proposed an open-enrollment system that would allow students to attend any public school in Minnesota. In both cases, the funds to pay for the student's education would follow the student to the institution of their choice. Students' movement would be hindered only if there was no room or it interfered with desegregation efforts; the latter was a concern in Minneapolis, which was under a 1972 court order to desegregate.[9]

Under Perpich's plan, the boundaries of school districts, which were often used to reinforce racial and economic segregation, would be largely meaningless. Although Perpich liked to talk about how his support for the idea of open enrollment arose when he and his wife had moved to find the right school for their children, he didn't come up with the ideas put forth in Access to Excellence. He received them from the Minnesota Business Partnership, a coalition of business executives. Ted Kolderie, a member and former longtime director of the Citizens League, a nonprofit public policy group, had bumped into Tom Triplett, a Perpich advisor, at a Citizens League meeting. "We're looking for an education program and we're not getting one," Triplett told him. The group sent him their ideas, and Perpich talked to legislators about them in a private meeting before the start of the legislative session. Connie Levi, Republican majority leader in the state house, said she would endorse the open-enrollment concept if Perpich supported postsecondary options.[10]

Access to Excellence faced stiff opposition from public school administrators and teachers. They feared public schools would lose money if high school juniors and seniors started attending college. Open enrollment could cause chaos, with some schools being forced to close if too many students fled. Marti Zins, president of the Minnesota Education Association, said the postsecondary program might not be constitutional—what if a student took their tax dollars to a religious college?—and it could open the door to paying for private education.[11]

With bipartisan support, the postsecondary options passed in 1985. Perpich was forced to retreat on open enrollment, though, after fierce opposition from within the public school system. The next year, as he faced reelection, Perpich backed off the idea again, but he asked school superintendents to consider doing it on a voluntary basis. He suggested that allowing open enrollment would hold off interest in school vouchers. "All the talk about vouchers would disappear. I think it would be one of the smartest things we could do," he said.[12]

President Ronald Reagan and his advisor, Milton Friedman, who had won the Nobel Prize for Economics in 1976, were keeping the issue of school vouchers alive. Reagan proposed another voucher plan in 1985, worth about $630 per child on average. His new, hard-charging education secretary, William Bennett, described the plan as "more far-reaching in its effect than anything we've yet proposed." The idea of "school choice"—that every student should be able to choose their school—also was getting increased attention. The National Governors Association released a report in 1986 that said choice plans "unlock the values of competition in the educational marketplace." Many of the governors, including Bill Clinton of Arkansas, a Democrat, and Lamar Alexander of Tennessee, a Republican, rejected private options but said, "Parents should have more choice in the *public* schools their children attend."[13]

After a successful reelection bid, Perpich secured a watered-down version of his open-enrollment plan, which made it voluntary for school districts. It wouldn't be long before the legislature made it mandatory. Thomas Toch, a prominent education writer, framed what Perpich achieved in Minnesota as something different than what Reagan championed. This was a marketplace within the public schools, or school choice for those who "aggressively opposed the Reagan administration's calls for vouchers and tuition tax credits as a way of fostering such competition."[14]

SHANKER, WHO HAD been head of the American Federation of Teachers since 1974, had been one of the few within the education establishment to embrace the overarching view of *A Nation at Risk*. He didn't favor all the solutions proposed in the report—he opposed merit pay for teachers and a longer school day and year, for instance—but he appreciated that the report elevated the importance of education nationwide. Shanker also felt the political winds shifting, wrote Richard Kahlenberg in his book *Tough Liberal: Albert Shanker and the Battles over Schools, Unions, Race, and Democracy*. The teachers' unions and other opponents had beaten back Reagan's proposals for school vouchers and tuition tax credits so far, but Americans' growing dissatisfaction with public schools couldn't be ignored. (Shanker noted, too, that none of Reagan's favored education policies were included in the report's recommendations.) He felt teachers needed to embrace reform before bad ideas were imposed upon them.[15]

In a speech at the National Press Club in Washington, DC, in the spring of 1988, Shanker proposed a major reform idea. He made what was an astonishing comment in light of his position as president of a national teachers' union. He said the nation's public schools were failing the majority of students, and he identified part of the problem as the uniformity of American education: "Essentially, we have one remedy, one pill, one way of reaching kids. And then we say that something is wrong with the kids if they don't respond to our remedy." He proposed a new type of school reform: Teachers, in groups of six to twelve, would be allowed to create their own school or autonomous program to experiment with novel ways to reach students who weren't succeeding. The new schools would be authorized and run under the supervision of the school district. Teachers involved in their creation would be unionized and have greater involvement in decision-making.

The model would acknowledge that "we really do not know just how to reach the 80 percent of these kids; that nobody has ever really educated all of them, and that therefore we are engaged in a search. It's a lot like trying to find a cure for the common cold, or for AIDS, or for cancer, or for a chip that we don't yet have," he said.[16] The idea was not unlike what Christopher Jencks had written more than twenty years earlier in his article "Is the Public School Obsolete?"

Shanker told his audience that two movements of education reform were underway across the country. The first and largest was the wave of accountability policies that had passed since *A Nation at Risk*. The second he described as "radical and tiny." He said it was happening in only a few places in the country, where educators were trying to "build something new" to reach the students. He pointed to New York City, where some teachers had created small "school within a school" programs to serve low-income students in Harlem. Similarly, he described the concept he was pitching as the teacher-led creation of a "different type of school."

Although the idea was similar to what Jencks had proposed years before, Shanker adapted it from a scheme described in the 1970s by Ray Budde, an education professor at the University of Massachusetts. Later, in a 1988 book, Budde expanded on his idea, suggesting that school boards could issue "educational charters" to teams of teachers to create new departments or programs. Shanker read Budde's book and also visited an "innovative teacher-led" middle and high school in Germany in 1987 in which teachers were given a great deal of flexibility.[17]

After the speech, a moderator asked Shanker if his new school model would create a "form of educational anarchy." In his response Shanker slipped into the language of the market-based reformers he disliked and said, "If there's anarchy, the customers will be gone in no time at all; so it will take care of itself." In a story in the *New York Times* that ran the day after his speech, Shanker's idea received a mixed review from the Reagan administration. William Kristol, the education secretary's chief of staff, said his department "didn't have problems" with the proposal, but "we think there is lots of evidence that traditional methods are working." The *Times*'s headline was forgettable too: "Shanker Asks Greater Autonomy for Teachers and School Officials."[18] But his pitch coincided neatly with the growing popularity of public school choice. "This would be a school of choice," Shanker told his audience.

BY THE SPRING of 1988, when Shanker made his pitch for a new type of public school, he was one of the most recognizable figures in education in the country. At age fifty-nine, he had been a union leader for about a quarter century. His efforts to get more bargaining rights for teachers in New York City had emboldened teachers' unions across the country. He was admired and reviled. He had been the punch line in a Woody Allen movie. Shanker had gone to jail to stand up for the rights of teachers, leading a teacher strike when it was illegal. But he had also opposed giving communities greater control over the public schools in New York City, where half the students were Black and Latino and most of the teachers were white. The 1968 strike he led caused widespread chaos in the country's largest school system and "stirred up racial animosity, particularly between Black parents and Jewish teachers," Kahlenberg wrote.[19]

Shanker used his national stature to draw attention to his idea for creating a new type of public school. He wrote about it in the *New York Times*, where he had a regular column that ran as a paid advertisement. In July 1988, in a piece titled "A Charter for Change," Shanker began calling the new brand of school he envisioned a "charter," a term he took from Budde. (Budde didn't know his idea had been featured in the *New York Times* until his wife told him.) The same month, Shanker pitched the proposal to three thousand delegates at the union's convention in San Francisco, winning their endorsement.[20] Then in the fall, he went to Minnesota, where he discovered that influential policy groups were already at work on a similar idea.

Perpich's efforts to transform public education had given Minnesota a growing national reputation for educational reform. The Minneapolis Foundation hosted the Itasca Seminar in the fall of 1988; the topic was public education. The seminar attracted a mix of educators, lawmakers, and businesspeople. Members of two influential groups also were in attendance: the Minnesota Business Partnership and the Citizens League. Sy Fliegel, a teacher and school superintendent, talked about efforts to turn around low-performing schools in Harlem via "school within a school" programs. Shanker talked about charter schools. He repeated his assertion that most students weren't succeeding in American public schools despite the so-called excellence movement of the preceding five years. He suggested to the group that teachers could be part of the solution by creating innovative educational methods in "charter schools."[21]

Shanker didn't know that members of the Citizens League already had spent some time thinking about how to create a new public school. The group had released a report the year before in which they had proposed "cooperatively managed schools," with greater flexibility for schools, and more power and autonomy for teachers. In exchange, teachers would then be held accountable for student achievement.[22]

Kolderie and Joe Nathan, a former teacher who had worked with the National Governors Association, were struck by some of the similarities between the Citizens League's idea and Shanker's proposal. Shanker's speech also caught the attention of Minnesota lawmaker Ember Reichgott. As vice chair of the state senate's education committee, she had sponsored the legislation that had made open enrollment mandatory for school districts. When it was time for Shanker to leave the seminar, Kolderie drove him to the airport. During the long drive, Kolderie told Shanker about the Citizens League's policy proposal, and the two men promised to keep in touch.[23]

A month later, the Citizens League released a new report, titled *Chartered Schools = Choices for Educators + Quality for All Students.* Teachers would be empowered, and the schools would be racially and economically integrated. (The report left some wiggle room for schools that were predominantly Black or Latino if the wish of the school community was to have a culturally affirming school.) But they made one detail clear: "The committee's vision for chartered public schools is that they must, like any public school, serve all children."[24]

7

"If We Do This, I Want to Win"

I N December of 1987, Annette "Polly" Williams met with Wisconsin's new Republican governor, Tommy Thompson, about an idea he was unlikely to support. Williams, a Democratic state representative, wanted to create a new school district out of the predominantly Black schools in Milwaukee's inner core, effectively ending the practice of busing Black students for school desegregation. She had taken the idea from Howard Fuller, a civil rights activist and her former classmate. Fuller wanted the city's Black residents to control their neighborhood schools, and to be given the power and money to address chronic problems of low academic achievement, discipline issues, and the troubling dropout rate among Black boys. Williams was among a small circle of political leaders in the city who were increasingly opposed to school desegregation plans that put the burden of integrating schools largely on Black families. In a poll taken in Milwaukee that year, 75 percent of Black residents in the city preferred integrated schools. But Williams believed that Black power was diminished by sending Black children out of their neighborhoods. She had been a longtime critic of busing and had held community meetings under the slogan "Integration is not education."[1]

In a manifesto he had cowritten that proposed an all-Black district, Fuller also rejected integration as a solution for the academic plight of Black children in Milwaukee. The paper began with a 1935 quote from the Black writer and activist W. E. B. Du Bois: "The Negro needs neither segregated schools nor mixed schools. What he needs is Education." The writers argued that the key difference between neighborhood schools and their proposal for a Black school district was that under their plan parents would have choice and power. The paper read, "In other words, no child would attend a school in this district if his or her parent did not make that choice. . . . For most of the parents, it would be either their first opportunity to have real power over the education of their children, and therefore, the future of their children."[2]

About eighty miles from her home in Milwaukee, at the governor's mansion in Madison, Williams made her case to Thompson. Fuller, education dean at Milwaukee Area Technical College, and George Mitchell, an educational consultant known for serving on the previous governor's education panel, also attended the meeting. The group told Thompson there were good schools serving Black and Latino students in the city's low-income neighborhoods, but they were all private schools. For many families, the schools were out of reach financially. "If those schools are doing such a good job, why not let the children attend those schools?" Thompson later recalled asking the group.[3]

Thompson, a white Republican from rural Wisconsin, had little to gain by supporting the creation of a predominantly Black school district. His Republican base was largely white and located outside Milwaukee's urban core. Democrats, who controlled the legislature, weren't likely to support the idea, even if it had been proposed by a member of their party. Williams hadn't introduced a bill yet, but she, Fuller, and other supporters were being called separatists who wanted to go back to the days of legal segregation. The NAACP had come out against the new school district, calling it "urban apartheid."[4]

Williams and Fuller had gotten some support from people who saw the unfairness of a public school system that allowed affluent parents to choose better-resourced public schools by moving to wealthier neighborhoods. Derrick Bell, a civil rights activist and law professor at Harvard University, penned an op-ed in favor of the plan in the *Milwaukee Journal*, calling it a "dramatic response to a critical situation." He wrote, "Let us be honest. Can we whose children are not required to attend inner-city schools honestly condemn the Manifesto writers and their supporters? After all, when middle-class parents— black and white—lose faith in the administration of a public school, we move to another school district or place our children in private schools."[5]

Bell's argument could be made in support of a wholly different educational reform: school vouchers. Except the concept hadn't gotten any traction. President Reagan had proposed a federal voucher program, and even some conservatives hadn't supported him. Fuller thought that vouchers were intriguing. Williams wasn't ready to give up on the idea of a school district run by Black people for Black children, and she was suspicious of Thompson, a frequent political opponent.

WILLIAMS HAD REASON to be wary of Thompson. They had little in common. Thompson had served twenty years in the legislature. As Republican minority leader he had earned the nickname "Dr. No" for consistently opposing the Democratic agenda. In the race for governor in 1986, Thompson highlighted his country upbringing. He had grown up in Elroy, a community with fewer than two thousand people, where his father owned a grocery store and his mother worked as a schoolteacher. He ran for governor on a campaign of welfare reform, dubbing Wisconsin a "welfare magnet." Williams, a divorced mother of four who had been on welfare at one time, believed Thompson's policies hurt people living in poverty.

Elected to the state assembly in 1980, Williams had served with Thompson for six years and disagreed with him about nearly everything. She often was at odds with her own party too; her focus on race made some white liberals uncomfortable. She wanted Black people to control the public institutions that shaped their lives, and she was unapologetic about it.

Williams had moved to Milwaukee when she was a young girl, after her family fled Mississippi following World War II. Like millions of Black people during the Great Migration, her family left the South looking for safety and jobs in northern cities. Her father and uncle were laborers in Milwaukee's tanneries, where the work of washing, beating, and stretching the animal flesh into leather was hard, dirty, and dangerous. Hides, shipped by train from the stockyards in Chicago, were soaked in fetid vats of urine, lime, and dung to stop them from rotting and to remove the hair and fat. A large, steaming iron pressed them into shape. Despite her father's backbreaking labor and the city's racial segregation, Williams recalled her early years in Milwaukee with fondness. A vibrant Black community lived in Bronzeville, on the north side, in the 1940s and 1950s. Williams described Walnut Street, with its cluster of Black-owned businesses, as "beautiful." It had "anything you could think of . . . beauticians, barber shops, ice cream parlors, movie theaters, churches," she said.[6]

Williams worked as a cashier, clerk, and typist to put herself through the University of Wisconsin–Milwaukee. She was well into adulthood when Milwaukee's economy began to collapse in the 1970s, even as greater numbers of Black people arrived from other northern cities and the South. She worked for several federal programs for urban cities, including an employment program and a mental health program, and she saw the despair in her community. By the time she became a state representative, many Black families in Milwaukee were worse off than they had been in her girlhood. Bronzeville had been ruined by highway construction.[7]

LIKE WILLIAMS, HOWARD Fuller had moved to Milwaukee as a small child, relocating with his mother and stepfather to the city from Shreveport, Louisiana. The family settled in a segregated, working-class neighborhood. His stepfather worked at a meatpacking plant. His mother, Juanita, found a job at a Kex factory, where she and other women washed and folded industrial towels. The job involved long hours of physical labor, with the women on their feet all day, repeatedly bending to load towels into the washers and dryers. By the end of the day, lint covered their bodies. On weekends Juanita earned extra money styling hair. In summers Fuller visited his grandmother in Shreveport, where he saw what life would have been like had the family stayed in the South. He drank from "colored" water fountains and rode in the back of the bus. As Williams had, Fuller saw some of the benefits of living in a segregated neighborhood in the North: Black people of all socioeconomic classes lived together, which provided a sense of unity and gave children from low-income families like his access to Black professionals. But Fuller harbored no romantic illusions about segregation.[8]

For preschool in Shreveport and elementary school in Milwaukee, Fuller attended Catholic schools. Donations covered his tuition. In the 1940s at St. Boniface Catholic School, on the north side of Milwaukee, Fuller was the only Black child in his third-grade class. When he grew old enough, Fuller convinced his mother to let him attend public schools with his neighborhood friends. For high school, that meant North Division High, which was 65 percent white during his freshman year. Williams was a couple of years ahead of him at North Division. When Fuller graduated in 1958, North Division had become majority Black. Five years later the high school had about thirteen hundred Black students and just eight white students.[9]

IN THE 1988 legislative session, Williams and Thompson moved forward with separate proposals. She cosponsored a bill to create the new North Division School District, named after her and Fuller's alma mater, now the area's historic Black high school. Black students would be allowed to transfer out of the new district, if they wished, and other students could transfer into it. If the legislation passed and was signed by the governor, the district would be one of Wisconsin's largest school districts, with about eight thousand students. Thompson separately announced a proposal for a school voucher program in Milwaukee, which would give one thousand low-income students the option to use tax dollars to pay for tuition at private schools, including religious ones, for a trial period of five years. Students' tuition would be paid for out of the state money that would have gone to the public schools. Jeffrey Bartzen, the governor's education advisor, said the proposal would give poor children the same choices as their wealthier classmates. Thompson included it in his proposed budget. Immediately he met with staunch opposition from public education officials, the teachers' union, the NAACP, and the American Civil Liberties Union. Bert Grover, the state superintendent of public instruction, described the proposal in one word: dead. The Freedom from Religion Foundation called the inclusion of religious schools a clear violation of the First Amendment's separation of church and state. Milwaukee's school superintendent said such a plan would degrade the public schools.[10]

Within the Black communities of Milwaukee, however, both plans generated interest. The *Milwaukee Community Journal*, the state's largest Black newspaper, wrote a small editorial in support of school vouchers and ran several articles that framed vouchers as an alternative to public schools. Mikel Holt, the paper's editor, wondered whether school vouchers would achieve the same goal as an all-Black school district. If enough students applied for vouchers, it could create a separate school system of sorts, he wrote. Williams remained skeptical about the governor's intentions. Fuller, who recalled the value of his early Catholic education, offered public support. When asked by a reporter what he thought of Thompson's proposal, he echoed the governor's advisor: "It's giving poor parents the option that people with money already have, and that is voting with their feet and taking their resources with them."[11] In an article about the plan, *Education Week* described it as similar to President Reagan's last voucher proposal.

Both Thompson and Williams suffered stinging defeats when the legislative session started. Democrats removed Thompson's proposal from the budget without discussion. Williams's bill made it out of the state assembly, a surprise in its own right, but it died in the senate.

THOMPSON DIDN'T STOP working on his school voucher plan. He asked another education advisor, Tom Fonfara, to put together a coalition of supporters to craft a plan that might stand a chance in a Democratic-controlled legislature. Thompson also reached out to the new superintendent of Milwaukee Public Schools, Robert Peterkin, the city's first Black schools leader. Peterkin had come from the public school system in Cambridge, Massachusetts, which had a "controlled choice" plan to integrate schools. Controlled choice gave parents the ability to rank their top picks for schools, and then the school system ensured that student assignments reflected the district's overall racial demographics. One of Peterkin's first moves as superintendent in Milwaukee had been to invite a professor from Harvard to study how the city could lessen the effects of busing on Black students. Thompson suggested to Peterkin that there was some precedent for school vouchers in the city: MPS already contracted with private, nonreligious schools to enroll about 350 "at-risk" students. What Thompson wanted, however, didn't appeal to Peterkin, and the superintendent began drafting his own separate proposal.[12]

As historian Jim Carl wrote, Thompson continued to court Williams's support, inviting her to an education workshop at the White House in January 1989, where he planned to leak details of his latest voucher proposal. This time he would leave out religious schools. His advisors thought he had a better chance of getting a small pilot program passed if they sidestepped some of the trickier legal questions, at least initially. Thompson believed he could expand the program later.

At the White House, Thompson told a small audience about his new plan, which would allow low-income children from kindergarten to sixth grade to attend any public or nonreligious private school in Milwaukee County. He said his proposal was "designed to help" the public school system. A member of the audience asked why Thompson had backed off the inclusion of religious schools. "Why not include religious?" he said, repeating the question. Because "I want to win."[13] At the conference, Williams listened but didn't offer her support. She told participants about one of her ideas, which would require the Milwaukee school district to get parental consent before busing children out of their neighborhoods.

Back in Wisconsin, Thompson started to market the broader idea of "school choice," with the support of the Lynde and Harry Bradley Foundation, the country's largest conservative philanthropic organization. Carl wrote that the foundation was forbidden from any "attempt to influence any national, state or local legislation" in order to keep its tax-exempt status, but under its president, Michael Joyce, a Republican who had worked for Reagan, the foundation began pushing school vouchers. In a survey created that spring by the Wisconsin Policy Research Institute, which was funded by the Bradley Foundation, 59 percent of Milwaukee residents expressed support for a state-funded voucher program. Pollsters asked this question: "Many people believe that poor children in urban areas are having problems in the public schools. One idea to improve their educational opportunities is for the state to give tax money to poor parents and allow them to choose which public, private, or parochial school to send their child to. This idea would not cost more than current public education. Would you like to see this idea adopted in Wisconsin?"[14]

Thompson's staffers also organized a conference about educational reform at the Milwaukee Area Technical College in March, drawing more than four hundred people. Fuller agreed to participate. At the event, Walter Farrell, an education professor at the University of Wisconsin–Milwaukee, challenged Fuller on vouchers. Fuller said that school vouchers could empower Black parents. Farrell countered that vouchers wouldn't solve the larger problem, which was the poor quality of education received by Black students in Milwaukee. Afterward, Felmers Chaney, president of the Milwaukee branch of the NAACP, expressed serious doubts about vouchers and their white conservative supporters, saying the "whole idea smacks of racism." He added, "And if the Republicans are for it, that's what it is."[15]

Thompson included his new proposal for school vouchers in the 1989 state budget. As in the previous year, Democrats cut it out of the budget without discussion. If the governor wanted to pass a school voucher program, it looked as though it would have to be in partnership with MPS.

⇥⇤

PETERKIN, THE NEW superintendent of MPS, had been meeting with representatives from the city's prominent nonreligious private schools. Urban Day School, Bruce-Guadalupe Community School, Highland Community School, Harambee Community School, and others had opened in Milwaukee during the upheaval of the 1960s and 1970s, as white families fled the city for suburbs. Black and Latino education advocates pushed to open new private schools where predominantly white private schools had closed. Those schools that survived became alternatives for middle-class Black and Latino students who didn't want to attend the city's public schools, Carl wrote. For a couple of the private schools, staying afloat financially was a constant struggle. Bruce-Guadalupe and Highland were near bankruptcy when Peterkin approached them. Some of their leaders were interested in partnering with the school district—not only to stay solvent but, in the case of Urban Day, to expand.[16]

Peterkin and some school board members saw it as an opportunity to get control of a program that represented a threat to the public school system, and the proposal his staff came back with was off-putting to some private school leaders. It called for MPS to contract with five to seven private schools to enroll up to a thousand low-income students who were considered "at risk" because of their academic or behavioral records. The private schools would have to prove that the children they accepted were progressing one grade level each year.[17] MPS would pay for a voucher worth 80 percent of its per-student funding and keep the remaining 20 percent as an administrative fee. A district director described the private schools as operating like an "extension" of the public schools. Peterkin called the proposal "Milwaukee Choice." Thomas Seery, a Democratic state representative, agreed to sponsor the bill. But some of the private schools feared they would become de facto satellite public schools under the legislation and withdrew their support.

Williams viewed the proposal as a way for the school system to dump its neediest children on private schools and get paid for it at the same time. When she learned that Thompson would support Seery's bill, she moved quickly to come up with her own version—with important changes. She removed MPS altogether. There would be no oversight role for the school district and no administrative fee. To be eligible for a school voucher under her plan, students only had to qualify as low income. Suddenly there were two school voucher bills sponsored by Democrats, a surprising turn of events. On July 5, 1989, the dueling bills reached the floor of the state assembly. Both bills were voted down, but Williams lost by a narrower margin. Some of Seery's Black supporters accused her of splitting the vote.[18]

Furious, Williams called Holt, the newspaper editor, and told him that some of the private school leaders had asked her after the vote to try again to pass her version of the bill. She wasn't sure what to do. She had tried and failed repeatedly to force change on MPS. Even as her voucher bill was voted down, Williams had succeeded in getting another bill passed, which would end busing for desegregation in Milwaukee. She had been triumphant, only to watch the senate reject her bill in committee. School vouchers were starting to seem like a viable experiment, one guaranteed to put pressure on the public schools. But she didn't want to be on the losing end of another vote.

"If we do this, I want to win," she told Holt.[19]

8

"Let Education Be the Focus"

G OVERNOR TOMMY THOMPSON STOOD IN FRONT OF SEVERAL
hundred people at a historic hotel in downtown Milwaukee, not
far from Lake Michigan. "Don't let me or my party be the focus. Let
education be the focus," he said. Thompson said Black children living
in poverty in the city deserved the same educational opportunities as
affluent white children living in the suburbs—and that was the goal of
the latest voucher bill crafted by State Representative Polly Williams.
In another year, Thompson's appearance at the conference for the Black
Women's Network, one of the most influential Black organizations in
Milwaukee, might have been considered strange. Thompson was hardly
a popular political figure in Black communities in Wisconsin. Many of
his social welfare policies were viewed as punitive, and they targeted
Milwaukee while exempting rural and largely white areas of the state.
When he ran for governor in 1986, Thompson received just 8 percent
of the Black vote in Milwaukee.[1] Yet here he was, four years later, lob-
bying for Black residents' support for a new school voucher bill for the
city's low-income children.

Both Thompson and Williams were determined to win this latest legislative battle, each for different reasons. Williams had grown frustrated with members of her own party and was open to what she considered an educational experiment. Thompson wanted Wisconsin to develop a national reputation for education reform, much like its neighbor, Minnesota, had. Unlike Minnesota, however, where Democratic governor Rudy Perpich had focused on creating more competition and choices within the public school system, Thompson was walking into a political hornets' nest with a voucher proposal. His advisors warned him that Reagan's pursuit of vouchers and tuition tax credits had largely backfired, forcing the president to back down. President George H. W. Bush, who took office in January 1989, hadn't shown the same interest in the issue as his predecessor. During his campaign, Bush adopted a gentler tone on education and declared his intention to be the nation's "education president." He said he didn't support public dollars for private education. Thompson knew he needed a broader base of support in Milwaukee. His effort to build a coalition with the Milwaukee school district had failed. This time he would align with Williams and rely on her to secure backing among Black families and Black political leaders in Milwaukee. Williams didn't agree with Thompson on much, but she was a shrewd and experienced politician. At an event in 1990 she explained her political philosophy: "If you're drowning and a hand is extended to you, you don't ask if the hand is attached to a Democrat or a Republican. From the African American position—at the bottom, looking up—there's not much difference between the Democrats and the Republicans anyway. Whoever is sincere about working with us, our door is open."[2]

To pass a voucher bill, Williams needed fifty of the ninety-nine legislators in the assembly to vote in favor. Thompson could bring Republicans on board in both chambers, but Williams would also need the support of several key Black Democratic politicians, some of whom already had made their opposition to vouchers known. In particular, she needed State Senator Gary George, who was the head of a critical committee.[3] She knew it was an uphill fight. But in some ways, this was the perfect moment and the perfect city in which to pursue a school voucher program.

MILWAUKEE, LIKE OTHER Midwestern cities in the years following World War II, became a destination for Black families fleeing the brutal racial oppression in the South. Williams's family found refuge there, as did Howard Fuller's. But Black families soon learned that Milwaukee had its own problems with racial discrimination. As the Black population grew, Milwaukee Public Schools tried to contain Black students within their own neighborhood schools, which led to overcrowding and segregation. Even as white families fled the city for the suburbs, the school district continued building new schools in white neighborhoods and upgrading existing facilities for white students. As the schools in Black neighborhoods became old and run-down, district leaders resisted changing school boundaries or building new schools.[4]

Historian Bill Dahlk wrote that the neglect to predominantly Black schools became obvious over time. Black schools were older and had inadequate teaching materials and equipment. By the early 1960s, elementary schools that enrolled predominantly Black students were seventy-two years old, on average, while the elementary schools with white students were thirty-three years old, on average. Instead of building new schools in Black neighborhoods, district leaders remodeled basements and storage rooms to create additional classrooms, according to Dahlk. When students had to be moved because of construction, officials would bus an entire class of Black students to a white school, where Black students would have access to a single classroom. To keep the students separate from the white children on campus, the city would bus the Black students back to their own school for lunch and recess. (Some white classes also were bused, though they were sent

to white schools.)[5] Despite opposition from Black families, district officials continued the practice until 1971. In the face of such blatantly
racist practices, district officials insisted segregated schools were simply
the natural result of housing patterns.

Black civil rights activists, who fought for desegregation of the city's
public schools in the 1960s and 1970s, shared the same vision—a better education for Black children—but they didn't necessarily agree on
how to achieve their goal. Some didn't care about the demographics of
a school's student body. They wanted Black schools to have more Black
teachers, compensatory programs, and increased academic expectations. Others believed equality could only be found in integrated school
settings. Lloyd Barbee, a lawyer who was a key player in Milwaukee's
desegregation battles, believed that improved facilities and education
weren't enough if schools remained segregated. "Upgrading of courses
or hiring of more teachers is the old Southern doctrine of 'separate but
equal,'" he said.[6]

In 1976, a federal judge ruled that MPS had deliberately maintained a segregated school system. He noted that of sixty-three board
decisions involving boundary changes, only one had resulted in more
integration. He ordered district officials to desegregate schools. By
then, Milwaukee's school system had become one of the most racially
segregated in the North. More than 100 of its 158 schools had a student body that was 90 percent one race. To solve the problem, the
superintendent thought he could convince white families to mix volun-
tarily, primarily by converting existing schools to magnet schools with
appealing academic programs.[7]

State leaders created a program in 1976 called Chapter 220 in
which white suburban schools would be paid to enroll small numbers
of Black students from the city; suburban students also could enroll in
Milwaukee's public schools. The voluntary program did little to desegregate Milwaukee's public schools. The US Supreme Court had ruled
a couple of years earlier, in *Milliken vs. Bradley*, that school districts

weren't responsible for segregation across district lines, effectively limiting many metropolitan areas from meaningful integration.[8] In other words, the suburban school districts, to which so many of Milwaukee's white families had fled, had no legal obligation to address school segregation in the city.

Milwaukee's district officials put the burden of desegregation on Black families, closing some predominantly Black neighborhood schools. New magnet schools resulted in fewer choices for Black students because most of the seats were reserved for white children. Black students were forced to travel to predominantly white schools in other parts of the city. Larry Harwell, a community organizer who would later work for Williams, created a group called Blacks for Two-Way Integration to draw attention to the issue. The city's school superintendent, Lee McMurrin, didn't see the problem: "Is it a burden to ride the bus to better facilities? Is it a burden to seek better opportunities?"[9] Despite continuing inequities, the message seemed to be that Black families should be grateful.

Even as civil rights activists fought the city over school desegregation, a small number of independent private schools opened to serve Black and Latino students. Some had been Catholic schools that were now nearly empty because of white flight. Urban Day, Harambee, and Martin Luther King Community School were predominantly Black; Bruce-Guadalupe was primarily Latino. The schools built a reputation for educational excellence, and many middle-class Black and Latino families enrolled their children in them.

By the mid-1980s, Milwaukee was a changed city. It had remained majority white, but its public schools had not. Critics of the school district, including Howard Fuller, pushed for transparency about Black student achievement in the public schools. As Dahlk wrote, Democratic governor Anthony Earl created a commission in 1984 to study academic achievement in MPS and the surrounding suburban districts. A year later, the results came out, and they were damaging to MPS.

Students in suburban schools were, on average, outperforming students in the city's public schools on standardized tests, grade-point average, and completion of courses. The district's dropout rate was five to six times higher than the rate in most of the suburban districts and was increasing in grades seven to nine. For critics of desegregation policies, one statistic jumped out: the dropout rate for Black students was highest in the most integrated schools.[10] What good was integration if it wasn't helping Black students?

Some researchers disagreed, however, about the role that poverty played in the results. Students in the district's magnet schools were generally on par with students in suburban schools, and both sets of schools enrolled more affluent students than Milwaukee's neighborhood schools. One commission member said, "The suburban schools are not successful because they somehow give a better education or function more efficiently. They simply have fewer poor children." Other commission members argued that poverty could be blamed for only a small degree of the difference in results.

Regardless, the commission's report gave fuel to critics, particularly after test scores released the following year showed that the gap between white and Black students had grown. Fuller told a newspaper reporter the results were tragic. "Now may be the time to talk about doing something totally different," he said.[11]

By the time Thompson and Williams proposed a school voucher program, Black families in Milwaukee already had a long tradition of looking for alternatives to the city's neighborhood schools, though their flight had garnered less attention than that of white families. Those who could sent their children to magnet schools, independent schools, and suburban public schools through the state's Chapter 220 program, which allowed Black students to attend predominantly white schools in the suburbs.

Williams had been one of the parents looking for options. She sent her children to Urban Day School, which enrolled students in kindergarten through eighth grade. To help pay their tuition, Williams did administrative work for the school. Later, she fought for her children to attend an integrated public high school, hoping it would guarantee them a better education. Initially she was told no, the school's racial quota had been met. She never forgot the rejection.[12]

>‹

WILLIAMS AND HER aide, Larry Harwell, relied on Milwaukee's independent schools to build a network of supporters for the school voucher bill. This time, vouchers wouldn't be framed as a conservative issue or Thompson's pet issue. This wasn't about Milton Friedman. Williams cared little about the free market, and Howard Fuller hadn't heard of the economist when they started the campaign. The issue, as Williams and Fuller saw it, was this: Black students in Milwaukee, particularly low-income children, weren't getting a good education in the city's public schools. School vouchers could help some of them escape low-performing schools, and in doing so could push the school district to make broader changes.

Often working out of the offices at the private Urban Day School, Williams and Harwell created a phone tree to spread the word about the latest developments. Mikel Holt covered the issue extensively in his newspaper, the *Milwaukee Community Journal*. As he wrote later, the group had "weekly training sessions . . . briefings, strategy meetings, and work assignments." He noted how Williams made sure to get the concept of "school choice" into greater circulation in the Milwaukee area through events and conferences: "Not a week went by without a voice proclaiming support for school choice." One of the most prominent examples was the Black Women's Network Conference, which that year was titled Parental Choice: Making Choices in the 1990s. Holt wrote that Thompson's speech at the event guaranteed media coverage while making it clear that "choice" had support from prominent members of Milwaukee's Black communities.[13]

Before Williams backed the voucher concept, the Bradley Foundation had sponsored an education conference in Madison in 1988. At
the event, an assistant secretary for education in the US Department of
Education said the cry for "freedom of choice" was coming from the "nation's poorest students." At that moment, the cry for choice was largely
coming from far-right conservatives. Now, with Williams pushing the
issue in Milwaukee, that had changed.[14]

><

WILLIAMS'S SCHOOL VOUCHER bill had been held up in committee, a
strategy designed to kill legislation without the inconvenience of noisy
opposition. A member of Williams's party, State Representative Barbara Notestein, had the power to release the bill for a public hearing,
but she was waiting for MPS to create its own proposal, as it had done
previously.

Williams's allies soon convinced Notestein to move on the issue. At
a rally held at a church, Mikel Holt compared Notestein to Bull Connor,
the southern segregationist who had set fire hoses and police dogs on
Black men, women, and children protesting for civil rights in Birmingham three decades before. Holt asked in an editorial whether any of the
"so-called liberal politicians" wanted to give Black people a way out of
their "enslavement." Notestein scheduled a public hearing on a weekday
morning at the administration building for Milwaukee Public Schools.
(Notestein later said she wasn't responding to public pressure; she was
asked to schedule the bill by then Speaker Tom Loftus.) Using their
phone tree, Williams's volunteers mobilized parents and other supporters to attend and arranged transportation for those who needed it. The
bill, altered somewhat from its original version, cleared the committee
on a 7–6 vote. A headline in Holt's newspaper proclaimed, "Lawmakers
Bombarded with Support for Choice Proposal."[15]

When the bill reached the state assembly in the spring of 1990,
Williams and her allies made sure that about two hundred Black par-

ents, children, and community leaders were in the state capitol to show their support. She believed that lawmakers whose jurisdictions weren't affected by the bill might be persuaded when faced with children and parents. When the bill passed out of the state assembly, Williams called it a "truly historic occasion"—but she had come this far with other bills only to see them fail in the senate.[16]

One key difference this time was that Williams had a groundswell of support, including nearly all the state's Black legislators. State Senator Gary George now supported the bill, as did Jared Johnson, a Black school board member in Milwaukee and a graduate of a Catholic high school. Milwaukee mayor John Norquist, a white conservative Democrat, had thrown his support behind it. Williams's unlikely political alliance with Thompson had grown to include Black Democrats, some key conservative white Democrats, and a lot of Republicans; the alliance had the financial and political backing of the influential Bradley Foundation. A small but committed group of Black parents in Milwaukee supported the legislation too.

Thompson had outgunned some of the opposition. He persuaded the state teachers' union, the Wisconsin Education Association Council, to drop its opposition by promising not to use his line-item veto power to expand the program if it passed. That assuaged concerns that Thompson might extend the program beyond Milwaukee. MPS superintendent Robert Peterkin had released a counterproposal—again taken up by Democratic representative Thomas Seery—but it was introduced too late for serious consideration.

Of the supporters Williams and Thompson had won over to their side, George became the most important when the proposal reached the state senate. George cochaired the powerful joint finance committee. Some of George's colleagues in the senate made it clear the legislation would be dead on arrival if it came as a stand-alone bill. Trying to save it, George attached it to the budget bill. Other senators then watered down the provision with amendments, including one stipulating that

children already enrolled in private schools were ineligible for the program. It was a major blow to many supporters who either worked for
or had children enrolled in Milwaukee's independent schools. (Within
days, the Bradley Foundation would donate $2 million for private
scholarships to families affected by the amendment.)[17]

Williams was sure the provision could be changed after the program started, but she feared that if the legislation failed now, it wouldn't
be resurrected. Thompson had failed three times before. She had failed
once. This version had the most community support and the most legislative support. It had momentum and less than expected opposition.
The time was now. She gave George her blessing to broker whatever
deals he needed to make to ensure its passage. On March 22, 1990,
the budget bill, with the country's first modern school choice program
buried inside, passed.[18]

Ten days later, Williams told the *Chicago Tribune* that she had taken
"an elitist concept and remold[ed] it so that low-income students of
color could benefit." Williams's view of school vouchers as a tool to up-
lift disadvantaged students of color was largely in line with that of early
progressive supporters, like Christopher Jencks, Theodore Sizer, and
John Coons, who had called for vouchers for poor children in the 1960s
and 1970s. It was not, however, a view shared by longtime voucher
advocate Milton Friedman, who liked to say that he viewed any program specifically for the poor as a "poor program."[19]

9

"The Unholy Alliance"

IN THE SPRING OF 1990, CLINT BOLICK SPOTTED A SHORT ITEM buried in the B section of the *Washington Times*. The headline read, "Plan Will Send Kids to Private Schools." Dateline: Milwaukee. With interest, Bolick read, "Gov. Tommy Thompson plans to sign a first-of-its-kind bill that would let 1,000 low-income Milwaukee students use public education funds to enroll in private schools. . . . The amount spent would be subtracted from the budget for the city's public schools, which have nearly 100,000 students."[1]

This was exactly what Bolick had been waiting for. Young, idealistic, and conservative, Bolick had come to Washington, DC, two years earlier to open a branch of the Landmark Legal Foundation, a conservative public interest law firm, with start-up money from the Bradley Foundation. It was a one-man operation in the basement of a townhouse near the US Supreme Court. He didn't have filing cabinets or an assistant. In his first week, the basement flooded. Still, for a then thirty-year-old attorney hoping to practice law in the nation's capital, it was a dream.

His first case had been a surprising success. Ego Brown, an entre-preneur and shoeshine man in Washington, was known for two things: he shined shoes in a tuxedo and he employed homeless men. By the mid-1980s, he ran shoeshine stands on four street corners, earning about a hundred dollars a day. An "Ego Shine" cost five dollars. Then the city's police officers arrested him.

Bolick, who read about the arrest in the newspaper, thought Brown's predicament had the makings of a great lawsuit, one that ex-emplified Bolick's libertarian ideals and the types of cases he wanted to pursue. Here was Brown, a successful businessman, and yet he had been regulated nearly out of operation. Unlike other street vendors who sold hot dogs or tourist merchandise, bootblacks were prohibited from operating on public streets. Shoeshine stands were the only street vendors banned, courtesy of a law passed in 1905. After his arrest, Brown took his business indoors, into barber shops and law offices, but the move reduced his income to the point that he could no longer support himself or employ others.[2]

Bolick found Brown at one of his indoor shoeshine stands and offered to work the case for free. He argued that the 1905 statute was a relic of the Jim Crow era, enacted at a time when most shoeshine operators were Black. It turned out to be an easy win. The district judge in 1989 ruled the law unconstitutional. Bolick was ecstatic, and the case received widespread media attention. Brown's triumph—and Bolick's—made ABC's *World News Tonight*. Anchor Peter Jennings closed his segment with these words about Brown: "He's made us all a little bit freer." The case, the media attention—they were everything Bolick had hoped for.

Nearly a year later, he saw the story about Milwaukee's new school voucher program in the *Washington Times*. It had been more than three decades since Milton Friedman had written "The Role of Government in Education." Southern segregationists had enacted voucher programs to dodge *Brown vs. Board*. Conservative and liberal advocates had toyed with different models. But not since Alum Rock had anyone created an actual on-the-ground voucher program, and for conservatives, Alum Rock hardly counted. For Bolick, it was a thrilling, historic moment—and it was sure to be followed by a lawsuit, one that would put what was among the most controversial concepts in the history of American education into the court system. He desperately wanted to be part of the action.

Except Polly Williams wanted nothing to do with Bolick. He called. She ignored him. Finally, he found an intermediary to reach out to Williams on his behalf and got her on the phone. He asked if she was ready for the lawsuit. "What lawsuit?" she responded.[3]

It was an inauspicious start. Bolick flew to Milwaukee to meet with Williams and her legislative aide, Larry Harwell. Neither seemed impressed by him, a white, conservative lawyer from Washington, DC, with outsize ambitions that had nothing to do with Milwaukee. Harwell questioned Bolick for two hours, took him on a tour of the neighborhood, and then sent him back to Washington to wait.

ON APRIL 27, 1990, Governor Tommy Thompson signed the law creating the Milwaukee Parental Choice Program. He made one final change to the bill: using his line-item veto, Thompson crossed out the provision that would have made the program a five-year pilot. As promised, he had not expanded the program, but now it had no sunset. For Thompson, an ambitious Republican governor, it was a triumph: Wisconsin had the country's first modern school voucher program. President George H. W. Bush called it "one of the most interesting experiments in educational reform in the country." Williams said Milwaukee's vouchers would empower low-income families, and she had fiery words for the city's public schools: "If you all are worried about your jobs, try doing them better."[4]

A month later, five organizations, including the teachers' unions, filed suit against the program. They were soon joined by the Milwaukee branch of the NAACP. They attacked the program on multiple grounds. It violated the uniformity clause of the state constitution by giving public dollars to private schools. (The constitution called for a system of uniform and tuition-free public schools.) It violated the public purpose doctrine, which requires accountability for public money. And it violated a provision in state law that called for some legislation to be considered as a stand-alone bill.[5]

With the NAACP on one side and Williams, a Black nationalist, on the other, racial politics loomed over the litigation. Felmers Chaney, president of the Milwaukee chapter of the NAACP, said vouchers were reminiscent of the "freedom of choice" plans in the South that were designed to prevent school desegregation. He said he was "a little shocked" by the alliance of Black Democrats and white Republicans that had formed to pass the program. He also didn't believe that conservatives intended to keep the program small. "I'm willing to wager that if it goes through and we can't stop it . . . in another year they will expand it to another 1,000 students and they'll keep expanding it," he said. Williams, in characteristic fashion, said she wasn't an "integrationist," and "I don't chase after white people." She didn't care who embraced the voucher model. "I think it's time that black people begin to look out for ourselves. It doesn't matter if conservative racists and bigots have the same idea." A headline in the *Los Angeles Times* read, "Milwaukee School Choice Proposal Ignites Bitter Racial, Political Battles." Williams would later refer to the coalition she had made with Thompson as the "unholy alliance."[6]

The legal landscape also got ugly fast. Bert Grover, the state's superintendent of schools, had been a vocal opponent of the legislation. Now Grover had regulatory authority over a program he loathed. He immediately added regulations to address what he considered some of the program's biggest flaws. To participate and receive taxpayer dollars,

private schools would need to comply with state rules for teacher certification, testing, and evaluation, as well as for due process for employees, and would have to provide services for children with disabilities.
Private school operators, who were incensed by the new regulations,
sued Grover in late June.[7]

With a few months before the start of the new school year, legal
challenges seemed to be coming from all sides. Private schools wouldn't
commit to offering the vouchers if the new regulations stood, and some
families didn't want to sign on to a program that could end at any time.
It was a mess and about to get messier—but Bolick had a case.

ONE LONG-STANDING SCHOOL voucher advocate didn't live long
enough to see Milwaukee's program enacted. The Reverend Virgil Blum
died of cancer in April 1990 at age seventy-seven, just weeks before
Thompson signed the legislation into law. But in his final years, Blum
had observed the developments in Minnesota and Wisconsin with cus-
tomary irritation. Three decades had passed since he had written his
book, *Freedom of Choice in Education*, and yet none of the latest efforts
to expand parental choice addressed what he felt was the heart of the
issue: religious freedom.

In a 1989 piece for a Catholic newspaper, Blum wrote, "Everybody,
it seems, is talking about parental choice of schools. . . . Yet President
Bush, Governors Perpich and Thompson and other 'choice' advocates
would violate the religious freedom rights of parents in the education of their children." Blum's focus had been on state aid for religious
schools for so long that he couldn't conceive of school choice without it
or see Milwaukee's program as a stepping stone. The title of his article
was "'Choice' Education Programs Suppress Rights of Parents."[8] It was
classic Blum, irascible and wholeheartedly committed to his beliefs.

Blum used his approaching death to raise money for the Catholic
League, the founding of which he viewed as among his most important

life's work. He wrote a letter to supporters in which he quoted scripture: "I am already being poured out like a libation, and the time of my departure is at hand. I have competed well; I have finished the race; I have kept the faith." The words "have seemed especially meaningful to me in these past few weeks as I reflected on my final days with the Catholic League," he wrote.[9]

An official at Marquette University, where Blum had taught for many years before his retirement, said the priest's politics "perfectly reflected his integral view of a faith which must in part manifest itself in work for the common good."[10]

BOLICK HAD A knack for publicity and an innate understanding of how important public opinion could be in the sometimes dry matters of law and public policy. He naturally looked for the story he could tell—to the media, to the judge, to the public—and he was shameless about promoting whatever angle helped his case. He saw the potential to make the issue about civil rights, as school vouchers in Milwaukee would largely go to low-income Black and Latino students, and he identified an enemy in Grover, the state's vocal school superintendent. He called John Fund, a friend from college who worked as an opinion writer at the *Wall Street Journal*, and encouraged him to write about the case. In late June, the newspaper ran an editorial comparing Grover to Southern segregationists "blocking the schoolhouse door" against Black children in Milwaukee.[11] The attack accomplished both Bolick's goals. Grover toned down his public comments about school vouchers, and the *Wall Street Journal*, a national newspaper, linked the concept of school choice to the civil rights movement. Bolick's strategy, though also employed by Mikel Holt, the newspaper editor in Milwaukee, didn't sit well with some voucher proponents. Howard Fuller, who had fought for civil rights in the South, thought Bolick risked alienating civil rights activists by co-opting their struggle. School choice had to stand on its own merits or not at all, he argued. It was an argument that would continue for years to come.

To defend the Milwaukee Parental Choice Program in court, Bolick first had to involve himself in the case. Technically, it was the state's job to defend its program against the lawsuit. Because Bolick was not admitted to practice law in the jurisdiction, he needed a local attorney to vouch for him. He also thought it was crucial for families to be directly involved in the lawsuit. He retained Anne Sulton, a lawyer for the Madison chapter of the NAACP. He wanted Sulton in particular because she was Black, a requirement of Williams's, and Sulton's affiliation with the NAACP mitigated the effect of having the Milwaukee branch of the NAACP named as a plaintiff on the lawsuit. Then Bolick filed a complaint against Grover's regulations, with a motion to intervene in the union's lawsuit as defendants. He also pushed for the new voucher program to start before the cases appeared in court, reasoning that it would be harder for a judge to pull students from their new schools.[12] Both cases, one from the teachers' unions seeking to overturn the new program and one from parents against Grover's regulations, would be heard by the same judge in circuit court on July 28, 1990.

Bolick started to prepare arguments for the most important case of his life to date, one that could shape the future of American education.

IN THE SUMMER of 1990, as the Milwaukee Parental Choice Program faced its first legal challenges, a new book came out that argued America's schools were failing its children. The authors proposed a radical theory of school reform. A passage in the foreword to *Politics, Markets, and America's Schools* reads:

> By most accounts, the American education system is not working well. Children appear to be learning less in school today than they did a generation ago. Some 25 percent of the nation's high school

students drop out before graduating, and in large cities—whose poor and minority children desperately need a quality education—the figure can climb to 50 percent. . . . More troubling still, these problems have stubbornly resisted determined efforts to solve them. During the last quarter century, successive waves of education reform have swept the country—most recently in the wake of publication of *A Nation at Risk*—but, as a new century approaches, there are few signs of real progress. How can government work so hard to improve schools yet make so little progress? In this book, John E. Chubb and Terry M. Moe argue that government has not solved the education problem because government is the problem.[13]

Political scientists Chubb and Moe argued that the country's "existing system of public education" was inherently flawed. Individual schools performed better, they contended, when they have "clear goals, an ambitious academic program, strong educational leadership, and high levels of teacher professionalism"—characteristics they believed were more common in private schools than public. The authors argued that the school autonomy necessary to create those characteristics was undermined by the public school system itself, which was steeped in bureaucratic control. Only school choice had the ability "all by itself" to bring about the kind of transformation Chubb and Moe deemed necessary. "Taken seriously, choice is not a system-preserving reform. It is a revolutionary reform that introduces a new system of public education," they wrote. The book provided voucher proponents with a compelling new argument: school choice wasn't just an escape for low-income students from low-performing schools; it was a method of systemic reform for the nation's public schools.

Chubb and Moe pointed out that their proposal didn't require the inclusion of private schools or vouchers. They acknowledged that vouchers were considered by the educational community to be the "embodiment of everything that is threatening to public education."

Yet their proposed solution was essentially to dismantle public education, transforming public schools into de facto private schools with "minimal" criteria for operation (and that would still be called "public" schools). Religious schools could participate if they kept their "sectarian functions" separate "from their educational functions."

Chubb and Moe believed that their idea wasn't likely to take off nationwide. "To the extent the movement can be called a movement at all, it is an extremely fragmented and conceptually shallow one. It lacks mission," they wrote. But they were "cautiously optimistic" because "choice is highly popular among ordinary citizens and is gaining adherents among reformers and state officials, particularly governors." Still, they concluded, "Just a few years ago, the suggestion that choice might succeed in restructuring American education would have been regarded as pure fantasy. Times have changed."

><

STANDING IN FRONT of Judge Susan Steingass in Dane County Circuit Court, Patrick McDonnell, a lawyer for Milwaukee Public Schools, argued that Milwaukee's new choice program would deepen school segregation if the court allowed it to stand. "What the Legislature did is ignore 25 years of history of desegregating Milwaukee Public Schools," he said.

The day had come. The Milwaukee Parental Choice Program, which would allow one thousand students to attend private schools with public money, faced two legal challenges. Both would be heard by Steingass about a month before the program was expected to start. One lawsuit, brought by the NAACP and the teachers' unions, argued that the program was unconstitutional because it gave public dollars to private schools, violating the state constitution's requirement that the state provide a "uniform" public education. The suit also argued the program shouldn't have been attached as a rider to the budget bill. The other lawsuit, brought by supporters of the program, argued that the new regulations created by the state school superintendent were beyond the scope of the law.

Robert Friebert, a lawyer for the Milwaukee chapter of the NAACP, told Steingass that the new program didn't comply with the public purpose doctrine in the state's constitution, as it didn't allow the state to monitor the progress of participating students. "You can't have the public funds without the public controls," he said.[14]

Bolick, who had been eager to get involved in the history-making case, was a "nervous wreck," he would recall later. He had a flair for showmanship but little courtroom experience.[15] He had designed red-white-and-blue buttons bearing the words "School Choice" for families to wear to the courtroom, and he had arranged for a bus to take families to Madison. When they arrived, the group discovered that the courtroom, which had been opened on a Saturday for the hearing, had no air conditioning. The room was suffocatingly hot. Further, the dueling lawsuits against the program had created an unusual situation. Warren Weinstein, a lawyer for the attorney general's office, would argue for the state alongside Bolick that the new program was constitutional, but then Weinstein would argue against Bolick in defense of Grover's new regulations.

Weinstein argued it wasn't unconstitutional for the program to receive state funds, and the use of those funds would be scrutinized by Grover and a legislatively mandated audit of the program, which would occur in 1995. Bolick, who thought he saw Steingass glance at the group of parents and students, made his case that the vouchers allowed students from low-income families to have the same opportunities as their wealthier classmates. The case was about power for parents, he said: "It transfers power in the area of public education from the educational establishment to the parents."[16] After three hours in the hot courtroom, the lawyers, some with sweat rolling off their faces, concluded their arguments. Steingass had given nothing away during the hearing. Bolick had no idea if his arguments—or the families wearing their patriotically colored buttons—had made an impression.

A long story in the *Washington Post*, which ran a few days after the court hearing, described the case as one that could have "far-reaching implications for education in America." In the article, Grover warned that the new law, as it had been written, made it possible for anyone to start a school and receive state funds with little accountability for either the funds or the children's education. He also said he believed religious schools would soon be allowed to participate, and the eventual result would be "gutting the public schools in America." In the same article, Williams took aim at MPS. "These parents would not be taking their children out of the public schools if they were being educated," she said.[17]

Within two weeks, Steingass issued her ruling: the program was constitutional, as it served the public purpose of providing education, and Grover had exceeded his authority by enacting complicated regulations not included in the original law. It was a huge win, but the court battles were just beginning.

10

Two Dueling Education Ideas

FIVE YEARS AFTER MINNESOTA STARTED EXPANDING ITS PUB-
lic school options, Ted Kolderie proposed a bold idea. The influential political theorist wanted states to allow for the creation of new
public schools outside the jurisdiction of local school districts. In a
short memo he published in the summer of 1990, Kolderie argued that
America's system of public education had no incentive to improve because it was "organized as a pattern of territorial exclusive franchises."
To make his case, he invoked Albert Shanker, president of a national
teachers' union and a staunch defender of public education. "As Albert
Shanker told the Itasca Seminar in Minnesota in 1988: 'This is a system that can take its customers for granted.'" What Kolderie was proposing, however, was not what Shanker envisioned. Shanker wanted
new options within the public school system, while Kolderie believed
the system itself was part of the problem. Kolderie, a senior fellow at
the Hubert Humphrey Institute of Public Affairs in Minneapolis,
wrote, "It is time to say this: Our system of public education is a bad
system. It is terribly inequitable. It does not meet the nation's needs. It

exploits teachers' altruism. It hurts kids."[1] His argument echoed some of the sentiments in Chubb and Moe's influential book.

Minnesota made it possible for any student to move to any public school in the state, but Kolderie felt the option was limited. Families were unlikely to select a school too far from home. But by allowing high school juniors and seniors to enroll in college, Kolderie believed that Governor Rudy Perpich had established a powerful precedent: someone other than the school district could provide public education.

IN MILWAUKEE, THE idea that public education could be provided outside the school district was already in play—with school vouchers. On the first day of the school year, State Representative Polly Williams welcomed students to Urban Day, one of seven private schools participating in Milwaukee's new school voucher program. Of the school's five hundred students, about a hundred were having their tuition paid for with tax dollars. Williams, whose own children had attended Urban Day, said the moment gave hope to the city's low-income children. "These kids are getting something out of these schools they can't get in the public school system. Every child who walks through those doors is expected to achieve. It's going to make a difference in the lives of a lot of children," she said. Yvette Harris, who enrolled her seventh grader at Juanita Virgil Academy, said it was a privilege to participate in the new program. Without the voucher, "I couldn't afford the tuition at all," she said.[2]

America's first modern school voucher program had begun, with fewer than four hundred students, intense media attention, and the threat that the state court of appeals would strike it down in the middle of the school year. A state judge upheld the program before school started, but Clint Bolick, one of the lawyers defending it, feared legislators might have run afoul of the "private or local bill" provision in state law. The provision required certain kinds of legislation to be considered on its own, rather than attached to a larger bill, to ensure that issues were debated in front of the public. Milwaukee's voucher program had been subject to public debate, but it had also passed as part of the state's budget. As students settled into their new private schools, Bolick prepared his latest defense. If the case turned on arguments about equity, he thought he had a shot. If the justices focused on the private or local provision, he might be sunk.

Part of the fascination with Milwaukee's program arose from Williams herself, a fifty-three-year-old, sharp-tongued politician who couldn't be put into a neat political box. Williams was often described in the media as a grandmother, a former welfare mother, and a "gutsy" legislator. She had quickly turned into a darling of the right. She participated in events across the country and gave speeches for conservative organizations. A conservative donor flew her on a private plane to appear with Republican representative Newt Gingrich. An op-ed in *Newsday* ran with the headline "Poor People Hoping for Help, Try Looking to Your Right." In it, Elaine Ciulla Kamarck, a senior fellow at the Progressive Policy Institute in Washington, DC, wrote that Williams "took on the entire liberal establishment of Wisconsin and beat them." *Crain's Chicago Business* titled a story "How 'Conservative' Won Vouchers," which attempted, rather badly, to describe Williams's political views, saying she "retained an unmistakably left-wing slant on social priorities that is offset by strong libertarian impulses for self-determination fused with neoconservative notions about the welfare state." Not all the attention was positive. The *Milwaukee Journal* ran a controversial editorial cartoon depicting Williams as a burglar, holding up the school superintendent with a gun, while behind her a white man stood with a bag labeled "Milwaukee private schools." The *Wall Street Journal*'s editorial board wrote about "The Polly Williams Backlash." For her part, Williams seemed to enjoy the attention, positive and negative. She told the *Journal*, "You'd think I dropped a bomb near the teachers' unions." And then, laughing, "Well, maybe that wouldn't be so bad." At the conservative Heritage Foundation, she joked, "God will strike you dead if you Black and you associate with Republicans."[3]

Despite the dramatic rhetoric surrounding the program, what was happening in Milwaukee was what Williams intended: a limited experiment. To participate in the program, students met income requirements that put them at 175 percent of the poverty line or lower, and they had to be entering kindergarten or already enrolled in one of the city's public schools. These provisions ensured that vouchers were an escape for low-income students in public schools and not a mechanism to pay tuition for students already in private school. Lawmakers capped participation at 1 percent of Milwaukee Public Schools' total enrollment, which meant the entire voucher program could enroll about one thousand students. Participating private schools had to be secular, in a city where most private schools were religious, and voucher students couldn't account for more than 49 percent of a single school's student body. A voucher was worth about $2,500, and the voucher money came directly from the district's budget. Williams described the small program as "just a step, an attempt to try to address a need that's not now being addressed in the public school system."[4]

Within only a few months, however, it appeared Bolick's fears had come true. The appeals court ruled in November that the program was unconstitutional on the grounds that it should have been considered as a stand-alone bill, not attached as a rider to the budget.[5] Students in the program could stay in their school until the end of the school year. The next stop was the Wisconsin Supreme Court; with no federal issues in play, a loss there likely meant the end of the program.

Not long after the court ruling, Juanita Virgil Academy shut down because of financial problems. Dozens of students using vouchers were stranded in the middle of the school year. Many returned to the public school system because other participating private schools didn't have room for the influx. The school closure represented everything the program's critics had warned against: the state had given tax dollars to a private school with precarious finances, and now, months into the school year, public schools had to find spots for stranded students. Advocates for Milwaukee's program tried to argue that this was the free market at work—with bad schools closing and good ones staying open—but Bolick knew it was a public relations nightmare.[6] Did parents really want to entrust their children's education to the vagaries of the market? No one, it seemed, had given much thought to what would happen if a private school funded with public dollars closed midyear.

><

IN MINNESOTA, EFFORTS to create a new type of public school—one outside the traditional system—were running into problems. By early 1991, charter school legislation already had failed twice in the state.

Some of the same people who had attended the Itasca Seminar in 1988—State Senator Ember Reichgott, Ted Kolderie, and Joe Nathan—were now key players in efforts to pass legislation that would allow for the creation of "chartered schools."

Reichgott had crafted legislation in 1989 based on the recommendations of the Citizens League, which had released a report after the Itasca Seminar. The group envisioned charter schools as part of the state's public education system. The schools would be open to students of all achievement levels, meet desegregation guidelines, and be run by licensed educators. The league defined a charter school as "one granted a 'charter' by either a school district or the state to be different in the way it delivers education, and within broad guidelines, to be autonomous. It need not be in a school building. It may result in several schools in one building. It is the process of schooling and not the building itself that will differentiate a chartered school from a conventional one." The word "process" was underlined, and the report made it clear the "schools could not select only the best and the brightest students or the easiest to teach."[7] The report also called for schools to hire more teachers of color and use curricula that reflected diverse cultures.

As Reichgott (later known as Ember Reichgott Junge) wrote in her 2012 book, *Zero Chance of Passage: The Pioneering Charter School Story*, she feared charter schools were too controversial for the legislation to pass on its own.[8] Instead she wrapped it into a comprehensive education package, which included mandatory statewide testing and a requirement that school districts collect data to help parents make informed choices about open-enrollment options. Still, when the legislation moved to committee, it quickly became clear that other lawmakers didn't favor charters. She then tried to attach a pilot program to the omnibus education budget. It would be an extremely limited program in which the state would allow for the creation of two charter schools, one in Minneapolis and the other in Robbinsdale Area Schools, her home district. After 1992, the state board of education could grant charters to applicants who were rejected by those two school boards. Teachers who worked at the new schools would be included in collective bargaining.

Even with those stipulations, the pilot failed to make it out of committee. Reichgott tried again in 1990 to attach the idea to the budget bill—and again, it was removed from the final version. The concept of charter schools was going nowhere.

Kolderie pressed the state's commissioner of education, Tom Nelson, a former Democratic state senator, to create a committee to work on a third draft of legislation. This time, charter schools would be called "outcome-based schools," a bid to appeal to the national focus on standards and accountability. The schools could organize as nonprofits or cooperatives, and charter authorizers included school districts, the state board of education, and colleges. Kolderie presented the idea to Betsy Rice, senate counsel, who said, "These are not public schools." He countered, "They are part of the state's program of public education."

REICHGOTT OPPOSED SCHOOL vouchers, but as she tried and failed to pass the country's first charter school law, the Democratic senator kept hearing her proposal compared to vouchers. The lobbyist of the Minnesota School Boards Association said her latest bill would create "an alternative system of private schools with no rules that is publicly funded." Robert Astrup, president of the Minnesota Education Association, called charter schools a "hoax" that would take resources from the state's public schools. Sandra Peterson, president of the Minnesota Federation of Teachers, said, "It's just vouchers in a disguised form."[9]

Reichgott had started pursuing the idea at the same time that Governor Tommy Thompson and State Representative Polly Williams were pushing a voucher program in Milwaukee. Both ideas were controversial, opposed by teachers' unions, and in some respects similar: charter schools and school vouchers sought to give students a publicly funded option outside the traditional public school. But Milwaukee's voucher program passed and hers didn't, pushing vouchers into a "raging national debate." To navigate the political landscape, she emphasized charter schools as an educational reform within the public system.

By the spring of 1991, as Reichgott made her third attempt to pass a bill, she had built some bipartisan support around the idea. The opposition, however, was fierce, and it came largely from the local teachers' unions. The Minnesota Federation of Teachers warned that charter schools could "jeopardize seniority rights as well as salaries and benefits, [and] subtract dollars from public school districts' general funds." The Minnesota Education Association called the entire concept "insulting," as it "implies that beneficial change cannot be brought about within the existing system of public education, and says that it is necessary to create an additional, untested, competing system." The unions also said charter schools "provide an open door to vouchers." State Representative Becky Kelso, a Democrat who wrote the house's version of the bill, countered that it was a "wonderful opportunity" for the public schools. Minnesota, she said, was not Wisconsin: "We're not like Milwaukee, where public schools are so terrible that they have to give kids the option to go to private schools."[10]

Reichgott's supporters in the Democratic Party faced enormous pressure to drop the issue. State Representative Ken Nelson, who had supported Reichgott's efforts in each of the previous years, was chair of the house's education finance division, and he represented south Minneapolis, a deeply liberal area. Nelson, who planned to retire soon, decided to support the proposal—with some compromises. In a memo, Kolderie had warned Reichgott that the "killer amendment" would be to "limit the sponsor to the local board" and to "agree that no significant number of charters could be issued." Nelson's compromise did just that. It called for a charter school to get approval from both the local school district and the state board of education. It limited the number of charter schools that could be opened statewide to eight, with only one or two allowed per school district. It said only licensed teachers could operate a charter school, and teachers employed at the school had to make up the majority of the school's board of directors. Nelson believed his amendment was closer to Albert Shanker's original vision, and it had a chance of actually passing the house and senate. Nelson was right. The proposal moved through the legislative process, and on May 20, 1991, it passed as part of the omnibus budget bill. Governor Arne Carlson, a Republican, signed it into law the following month, making Minnesota the first state in the country to allow charter schools. Far from overjoyed, Reichgott was "deeply disappointed." So were Kolderie and Nathan. The resulting legislation was far more restrictive than what they had envisioned.

Shanker, who had done so much to elevate the idea of charter schools, wrote in a note to Kolderie that he, too, was disappointed— disappointed that the bill had passed. Shanker said teachers who wanted to work in a charter school would have to "give up most of their rights," which was "hardly an incentive." He wasn't at all surprised that the state's teachers' unions had worked hard to stop its passage. He wondered if the law could be "shaped up." Shanker also feared that Minnesota's law would become a template for other states.

11

School Choice, Public or Private?

MORE THAN A YEAR AFTER MINNESOTA PASSED THE COUN-
try's first law authorizing charter schools, City Academy opened
in St. Paul. Two teachers, Milo Cutter and Terry Kraabel, started the
nation's first charter school in 1992 on a shoestring budget in a city
recreation center with the goal of reaching students ages sixteen to
twenty-one who had dropped out of the public school system. In
some ways, the small school, with about fifty students, fit the model
originally proposed by Albert Shanker four years prior. Created by
teachers, the school met a critical need. Cutter and Kraabel kept the
school small by design and emphasized hands-on projects and programs tailored to each student. They were most interested in serving
students who had the least chance of success, those who had dealt
with poverty, drug abuse, and violence before dropping out. Before
the school year started, the two teachers recruited students who were
living on the streets and took referrals from the St. Paul school district, which authorized the school's charter. A quarter of the first class
was homeless.[1]

Cutter, an experienced teacher, had grown disillusioned by classrooms crowded with forty students seated in rows. For a time she had worked in a public school that was designed to be a small and close-knit community, but after the principal died the school began to change. She had heard of the Citizens League report about charter schools and was intrigued by the idea. She talked to the state's education commissioner and then the superintendent of St. Paul's public schools. The superintendent suggested she run a contract program in the summer. She did, but then she learned district officials wanted the program to continue with hand-selected special education students. Cutter wasn't interested. She returned to the idea of opening her own school with a focus on at-risk students, an "obvious need" in the school district. "The district hadn't met with success, the students hadn't met with success. What was the harm in trying another way?" she said later.[2]

Some students who found their way to City Academy weren't considered "at risk" at all. They were just looking for something different from the traditional public high school. Melinda Sjoblom met Cutter through a friend and was drawn to her open, engaging style. Cutter, whom everyone called by her first name, seemed genuinely interested in students' interests and dreams for themselves. Sjoblom enrolled. She convinced her boyfriend, Tom Gonzalez, to do the same. "You have to come and meet Milo," she kept telling him. He finally did and found himself drawn in by a school that was "so different than anything I had ever seen." Many of his classmates were seen as "brown kid troublemakers." Gonzalez had done well enough in his public school, but as a Latino kid he also felt stereotyped. A guidance counselor at his high school encouraged him to become a car mechanic rather than go to college, even though Gonzalez had no interest in cars. When he first met Cutter, she asked him what he wanted to do with his life. She listened. Gonzalez was sold. He enrolled in City Academy as a sophomore.[3]

><

THE YEAR CITY Academy opened, the presidential election pitted an "education governor" against an "education president." Education had never taken center stage during a presidential election before, but it ranked in the top five policy issues in 1992. President George H. W. Bush and his Democratic challenger, Governor Bill Clinton of Arkansas, agreed on many education policies, including expanding a federal preschool program called Head Start, and making the certification process for teachers more flexible. They both wanted national standards and testing. But on one issue they drew a sharp line between them: Bush supported school vouchers and Clinton did not. They both were for school choice, but Clinton would support choice options that were only within the public school system.[4]

At the start of his presidency, Bush had distanced himself from Reagan's education agenda. Over time, though, he had come to embrace one of Reagan's most extreme ideas: the school voucher. The summer before the 1992 election, Bush unveiled a bold new federal education plan. At a gathering at the White House, he declared, "A revolution is underway in Milwaukee and across this country, a revolution to make American schools the best in the world." His so-called GI Bill for children would provide students from middle-class and low-income homes with $1,000 "scholarships" to attend the public or private school of their choice.

Bush had changed his mind about school vouchers. Or perhaps his mind had been changed for him. As political scientist Patrick J. McGuinn wrote, Bush campaigned in 1988 as the "education president," yet surveys showed most of the public didn't think he improved America's schools. In one poll, 72 percent of respondents said Bush had "just talked about it." Facing reelection, Bush didn't have much of a domestic record on which to run. His other memorable promise of the 1988 campaign had been to avoid raising taxes, but he agreed to a budget with new taxes. His slogan "Read my lips: No new taxes" had come back to haunt him. Education reform seemed like a place where he could still make a mark. (A failed 1991 education package included vouchers, too, though on a smaller scale.) Republicans explained Bush's change of heart on school vouchers as evidence of the poor state of American public schools. Chester Finn Jr., assistant secretary of education under Reagan, said, "There's absolutely no doubt that over four years Bush has changed on this issue. The continuing decrepitude of American education between 1989 when Bush was inaugurated and the present—and the mounting evidence that the reforms of the '80s have not worked—has radicalized me. I wouldn't be at all surprised if it's had a similar effect on Bush."[5]

For a Republican president facing a tough reelection battle, 1992 was a good year to become a supporter of school vouchers. In March, Milwaukee's voucher supporters secured a huge win when the Wisconsin Supreme Court upheld the landmark program in a narrow 4–3 ruling. A majority of the state justices overturned the lower court's ruling. In writing the majority opinion, Justice William G. Callow declared that "education of our citizens knows no boundaries and other states could benefit from the knowledge resulting from this innovative experiment." Clint Bolick, one of the lawyers who defended the program in court, said the victory could encourage other state lawmakers to act: "Clearly the court thinks this is a legitimate educational reform. I think other legislators will begin to model other plans based on the Wisconsin plan."[6]

When Bush announced the GI Bill for children, a $1.5 billion initiative that closely followed the Milwaukee model, he invited some of the major players from Wisconsin for the announcement at the White House. Among those gathered were Governor Tommy Thompson and Michael Joyce, president of the Bradley Foundation. In his remarks, Bush noted the absence of State Representative Polly Williams, who was home caring for her mother. "So it is our belief then that parents, not the government, should choose their children's schools. So today I am proposing that we take another giant step forward in this revolution," he said to those gathered around him. The administration had timed the announcement for the forty-eighth anniversary of the original GI Bill.

In his speech, Bush adopted the language of free-market support-ers. "For too long, we've shielded schools from competition, allowed our schools a damaging monopoly power over our children. This monopoly turns students into statistics and turns parents into pawns. It is time we began thinking of a system of public education in which many pro-viders offer a marketplace of opportunities, opportunities that give all of our children choices and access to the best education in the world." Clinton had been intrigued by Milwaukee's school voucher program, writing a short congratulatory note to Williams when it passed in 1990. "I'm concerned that the traditional Democratic Party establish-ment has not given you more encouragement," he said. "The visionary is rarely embraced by status quo." Two years later, as a presidential candidate, Clinton came out against vouchers. The forty-six-year-old governor embodied the so-called third way, a centrist strategy to help Democrats win after having lost three previous presidential elections. On the campaign trail Clinton talked about his education record in Ar-kansas, said American students were being outperformed by their peers internationally, and said he favored giving principals and teachers more autonomy. When he gave the keynote address at the convention of the Democratic Leadership Council in Cleveland in May 1991, months before he would announce his candidacy, Clinton said the Democratic Party could provide American voters with more choices, including public school choice. "I believe we should be for more choices," he said. "Choice is not a code word for elitism or racism."[7]

Although Clinton didn't mention charter schools in his speech at the DLC, the convention passed the New American Choice Resolution, which called on states to develop public school choice plans and said they should "consider giving entities other than school districts the op-portunity to operate public schools." The idea came from Ted Kolderie, the behind-the-scenes force for Minnesota's chartering legislation.

Kolderie had written a policy paper about the charter school concept in 1990 for the Progressive Policy Institute, a think tank founded by the DLC. In it, Kolderie wrote that the state must provide "choice of school as well as providing alternatives to public schools."[8] Here was an education reform Clinton could use to counter Bush's voucher proposals.

Clinton's attacks on Bush's education agenda seemed effective. He described school vouchers as an assault on the nation's public schools. Speaking at East Los Angeles College, a two-year school, during the campaign, Clinton said, "Now is not the time to further diminish the financial resources of schools when budgets are being slashed by states all across America." In a Gallup Poll, 87 percent of respondents ranked education as a "very important" issue in the election, just below the economy. Clinton linked the two, citing the importance of a well-educated populace able to compete in a global economy. Another poll, taken a month before the election, found that voters opposed school vouchers by a margin of almost two to one. Instead, they favored having greater options within the public school system.[9] Charter schools were about to have their moment.

CALIFORNIA IN 1992 had become a microcosm for the growing debate over school choice. In that politically influential state, a group of voucher proponents had been pursuing a ballot initiative to create a statewide school voucher program. Unlike Milwaukee's modest program, which was limited to a percentage of low-income students enrolled in a single city's public schools, Proposition 174 aligned closely with Milton Friedman's long-held ideal: vouchers for all. The initiative, which would make its way to the ballot in 1993, would give all parents the right to select a public or private school for their child and to pay for it with tax dollars.

Democratic state senator Gary Hart, a former public school teacher, saw the effort as a "full-blown effort to reconstitute public education in

California." (Gary Hart of California is not to be confused with former presidential candidate Gary Hart of Colorado.) A similar initiative was already in play in Colorado for a statewide program. Hart had seen other school voucher initiatives fail, but he worried the latest one in California could succeed. He cast around for an idea for education reform that included some of the appealing aspects of school vouchers— greater choice for parents, local control, and a perceived responsiveness to the "clients"—while preserving the basic tenets of public education, "that it be free, nonsectarian and nondiscriminatory." He settled on charter schools, an idea he had read about in Albert Shanker's *New York Times* column but that was still so new he struggled to explain it to his fellow lawmakers. Hart wrote later that Shanker's writing about charter schools gave the concept "greater credibility" and "spurred" him on. Charter schools seemed like a bold educational experiment, one that could help disadvantaged students, and it checked off the boxes he sought in an alternative to school vouchers.[10]

In crafting his legislation, Hart cast his eyes to Minnesota. The Midwestern state had passed the country's only existing charter school law the year before, giving the California legislator a template to use in his own state. He and Sue Burr, a legislative staffer, got to work. They soon met Kolderie through Eric Premack, another legislative staffer in California, who had grown up in Minnesota. Premack and Kolderie were family friends. Burr spoke to Kolderie many times as they prepared a senate bill. When the 1992 legislative session began, however, Hart's bill wasn't the only one to propose the creation of charter schools. Delaine Eastin, Democratic chair of the assembly's education committee, had written her own bill. There was a clear divide in their approach. Hart's bill, which would allow for the creation of up to one hundred charter schools, didn't guarantee collective bargaining rights for teachers or require teacher credentials. Eastin's did. The question of who would authorize charter schools also differed, with Hart's bill giving the responsibility to the local school board, while Eastin's required state approval and agreement from school personnel unions.

Although each wanted to see their version succeed, Hart and Eastin wrote a press release together to announce their efforts to create the country's second charter school law. In it, both insisted charter schools wouldn't threaten the public school system but would act as a vehicle for innovation within it. "The charter school approach would represent a major education reform which would stimulate and encourage such alternatives, while maintaining our traditional democratic commitment to public schools," Hart said. For those who remained concerned, the last line of the press release wasn't much of a comfort. In it, Hart echoed Ted Kolderie's 1990 memo, which said the public education system was "organized as a pattern of territorial exclusive franchises." The press release read, "Charter schools would send an important message to parents, teachers and the education community that there are new ways of operating schools that must be considered and that public schools can no longer be viewed as an exclusive franchise."[11]

The teachers' unions lined up behind Eastin's bill, while Hart's received the support of the California School Boards Association. Other groups were quiet, apparently waiting to see how the two pieces of legislation would shake out during the session. Hart and Eastin had a "gentleman's agreement" to let the bills go to a conference committee largely unaltered, with a plan to reach a compromise. But after both bills had gone through, Eastin called Hart and said there would be no compromise. The speaker of the assembly wasn't willing to allow Hart's bill to go any further. Angry at the apparent deception, Hart decided he would try to "sneak it through."

He waited for a lull during a floor debate about the year's budget, a contentious issue that commanded lawmakers' attention, and asked for his bill to be removed from conference for an immediate vote. It passed. Eastin quickly made the same motion for her bill, which also passed. Governor Pete Wilson, a Republican, suddenly had two charter school bills, largely unchanged from the original versions. Wilson signed Hart's.[12] California had become the second state to pass a charter school law, and with Wilson's signature it had bipartisan support. Two months later, Clinton was elected president, effectively ending the effort to create a federal school voucher initiative and putting a charter school supporter into the Oval Office.

⇥⇤

IN CALIFORNIA, THE teachers' unions were engaged in an aggressive political fight, but it wasn't over two Democratic legislators' dueling proposals for charter schools. The California Teachers Association, with about 230,000 members, was focused on defeating school voucher initiatives. An effort to get a voucher initiative on the 1992 ballot failed, giving the union time to build a large antivoucher coalition and raise money for an advertising campaign. To help fund the effort, the CTA charged each member an extra nineteen dollars.

Before Proposition 174 landed on the ballot for the 1993 election, some union members even made an effort to stop supporters from collecting signatures. Teachers and members of the state's parent-teacher association volunteered to stand near signature gatherers on street corners and in shopping malls. Most of the time volunteers were polite, but occasionally it got ugly. The *Los Angeles Times* noted "some reports of overzealous opponents shoving, arguing with and even forming a human chain around signature gatherers to prevent them from doing their jobs." CTA president Del Weber, who called the ballot initiative "evil" in a message to his members, defended the aggressive stance the union had taken. "People will defend their homes and their property. I will defend the right of kids of this state to have hope, to have education. If you say you're going to take that away, you have, in the Wild West, drawn on me. I'm going to draw back."[13]

Republican proponents tried to rally support from a diverse array of parents, targeting white parents whose children already attended private schools, Black parents who might be dissatisfied with their public school options, and Latino parents whose children were in Catholic schools. They also appealed to elderly voters, who might be persuaded that vouchers could be a cost-saving measure for the state. (The claim was dubious, however, as analysis showed that the initiative had the potential to pull more than $1 billion from the public school system in its first two years if the five hundred thousand children already in private schools used vouchers to pay tuition.) The ability of private schools to accept an influx of public school students also was limited—one survey found that only about 5 percent of California's students could be admitted.[14]

It soon became clear that voucher supporters had been outspent and outmanned as the CTA-led coalition raised more than $16 million for its advertising campaign. And numerous unanswered questions about how the program would affect existing public schools didn't help. In November 1993, Proposition 174 was defeated by a wide margin. Colorado's voucher initiative had met the same fate a year earlier.

CLINT BOLICK, WHO beat the initial legal challenges to Milwaukee's experiment, had come up with a bold idea: he wanted to sue struggling urban school districts for what amounted to educational malpractice against low-income students. The remedy? School vouchers. He based the strategy loosely on "educational equity" lawsuits in which school districts sued the state for more funding. In 1992 Bolick cast around for potential school districts, settling on Chicago and Los Angeles.

In court, the cases were a spectacular failure. But Bolick met with some success in the area where he so often shined: the court of public opinion. Such seemingly outrageous cases drew national media interest, with an editorial appearing in the *Washington Post* and coverage in *USA Today* casting a brighter spotlight on the still nebulous concept of "school choice." The *Post's* editorial, titled "School Choice on Trial," noted the shifting political landscape of the voucher concept, which had evolved from the economic argument outlined by Milton Friedman in 1955 into a fight to save vulnerable students from poor-performing public schools. "The new rationale is embedded in the language of class struggle, and it's decidedly more militant: Only school choice can 'liberate' disadvantaged parents and their children from inferior public schools. The buzzword . . . is 'empowerment.'" The writers concluded that private school choice was worth "watching," but it couldn't solve the "gross inequities that prevail among America's schools."[15] Still, Bolick considered the coverage a win because it introduced and elevated the concept of choice to a large national audience.

The following year, Puerto Rico's Democratic governor championed a voucher plan for low-income students that included religious schools—a first for the country—and Bolick's firm quickly moved to intervene in the lawsuit that followed its passage. He even drew up "Libre Seleccion" pins. In an op-ed for the *Wall Street Journal*, Bolick lauded Puerto Rico for leading the way on school choice.[16] But that case, too, ended in failure. In a 5–2 decision in 1994, the Supreme Court of Puerto Rico ruled that the program's inclusion of religious schools violated the commonwealth's constitution.

With voucher losses piling up, the political climate seemed to be shifting in favor of charter schools. Lawmakers in other states who were looking for education reform ideas were encouraged by President Clinton's support and the models that had come out of Minnesota and California. Premack, the staffer who had worked with Hart on the charter legislation, saw his phone light up with calls from Michigan, Massachusetts, Colorado, and Florida. Kolderie, who preferred to advocate behind the scenes, began traveling to state capitals across the country to talk to interested legislators. "The idea sold itself," he would say later.[17]

12

"Slippery Slope"

F IVE YEARS INTO MILWAUKEE'S VOUCHER EXPERIMENT, Governor Tommy Thompson announced his intention to expand the program to include religious schools. In his State of the State speech, he said "school choice" stood for more than any single program; it represented a broader educational philosophy: "It is the belief that parents will choose the best school for their child. That's education serving the public." Education serving the public, not public education. Thompson made it clear that his goal was a "complete redefinition of public education in Wisconsin." Thompson's words, though subtle, represented a dramatic shift in thinking about American education in the twentieth century—one that called to mind the nineteenth-century English philosopher John Stuart Mill, who wrote, "An education established and controlled by the state should only exist, if it exist at all, as one among many competing experiments."[1]

In 1995, Wisconsin stood on the precipice of having "many competing experiments" in education. The state's first charter school had opened, the result of a 1993 law Thompson had championed, and

Milwaukee still claimed the country's only modern school voucher program, with about eight hundred students participating during the 1994–1995 school year. The choice program went through a small expansion, approved in 1993, which increased the number of students who could participate but didn't fundamentally alter the program.[2] What Thompson wanted—what he had envisioned from the start—called for a radically different view of the purpose of state-funded education that would test the boundaries of the law. But now he thought he had the political power to pull it off.

Thompson proposed a dramatic expansion of the existing program that would allow religious schools to participate, eliminate the cap on how many students could enroll, and remove the requirement that an independent researcher evaluate the program every year. Another proposed change made it clear that one of the underlying justifications for the voucher program had shifted: students who were already enrolled in private schools would be allowed to participate, meaning the program would no longer be a means of escape for only students from public schools. As Thompson made clear, he believed that parents should have the chance to choose their children's school—and he wanted the state to pay for that choice, whether it was a traditional public school, a charter school, or a private school participating in a voucher program.

The implications of the proposal caused an uproar. Mordechai Lee, vice chairperson of the Wisconsin Coalition for Public Education, cited an apocryphal quote from the Vietnam War, comparing Thompson to the general who said a village had to be destroyed in order to save it. In this case, public education was the village to be destroyed. Mike Turner, a spokesperson for state school administrators, said Thompson's proposal was a "slippery slope." John Witte, a professor at the University of Wisconsin–Madison and the official evaluator of Milwaukee's program, warned that the expansion could cost the state more money and squeeze low-income families out of the program by opening it to a wider group. Testifying before a legislative committee in March 1995, he told lawmakers that allowing religious schools to participate could create pressure on legislators to expand school vouchers from a single city's troubled school system to a state-wide program for all private schools. "Are you going to provide vouchers for every religious school in Wisconsin?" he asked. As far as Thompson was concerned, that was fine. At a conference that month he suggested he would consider creating a statewide school voucher program in a few years. "If it works in Milwaukee, I think it will sell itself," he said. State Representative Shirley Krug, a Milwaukee Democrat, acknowledged the idea had a lot of support in other parts of Wisconsin. But she issued a warning: "It's not at all clear the state has enough money to finance its existing obligations to public education."[3]

Thompson, who had tried to enact voucher legislation as early as 1988, had been forced to move slowly in 1990, creating a coalition across the aisle with Democratic state representative Polly Williams and counting on her to bring along other Black lawmakers and to secure support from Black families in Milwaukee. With a Democratic-controlled legislature, the unusual coalition squeaked out a win by burying the proposal in the state budget with amendments that limited the program's scope. Now, seven years after his initial attempts to pass a voucher bill, Thompson had far more political muscle behind him. Republicans narrowly held the legislature, and Milwaukee's voucher initiative had a larger and more influential coalition of supporters. The base of support had shifted, though, from a small group of Black parents and Black elected officials—backed by white Republican lawmakers whose districts were largely unaffected by the program—to include predominantly white business leaders and religious groups in Milwaukee, some of whom had different ideas about the purpose and future of "school choice."

The influence of the Bradley Foundation also loomed large behind the changing coalition. The foundation's president, Michael Joyce, helped to persuade members of the business community to back school vouchers rather than focus on aiding the public school system, which enrolled nearly one hundred thousand students—about 125 times more than were using vouchers. Bradley money helped to fund the new Blum Center for Parental Freedom in Education at Marquette University in Milwaukee. The center had been named for the Reverend Virgil Blum, who had died in 1990. The center's founder, Quentin Quade, a retired vice president at Marquette, also pushed for business leaders to support school vouchers. The Metropolitan Milwaukee Association of Commerce, or MMAC, became one of the largest supporters of school vouchers, even hiring a consultant in late 1994 to work on proposed legislative changes that would expand the city's program. To explain his support for a larger voucher program, Richard Abdoo, chairman of the MMAC's education committee, painted a dire picture of the city's public schools: "We are creating an army of illiterates with no skills."[4]

The Bradley Foundation also laid the groundwork for a future expansion by funding scholarships for low-income children interested in attending private religious schools, an approach being taken in other cities, including San Antonio and Indianapolis. The nonprofit scholarship organization, called Partners for Advancing Values in Education, or PAVE, formed in 1992 with the help of Bradley funds. Some PAVE supporters believed the privately funded vouchers were a temporary measure until lawmakers could be convinced to expand the state-funded voucher program. PAVE actually awarded far more private scholarships than the Milwaukee Parental Choice Program. In 1995, the organization provided 2,649 scholarships to low-income students in Milwaukee, compared to about eight hundred in the city's voucher program. PAVE also claimed to have more than a thousand students on a waiting list. Dan McKinley, PAVE's director, made it clear he backed the governor's proposed expansion. In a memo sent to news reporters, he said, "Charity alone cannot help all the low-income families struggling to find good opportunities for their children. For this reason, we support the governor's budget proposal to expand the voucher program to include religious schools."[5]

The shifting alliance behind school vouchers in Milwaukee strained the support of Black politicians and activists who had supported the original experiment. The proposed expansion would likely change the demographics of the students served from predominantly Black to white, as the city's religious schools mostly enrolled white children. The inclusion of religious schools, which was a clear test of the First Amendment's separation of church and state, nearly guaranteed another protracted legal battle. Williams and State Senator Gary George supported the new proposal, while other Black representatives did not.

Howard Fuller, a prominent early supporter of school vouchers, was largely absent from the debate. He became superintendent of Milwaukee Public Schools in 1991, and as part of getting the job he agreed to tamp down his public support for school vouchers. Thompson's proposal put him in an awkward spot, and as superintendent he bristled when faced with harsh criticism of the school system. Responding to Abdoo's "army of illiterates" comment, Fuller called it an "an unfair characterization" and said, "We have made it clear that we know we have to improve student achievement, but to paint that type of broad brush is beyond the bounds of what is acceptable."[6]

Despite the powerful political support behind the program in 1995, one problem loomed: after five years, there wasn't much evidence that school vouchers improved educational outcomes for students in Milwaukee. When proposing the program in 1990, supporters had almost taken it for granted that students would do better academically in private schools. Many of the arguments for Milwaukee's voucher program rested on the notion that public schools were failing students. But after evaluating the program annually following its enactment, Witte, the professor at the University of Wisconsin–Madison, concluded that students using vouchers performed about the same on standardized tests as their public school counterparts. Parents in the program were more satisfied with their school selections, but the evidence for widespread academic improvement just didn't exist.

Other researchers disputed Witte's findings. Paul Peterson, a Harvard professor, argued that Witte's analysis didn't take into account that students using vouchers had lower test scores coming into the program than other low-income children, which was perhaps an indication that families using the program were truly among the most vulnerable. In that case, Peterson argued, private schools were raising students' achievement to the average level of their public school peers but for less money than district schools would spend. In Witte's response, he said Peterson made misinterpretations that "bewilder me."[7] In contrast to both Witte and Peterson, the state's audit bureau said no conclusions could even be drawn about the program because of its small size.

But now Thompson wanted to eliminate the annual evaluation altogether. It seemed the program's effectiveness would be based on demand from parents, not whether private schools could deliver on the promise of providing a better education to low-income students.

Milwaukee remained the site of the country's only school voucher initiative. Voucher legislation had been defeated in multiple states, including New Jersey, Kansas, Maryland, and Texas.[8] Voters in California and Colorado had soundly rejected statewide voucher initiatives. Puerto Rico's Supreme Court had knocked down a program with religious schools. Clint Bolick's recent lawsuits had come to nothing.

Despite the losses, Milton Friedman, now eighty-two years old, remained certain that his vision for education was correct and soon to catch on. In the *Washington Post* in 1995, Friedman called for public education to be "radically reconstructed" by "privatizing a major segment of the educational system." He made his position clear in the title he gave the column: "Public Schools: Make Them Private."

Such a reconstruction cannot come about overnight. It inevitably must be gradual. . . . It is essential that no conditions be attached to the acceptance of vouchers that interfere with the freedom of private enterprises to experiment, to explore and to innovate. . . . I sense that we are on the verge of a breakthrough in one state or another, which will then sweep like wildfire through the rest of the country as it demonstrates its effectiveness.[9]

Despite Friedman's confidence, school vouchers remained deeply unpopular. Both Democratic and Republican lawmakers were rushing to embrace a different type of choice: public school choice. Lawmakers in a variety of states adopted open-enrollment options similar to Minnesota's, which allowed students to cross district boundaries to attend school. Republican and Democratic governors signed laws authorizing the creation of charter schools. By 1995, more than a dozen states had passed charter school laws, including Massachusetts, Colorado, Michigan, New Mexico, Arizona, and Hawaii. President Clinton signed off on the creation of a federal program in 1994 to assist prospective charter schools with start-up costs, a potential hurdle for those opening a new school. Legislation for the federal Charter Schools Program was sponsored by Senator Dave Durenberger, a Republican from Minnesota, and Senator Joe Lieberman, a Democrat from Connecticut, another show of bipartisan support for the concept of charter schools.

Many of the first charter schools fulfilled the purpose of their creation, as espoused by Albert Shanker, president of the American Federation of Teachers, by addressing unmet needs in the public schools, focusing on vulnerable students, or offering new or unusual academic programs. Not all charter schools were brand-new academies of innovation, however. In California, one of the state's first charter schools opened after teachers at a public school in the Los Angeles area converted to charter status. The newly named Vaughn Next Century

Learning Center already had improved from one of the worst schools in the district and was considered a "model of innovation." As a public school, Vaughn pursued grants to offer additional academic programs and social services to its largely low-income and Latino student body.

Staff members supported the charter conversion in large part because they feared what would happen if the school lost its extra funding. "One of our first concerns was once those grants are gone, all of our programs are gone, because we won't have the blessing from the state to do things differently from what the district allows," said Annamarie Francois, a first-grade teacher at the school.[10]

Some of the key architects behind charter schools were pleased by how quickly the concept was spreading nationwide. But Shanker, whose early support was cited by lawmakers in Minnesota and California, had changed his mind. Many of the new schools would be competitors of the traditional public schools, not laboratories for innovative practices. Within two years of Minnesota's law passing, Shanker lumped charter schools in with vouchers as a reform "gimmick." In a 1993 column in the *New York Times*, he called them both "quick fixes that won't fix anything." Instead, he called for "clear and rigorous standards and a system of incentives with consequences for success and failure."[11]

Shanker's criticisms and the opposition of school boards and teachers' unions did little to slow the rapid spread of charter schools. Charter schools were free from some of the trickiest legal questions that plagued school voucher legislation, they had bipartisan support, and media coverage was largely favorable. News organizations often framed the concept as one of public school bureaucracy versus charter school innovation. A story in the *Star Tribune* in Minneapolis described how a number of early charter applicants were denied by school boards acting as authorizers. It began, "Minnesota's charter schools were supposed to free teachers and parents of school bureaucracy. But the bureaucracy isn't willing to let go." The *Washington Post* called charter schools the "hottest educational movement in the nation." The story described a scene at City Academy in St. Paul, Minnesota, in which three students crash-tested a model car in a stairwell, a "little burst of high-spiritedness" that might result in a "trip to the in-house suspension room" at a traditional public school. "At City Academy, it's seen as creative expression, and the grown-ups get as much of a kick out of it as the youngsters."[12]

The education reform sweeping the country like wildfire wasn't school vouchers. It was charter schools.

IN APRIL 1995, Howard Fuller resigned as superintendent of Milwaukee Public Schools after four years. His tenure had been rocky, with a failed tax referendum for money to repair old schools and build new ones, a bruising budget process, and a fight with teachers over frozen salaries. Then in 1994 he proposed that the school system contract with the Edison Project, a for-profit education management company, to run two public schools. The company promised to put about $3 million into the schools. As Fuller wrote later in his memoir, he didn't think it mattered that the company turned a profit if the arrangement brought in extra money for the schools. The teachers' union disagreed, and union officials accused Fuller of trying to privatize the school district. The issue consumed the next school board election. The union backed five school board candidates who would oppose Fuller if elected. When four of the candidates won—not a majority of the nine-member board but enough to make his job harder—he decided to step down. It was a difficult, emotional time.

In a speech at the school district on the night he announced his resignation, Fuller referred to the "scurrilous messages" the Milwaukee Teachers Education Association had raised during the election and said his agenda was about helping the city's children. He warned that the school system needed to be "transformed radically" and said it remained "fundamentally mired in the status quo." Afterward, the *Milwaukee Journal Sentinel's* editorial board defended Fuller and suggested that the school board election had been about "phony issues."[13] Taking a moment to consider his options, Fuller ruled out ever taking another job as superintendent. A longtime critic of Milwaukee's public schools, he had experienced firsthand how hard it was to reform the system.

13

"A Clear and Calculated Undermining of Public Education"

IN HIS PURSUIT OF SCHOOL VOUCHERS IN WISCONSIN, GOVERnor Tommy Thompson had been forced to take it slow, first passing a small experimental program and then pushing to expand it over time. Now another Republican governor in the Midwest was poised to go much further, much faster.

George Voinovich won the Ohio governor's office in 1990, with an endorsement from the Ohio Federation of Teachers, and he declared his intention to be an "education governor" and for Ohio to be the "education state." By 1995, in his second term, he had largely delivered, refusing to reduce the elementary and secondary education budget despite the necessity of either deep cuts or tax increases to fill a deficit. (He raised taxes because he would not "cut the guts out of secondary and primary education," he told a reporter.)[1] He had formed an education commission that proved influential in pushing myriad policies, such as grade-level tests in public and private schools, expanding early childhood programs, and shifting some state aid from wealthier districts to poorer ones. He also had endorsed the concept of a school voucher pilot, though legislation on the issue had stalled. In his 1994 reelection run, the state teachers' union declined to endorse him or his Democratic challenger, perhaps in part because Voinovich appeared poised for a landslide victory.

In Voinovich's first term, some members of his education commission had made it clear that any consideration of school vouchers, which were getting increased national attention, would be too divisive. State Superintendent of Public Instruction Ted Sanders said, "Every education organization, except those representing private schools, draws the line on this issue. If it's in, they're out."

Some Ohio lawmakers were already interested in school vouchers, however, and had been for years. Both State Representative Mike Fox, a Republican, and State Representative Patrick Sweeney, a Democrat, had sponsored failed voucher legislation decades earlier, in the 1970s, when it was still "far off the chart as a viable political issue," as Fox put it. In January 1992, they were among the sponsors of a bill that would allow low-income students to attend private schools with a school voucher. Similar to Milwaukee's voucher legislation, the proposal was framed as an educational experiment, one designed to compare the performance of the state's public and private schools. Only three thousand students would be able to participate, and the program would end after five years.[2] Unlike Milwaukee, however, sectarian schools were included; most of the state's private schools were religious.

The same year, Voinovich created a second commission, this time devoted to exploring choice options. The Governor's Commission on Educational Choice, established in the spring of 1992, included more than two dozen members. Its chairperson was David Brennan, a prominent Republican political donor, businessman, and Catholic. Brennan was not a neutral selection to run the commission. He was an ardent fan of Milton Friedman, and he wholeheartedly agreed with a

market-driven approach to education. Brennan made it clear the commission's task was to create workable voucher policies, not to explore
whether the idea itself had any merit. One member of the commission, a public school superintendent, later accused Brennan of having
a "vengeful attitude against public education," and suggested that if
Voinovich had wanted an "objective assessment" he wouldn't have selected Brennan as the chairperson. A few months after the commission
formed, Republican state senator H. Cooper Snyder offered to create
a senate version of Fox's bill, giving the issue more visibility and press
coverage. But the legislation went nowhere, as expected when the Democrats controlled the Ohio House.[3]

Voinovich asked the choice commission to have its proposals ready
by the fall. In December 1992, the commission formally recommended
the Ohio Scholarship Plan, a proposal for a voucher pilot program, which
included religious schools and wasn't limited to low-income students.
(It required participating schools to reserve 20 percent of the vouchers for low-income students.) Brennan savvily pushed to use the term
"scholarship" rather than "voucher" because it was less controversial and
more easily understood by the general public.[4] In 1993, Fox came back
with a new voucher proposal, one similar to what the commission had
recommended: a two-year experiment that included up to eight local
school districts. Again, the vouchers could be used at religious schools.
Again, Snyder offered a senate version. Again, the legislation faltered.

With increased talk of school vouchers, opposition steadily grew.
A variety of elected officials, parents, teachers, and education organizations across the state mobilized, forming a coalition called Citizens
Against Vouchers. John Brandt, of the Ohio School Boards Association, zeroed in on the core of the resistance, saying the state "has an
obligation to improve the public schools, not put public money into the
private schools and leave the public schools to slide."[5]

As he pursued reelection in 1994, Voinovich offered tepid public support for vouchers, taking a cautious approach even though he

was immensely popular and seemed sure to win. He didn't endorse the commission's recommendation, saying only that he would give it "serious review and consideration." His education reform package, an amendment to the 1993–1995 budget, didn't have a voucher pilot, and most of the policies it did include were supported by the teachers' unions. Fox told the newspaper in Dayton that Voinovich's strategy was deliberate. "The governor made a commitment to me," he said. "Basically it was: 'Don't raise hell about this prior to my re-election, and I'll put it in the [next] budget.'"[6]

In a letter to Brennan from the spring of 1994, however, Voinovich was clear about his intentions for his second term. He wrote that he was "very interested in a full-blown national pilot program (or pilot programs) in the area of Choice." He expressed a willingness to consider charter schools, which he said he didn't know much about, but his focus was on school vouchers. "In terms of Choice, I feel we are going to have to crawl before we can walk. I believe if we can *really* get it underway in one or two districts during my second term, we will have accomplished more than what has been accomplished thus far."[7] (Emphasis in the original.)

But school voucher advocates would need more than a Voinovich win to pursue their agenda, as the previous years' failures demonstrated. Republicans had controlled the state senate and the governor's mansion when voucher legislation failed but not the house. No influential Democratic politician had embraced vouchers the way Polly Williams had in Milwaukee; Patrick Sweeney had shown an interest, but he didn't seem likely to persuade the rest of his party. To have a real shot at passing legislation, they needed a Republican majority in the house, where Democrats held fifty-three seats to Republicans' forty-six.

Leading up to the 1994 election, one man thought he could make it happen.

➤✦

DAVID BRENNAN WAS known for a large ego and his height. He stood six feet five before he put on his iconic white ten-gallon Stetson. Called a bully by some critics, Brennan was determined, ambitious, and politically connected. He was a member of President George H. W. Bush's "Team 100," a club of 250 wealthy donors who each gave the Republican Party $100,000 during the 1992 presidential election. And he donated more than that to Voinovich's first campaign for governor.[8]

In 1992, when Voinovich put Brennan in charge of the choice commission, it seemed like the time might be right for Ohio to pursue a school voucher program. President Bush had become a supporter, pitching his GI Bill for children in the lead-up to the November election. Milwaukee already had its program. Political scientists John Chubb and Terry Moe, often referred to as a single unit, "Chubb and Moe," had elevated the idea that private schools were simply better than public schools and that school choice could be a panacea for all that ailed, or was perceived to ail, public education. But then Bush lost his bid for reelection, and voucher legislation in Ohio stalled. State Representative Bill Batchelder, a Republican who had been in the Ohio House since 1968, told Brennan he could count on maybe twenty-five votes for school vouchers out of ninety-nine members in the house.[9] Some Republican lawmakers were unwilling to support statewide vouchers because the concept wasn't popular with their rural or suburban constituents, many of whom liked their public schools. School vouchers were a solution without a problem.

Ahead of the 1994 election, Brennan put his money and influence to work in support of a slate of candidates he believed would be friendly to school voucher legislation. In January 1993, he told two major Republican donors in Ohio that they collectively needed to raise $2 million to "take back the House." He planned to target more than a dozen races in his quest. (Between 1991 and 1994, Brennan personally gave at least $580,000 to Republican candidates and causes, according to the *Akron Beacon Journal*.) In the months before the election, it appeared his strategy was paying off. Headlines in the *Columbus Dis-patch* proclaimed, "Democrats Expect It to Be Rough Election Year" and "Ohio House Control at Stake in Election" and "Ohio House: GOP May Take the Reins."[10]

In November 1994, the *Dayton Daily News* reported what Bren-nan had been working toward: "Voinovich, GOP Crush Opposition."[11] The election wins, propelled in part by Brennan's fundraising, secured Republican control of the governor's mansion, the state senate, and the house. Voinovich won with an astonishing 72 percent of the vote, while Republicans gained a tighter hold on the senate. In the house, where Democrats had held the majority for two decades, Republicans now led, with fifty-six seats to forty-three. It was a stunning reversal.

The editorial board of the *Dayton Daily News* offered Voinovich some support for the voucher pilot they assumed would be coming to Ohio with Republicans in control of state government—if it was for low-income families, not parents who could already afford private school. "He should be allowed his experiment—so long as it's directed to families who truly need the state's help."[12]

Republican wins in the house put some longtime voucher advo-cates in a better position to influence state education policy. Republican Mike Fox became chairperson of the House Education Committee, giving him an outsize role in setting the agenda. Patrick Sweeney, a Democrat who had cosponsored voucher legislation with Fox, became the house minority leader. But, as the Dayton newspaper noted, what really mattered was this: "Next year will mark the first time in two de-cades that the multibillion-dollar state budget will be drafted and han-dled in the General Assembly entirely by Republican leaders."[13]

As Voinovich started his second term, the path seemed clear for Ohio to pass the country's second school voucher program. But Repub-licans had underestimated the intensity of the opposition.

><

VOINOVICH SEEMED AN unlikely candidate to pursue dramatic changes to the status quo. A career politician, he was considered less ambitious than other Midwestern governors like Wisconsin's Tommy Thompson. He described himself as an "ordinary person" and his job as that of a manager. Writing about Voinovich's run for reelection in 1994, a journalist at the *Washington Post* described him as someone who "would easily blend into the crowd at any bowling alley in the state." The headline read, "Holding Hard to the Middle." A Republican in a battleground state who had been a two-term mayor of a Democratic city, Voinovich was adept at the political compromise. He supported state budget cuts but also a tax increase on people who earned more than $200,000 a year. He personally opposed abortion but selected a running mate in 1994 who was proabortion. At a time when many governors were emphasizing law-and-order politics, Voinovich declared his intention to be an "education governor." (He told a reporter that his biggest regret from his tenure as Cleveland's mayor was not doing more to influence education reform.)[14]

Voinovich's interest in school vouchers may have been more personal than political. As a Catholic, he had long been supportive of parochial education. His own children attended both public and parochial schools when he was mayor of Cleveland in the 1980s. As a state representative in the late 1960s and early 1970s, he supported state aid to Catholic schools, and he openly admired the parochial schools, saying many lawmakers "looked upon Catholic education as a yardstick by which to measure other schools."[15] Ohio already had a strong tradition of providing state support to private schools, supplying funds for secular functions such as bus service, therapies for students in special education, nonreligious textbooks, and technology. But Voinovich cast the idea of school vouchers as a simple educational experiment, not an effort to support religious schools.

Coming into his second term off a huge victory, Voinovich had far greater political power to create a pilot. But the opposition had only grown, spreading across the state. Citizens Against Vouchers, which included the Ohio Parents and Teachers Association, Ohio Education Association, Ohio School Boards Association, the NAACP, the Cleveland Teachers Union, and the Ohio AFL-CIO, fought hard against voucher legislation in the run-up to the 1994 election. Fox knew many Republicans had been leery of offending financial contributors and political power players, such as the teachers' unions, in an election year. School boards across the state also passed resolutions condemning vouchers and questioning the real goals of voucher proponents. In Columbus, school board member Bill Moss said voucher programs were a "clear and calculated undermining of public education."[16]

Even after the election sweep, some Republican lawmakers were reluctant to sign on to a statewide voucher program. Those in rural or suburban districts saw little reason to bring that fight to their communities, as most of their constituents supported the public schools or had moved there specifically for the perceived quality of the public schools. Fox realized he and other supporters would have to start smaller, similar to what Thompson had done in Milwaukee. One school district, Ohio's largest, seemed promising in the spring of 1995: a federal judge had just put Cleveland's troubled public school system under state control.

CLEVELAND'S BELEAGUERED PUBLIC schools had a history of racial segregation, declining enrollment, and poor academic outcomes. In the early 1990s, only about half the students graduated. That the school system struggled should not have been a surprise. Cleveland had seen some of the same problems as other large cities in the North in the decades following World War II, with increasing poverty, growing racial tension, and segregation. As Black families moved in, thousands of white families fled to the suburbs. Those who didn't leave tried to contain Black families to certain neighborhoods and schools, leading to financial distress and overcrowding. After a lawsuit by the NAACP, a district judge ruled in 1976 that the Cleveland school board and the state department of education had segregated the school system. School officials appealed and stalled, but eventually the district began busing students to create more integration. Some modest academic improvement resulted, and a 1983 survey found that high percentages of Black and white families believed school desegregation had improved education.

As historian Jim Carl wrote, meaningful integration was difficult to achieve, however, with thousands of white students leaving the public schools. By the 1990s, many Black families had become disillusioned with desegregation as a method of reform. Cleveland had grown smaller and more impoverished. By 1990, the city's population had fallen to about 500,000, down from 750,000 just two decades earlier. The city was divided almost evenly between white and Black residents, but the public school system was now majority Black as white students moved to private schools. Public school students were increasingly marginalized by poverty, both inside and outside the school system. By 1990, 94 percent of Black students qualified for subsidized lunch, compared to 60 percent in 1975. Two ballot tax measures to support Cleveland's schools failed. White voters were less likely to support additional taxes for a public school system many of their own children didn't attend. The *Plain Dealer*, the city's newspaper, reported that after years of neglect of the schools, some children were "trying to learn in barely functional school buildings with serious electrical hazards, leaking roofs, and cracked and buckling floors."[17]

A new school superintendent, Sammie Campbell Parrish, proposed providing families with more choices, including magnet schools—as other northern cities had done—instead of busing for desegregation. She framed the plan, which drew some opposition, as the school district's "last chance."[18] Parrish created some high-performing magnets, but those schools didn't drive widespread improvement. Often, they pulled high-achieving students out of neighborhood schools. After a falling-out with the mayor, Parrish quit in February 1995. A month later, a federal judge in the desegregation case ordered the state to take over Cleveland's public schools.

School voucher advocates saw in Cleveland's troubled district the means to launch a pilot program. What better place for an "educational experiment" than a school system where a federal judge ruled local officials could not be trusted to run the public schools? As Fox said later, "The school district was a mess, it was impossible to defend it."[19]

Despite the similarities, Cleveland was no Milwaukee.

In Milwaukee, Democratic state representative Polly Williams had passed a voucher initiative through an "unholy alliance" between white Republicans, Black Democrats, and a committed group of Black families. In Cleveland, the push for school vouchers largely came from white Republicans outside the city. With a few exceptions, including the mayor, most of the Black elected officials who represented Cleveland opposed school vouchers. Many advocated for more funding for public education. Democratic state representative C. J. Prentiss, a Black woman whose district included Cleveland, had blasted school vouchers in 1994, when lawmakers debated another voucher bill in the Ohio House. "Let's 'experiment' by fully funding education," she said. "The most draconian and dangerous idea of all is to take the taxpayers' dollars and educate a handful of children in private schools." US Representative Louis Stokes, who headed the Black Elected Democrats of Cleveland, said a voucher system would "guarantee the total collapse of the public schools."[20]

Amid the fierce opposition of most Black politicians in the city, Fannie Lewis, a Democrat on the city council, stood out as an unlikely supporter. As a young woman in the 1950s, Lewis had moved to Cleveland with her husband and four children from Memphis, Tennessee,

to escape racial oppression in the South. She soon gave birth to another child in Cleveland. A young mother of five, Lewis worked at a dry
cleaner while her husband started a trucking business. Lewis said she
struggled to get her children through Cleveland's public schools, and
she was open to ideas for education reform. Elected to the city council
in 1979, she represented Ward 7, a predominantly Black, working-class
area known for the riots that had engulfed the Hough neighborhood
in July 1966.[21]

After Milwaukee passed its voucher program, Lewis met with Polly
Williams and the Bradley Foundation's president, Michael Joyce. Intrigued, she invited Williams to Cleveland in 1994 to talk to her constituents about vouchers. She also invited Brennan to speak that year.
At the event he referred to public schools as "warehouses," while Lewis
said plainly that she was "looking at the voucher system as an alternative
to public schools." Unlike Williams, Lewis couldn't vote on a voucher
bill. She became an important advocate, however, as a highly visible and
well-known Black politician recognized for championing her constituents. (Asked once if she was concerned about wealthy families receiving
vouchers, Lewis quipped, "I can't worry about rich people right now because we don't have rich people in Ward 7.")[22] Republicans could point
to Lewis and some of her backers as "grassroots support," even as some
privately expressed concern that there wasn't the same groundswell in
Cleveland as in Milwaukee.

In his State of the State speech in late January 1995, Voinovich announced that he would include a voucher pilot program in the upcoming budget, calling for an "honest-to-goodness experiment in school
choice." He didn't identify a specific city, suggesting that several school
districts could participate. Critics accused him of hiding the initiative
in the budget in order to limit public debate. A month later, Lewis organized a group of three hundred parents and students to travel to Columbus in a show of support for a voucher program in Cleveland. One
of the parents on the trip, Genevieve Mitchell, said the city's public

schools were setting up Black children for failure. "The public schools are preparing Black children for prison, the welfare office or the grave-yard. As a Black parent, that's unacceptable." A headline in the *Columbus Dispatch* read, "Clevelanders Lobby for Voucher Plan." Another head-line read, "Storming the Statehouse: Local Voucher Plan Supporters State Their Case in Columbus."[23]

After Cleveland schools came under state control, Voinovich urged lawmakers to put the voucher pilot in the city, as some Republicans in the Ohio House had already suggested. One legislator said it would be an "easier sell." Mimicking Lewis's earlier trip to the state capitol, a Cleveland school board member led a caravan of opponents, includ-ing parents, to protest in Columbus. All twelve Black members of the Ohio House had already issued a joint statement to say they opposed the budget and its inclusion of school vouchers. An antivoucher rally in Cleveland drew 150 people. Stokes, the Cleveland Democrat, said if school vouchers came to the city they could spread across the country. "If you let it happen here, it can happen anywhere," he said. "The whole nation is watching us to see whether we allow it." In the face of strident opposition, Voinovich continued to describe the pilot as a simple ex-periment in education reform, one that could be cast aside if it didn't work. "I think what we need to do is look at this as another option on the education-reform smorgasbord, take it on, look at it, and see if it works. What do we have to be afraid of?"[24]

IN THE SUMMER of 1995, the Ohio House included a Cleveland voucher proposal in the state budget, despite a last-minute attempt by one Democratic lawmaker to derail it. But the senate stripped it from its version, a move the *Dayton Daily News* said was likely intended to send a message to the governor that he would need to pull some strings to get his favored program included when the house and senate met to reconcile the two budgets.

An editorial in the *Daily News* downplayed the potential effect of any voucher pilot in Cleveland, saying, "The voucher proposals on the table aren't a serious threat to public education, nor are they likely to promote dramatic reform. They are mainly a political statement that some people in power think public education is falling down on the job. . . . That message is worth sending, but there's no sense pretending that pilot voucher programs would force bad schools to get better fast."[25]

Lawmakers soon ended the stalemate and sent the biennial budget to Voinovich for his signature. It included what would eventually be called the Cleveland Scholarship and Tutoring Program, which would start in the fall of 1996 and offer school vouchers worth up to $2,250 to students in kindergarten through third grade. Students, who would be chosen in a lottery, would have 75 to 90 percent of their tuition costs paid for, depending on their household income, with priority for seats going to the lowest-income students. All private schools, including religious ones, could participate. Voinovich signed the budget on June 30.

Cleveland was now home to the country's second voucher program—one that included religious schools. Two decades earlier, the US Supreme Court had struck down a New York grant program because it gave state aid to religious schools. Cleveland's program would almost certainly face a legal challenge. The question was: What would the courts do?

14

Constitutional Insurance

WITHIN ONE MONTH OF EACH OTHER IN THE SUMMER OF 1995, Republican governors in Wisconsin and Ohio signed legislation allowing school vouchers to be used at private religious schools, setting the stage for a legal showdown that could end at the US Supreme Court. Governors George Voinovich of Ohio and Tommy Thompson of Wisconsin tried to "bulletproof" the legislation against legal challenges by tapping into a small network of conservative lawyers and strategists who were trying to create voucher programs nationwide. Like reading tea leaves, the lawyers combed past court rulings for constitutional clues. They eyed judges in the lower courts, looking for signs of a liberal or conservative viewpoint. And they kept a watchful eye on the Supreme Court. President Bill Clinton already had appointed two justices, Ruth Bader Ginsburg in 1993 and Stephen Breyer in 1994, and retirement rumors swirled around Chief Justice William Rehnquist and Justice Sandra Day O'Connor, both of whom were considered potentially friendly to voucher cases. Even with the current court, justices might strike down either Cleveland's or

Milwaukee's program, imperiling all future policies. Just one vote could make the difference.

Clint Bolick was among the strategists guiding Voinovich and Thompson. As the legislative proposals were drafted, he flew to Milwaukee and Cleveland to consult with lawmakers and other advocates, like Ohio's David Brennan. He urged them to include "constitutional insurance" in the bills based on past court cases.[1] Cleveland's new program or Milwaukee's expansion could run afoul of either state or federal law, but the biggest constitutional principle in play was the prohibition of government aid to religion. The First Amendment doesn't include the phrase "separation of church and state." The establishment clause, at the start of the amendment, is the basis for the well-known concept: "Congress shall make no law respecting an establishment of religion." Thomas Jefferson, the country's third president, also cemented the expression in American minds when he wrote in 1802 that the establishment clause built a "wall of separation between Church and State."[2] How could lawmakers determine, while drafting legislation, whether a policy would violate church-state doctrine? Bolick and other conservative strategists knew the most relevant case names, which spanned nearly seven decades of jurisprudence: *Pierce, Everson, Lemon, Nyquist, Mueller, Witters,* and *Zobrest.*

In *Pierce vs. Society of Sisters*, the Supreme Court established that private schools had the right to operate alongside state-funded public schools. The unanimous 1925 ruling struck down an Oregon law that required students to attend public schools. Though not a First Amendment case, *Pierce* became a rallying cry for parental rights when the court declared, "The child is not the mere creature of the state; those who nurture him and direct his destiny have the right, coupled with the high duty, to recognize and prepare him for additional obligations."[3] In other words, the state could require children to get an education, but it could not deny parents the right to decide the type of schooling. If *Pierce* established parents' rights to determine how and where their children were educated, the ruling said nothing about whether the government should pay for that choice if it fell outside the state-funded public schools. By 1995, seven decades after *Pierce*, no state opposed parents' right to select a type of schooling for their child. Every family could choose public or private education. The underlying question in Cleveland's and Milwaukee's policies was whether the state should pay for a public school system for all children and also pay for some children to opt out of that system, particularly if those children went to a religious school.

The constitutional basis for what Voinovich and Thompson had done was murky, but so was church-state law. The US Supreme Court had been ambiguous about what kind of financial support could flow from the state to religious schools, allowing some policies to stand while striking down others. In 1971, Chief Justice Warren Burger acknowledged how difficult church-state rulings were, writing, "We can only dimly perceive the lines of demarcation in this extraordinarily sensitive area of constitutional law." In 1947, the court declared in *Everson vs. Board of Education of the Township of Ewing* that the wall of separation between church and state was "high and impregnable."[4] But somewhat paradoxically, the 5–4 ruling upheld a program in New Jersey in which public dollars paid for transportation for students at private schools, even though 96 percent of those schools were Catholic. The majority found that the program didn't violate the First Amendment because public aid wasn't given directly to religious schools. Students at those schools were simply included in a "general program" to help all students get to school.

After declaring the church-state wall impregnable, the court waited more than twenty years to provide a litmus test to determine if a policy breached it. That came in 1971's *Lemon vs. Kurtzman*. The so-called *Lemon* test had three prongs: the law must serve a "secular legislative purpose," its "principal or primary effect" must not advance or inhibit religion, and it must not foster "excessive government entanglement with religion." Two years later, justices applied the *Lemon* test in a 6–3 ruling that strongly suggested the court wouldn't support most state aid to religious schools. In *Committee for Public Education and Religious Liberty vs. Nyquist*, justices invalidated three programs in New York that provided financial aid to religious schools and families attending religious schools. Writing for the majority, Justice Lewis Powell said the state sought to increase educational opportunities for low-income families—whose "right to have their children educated in a religious environment is 'diminished or even denied'" by financial constraints. But, he wrote, "In its attempt to enhance the opportunities of the poor to choose between public and nonpublic education, the State has taken a step which can only be regarded as 'advancing' religion."[5] The message seemed clear: families could choose a private religious education for their children, but they couldn't expect the state to pay for it, even if they lacked the means to do so themselves.

If *Nyquist* had been the last word from the Supreme Court, the matter would have seemed largely settled. But a decade later the court took up the issue again in *Mueller vs. Allen*, ruling 5–4 to uphold tax deductions in Minnesota for religious education. Rehnquist, who wrote the majority opinion, applied the *Lemon* test and, though the case was similar to *Nyquist*, found that Minnesota hadn't violated the separation of church and state. How were the two cases different in his view? In New York, the benefit of the tuition reimbursement only applied to private school parents. In Minnesota, all parents benefited, including those with students in public schools. Private school parents could deduct tuition, while public school parents could deduct money spent for textbooks and transportation costs. The "primary effect" was not to advance religion, Rehnquist said, because public money became "available only as a result of numerous private choices of individual parents of school-age children."[6]

The *Mueller* case highlighted two key principles: neutrality and indirect aid. A neutral public policy would offer something to parents at both public and private schools. With indirect aid, any financial support that went to religious schools got there only through the choices of parents. (*Nyquist* addressed that question, too, but with a different outcome. Powell called it "only one among many factors to be considered.") A few years later, the court ruled unanimously in *Witters vs. Washington Department of Services for the Blind* that a blind student could use public dollars, through a state program, to attend a religious college with the objective of becoming a pastor. The court found the program had a neutral purpose: to assist blind students. The principles of neutrality and indirect aid seemed to be reinforced by the court in 1993, when justices ruled 5–4 in *Zobrest vs. Catalina Foothills School District* that public dollars could pay for an interpreter for a deaf student who attended a Catholic high school, even though the interpreter signed both secular and religious instruction. Writing for the majority again, Rehnquist said the interpreter was "part of a general government program that distributes benefits neutrally to any child qualifying . . . without regard to the 'sectarian-nonsectarian, or public-nonpublic nature' of the school the child attends."[7]

Attempting to read between the lines of the various rulings, Bolick and other advocates made a number of suggestions for Milwaukee's and Cleveland's programs as the legislation was drafted. Some were included, others rejected. In Milwaukee, the legislation allowed voucher students to opt out of religious instruction and gave checks to parents who would then sign them over to the private schools—the former avoided advancing religion, while the latter was a nod to the concept of indirect aid. In Cleveland, the legislation offered tutoring for students who remained in the city's public schools and allowed suburban public schools to participate in the voucher program. But over Bolick's objections, both governors slipped their proposals into the state budgets, moves that opened the programs to legal challenges and signaled that neither governor believed the proposals could withstand public opposition as stand-alone bills.

By the summer of 1995, it was done—and there was a new case to consider. In late June, a day before Voinovich signed his state's budget, the US Supreme Court issued another 5–4 ruling on a church-state case. In *Rosenberger vs. Rector and Visitors of the University of Virginia*, the majority found that a university had to offer the same financial support to a religious magazine that it gave to other publications.[8]

Bolick took it as a hopeful sign and once again waited for the next chess move from voucher opponents. Milwaukee's program would likely be challenged first, as the expansion would start in the fall. Cleveland's program, scheduled to start in 1996, could face a legal challenge any time in the next year. How would the US Supreme Court rule? Only one thing was clear: it would be a close call. Many of the pivotal establishment clause cases—*Everson, Mueller, Zobrest*, and now *Rosenberger*—had been decided by one vote.

THE TWO LAWYERS at the heart of the courtroom battles to come could not have been more different from one another. Bolick, by then thirty-seven years old, left the firm he had started in Washington, DC, to cofound the Institute for Justice. The IJ, as it was called, opened with money from billionaire libertarian brothers Charles and David Koch, and the firm tackled cases with libertarian principles. Bolick had a jovial spirit but the soul of a fiery conservative, one deeply influenced by Justice Clarence Thomas, for whom he had worked briefly at the US Equal Employment Opportunity Commission.[9] For a lawyer, he often was idealistic and eager. As he had shown in his first voucher cases, Bolick would work any angle he could to win, packing courtrooms with students in neatly pressed school uniforms, handing out "school choice" buttons to supporters, and helping to organize rallies outside the courthouse. He was comfortable with reporters and always ready with a quick quote or sound bite.

If Bolick was younger and theatrical, his opponent was seasoned and narrowly focused on the law. Robert Chanin, sixty, was a well-known labor lawyer who had argued in front of the US Supreme Court and was credited with turning the National Education Association into a political force. He had been born in Brooklyn during the Great Depression. Having overcome a speech impediment in childhood by working after school with a speech teacher, Chanin now was a powerful orator. His father was a Russian immigrant, his mother the daughter of Russian immigrants. He pursued the law at the urging of his parents and started representing the NEA not long after graduating law school. (The NEA was a client of his law firm. He continued to represent the union after moving to a different firm in Washington, DC.) By 1995, he had served the union for three decades and was known for his extensive knowledge of national labor laws and union bylaws. In the courtroom, he often chewed on a toothpick until it was his turn to speak, and he wasn't afraid to be aggressive.[10]

Bolick poked fun at Chanin's Brooklyn accent and viewed him as an "obnoxious labor lawyer." Chanin disdained Bolick's bombast—his rallies, his buttons, his courtroom theatrics. He found it offensive when Bolick suggested teachers' unions weren't interested in the welfare of students. "Of course we care about the children," he said years later. "We care on a long-range basis. Vouchers, if they survive, are never going to be the way the vast number of children in our country are educated. Unless we improve the inner-city public school systems, we don't solve the problem." *Education Week* would later write about their frequent courtroom clashes under the headline "Bolick vs. Chanin."[11]

➤<

ONE MONTH AFTER Governor Thompson signed the budget bill that allowed Milwaukee's school voucher program to include religious schools, two separate lawsuits were filed to stop the expansion. In August 1995, the National Education Association and the American

Federation of Teachers filed two lawsuits, which were then consolidated into one action and joined by the ACLU, Americans United for Separation of Church and State, and later the NAACP. "You can't coerce taxpayers into funding support for religious ideas they don't agree with," said Christopher Ahmuty, director of Wisconsin's ACLU chapter, before the lawsuit was filed.[12] Chanin attacked the program on state and federal grounds, including, as Bolick had feared, the charge that the policy should never have been buried in the state's budget. A challenge based on the First Amendment was a given, but Chanin also could potentially sidestep a review by the US Supreme Court if the Wisconsin Supreme Court invalidated the program for state constitutional reasons.

Working with conservative strategists, Thompson considered how to defend Milwaukee's expansion. The state's Democratic attorney general, Jim Doyle, would be expected to defend it in court, but Thompson didn't want to leave the matter in the hands of a Democrat.[13] He brought in his own legal team, with the Bradley Foundation picking up most of the tab. He hired Ken Starr, a former federal judge and US solicitor general under President Bush whose national profile rose when he took over the Whitewater investigation into Bill and Hillary Clinton's real estate dealings. Here Starr would concentrate on the religious arguments, both state and federal, while Bolick would tackle the intricacies of the other state issues. Thompson asked the Wisconsin Supreme Court to fast-track the case, leaping over the trial court, and to allow his legal team to represent the state. The court agreed.

The timing of the legal challenge, though expected, coincided with the start of the 1995–1996 school year. Voucher advocates hoped to get students into their new schools, thinking that would make it harder for justices to stop the program. About eighty religious schools had agreed to participate in the state program, and about twenty-three hundred students wanted to use vouchers at religious schools. Opponents asked the court to halt state funding until the case could be decided.

If Bolick thought students starting at their new private schools would sway the court, he was quickly proven wrong. The Wisconsin Supreme Court agreed to the injunction in September 1995: the state could not fund the expansion until justices reached a decision, one that might be many months away.[14]

The move to halt the expansion after some students had already started class proved to be a potent public relations tool. The Bradley Foundation offered $1 million to pay for students' tuition, with $200,000 of it promised as a match to other donations. Smaller amounts, from $10 to $100, came rolling in, sometimes with notes from donors who valued their own religious education. National newspapers covered the fundraising drive, and $1.4 million was raised in the first week following the court's decision. The headline on a front-page story in the *New York Times* read, "Milwaukee Forces Debate on Vouchers: With Issue in Courts, Gifts Keep Needy Students in Church Schools." One mother, Joanne Curran, vowed to go to jail before allowing her kindergarten-age daughter to attend public school. The girl was one of sixty-five students with vouchers who still showed up at school after the ruling, the *Times* reported. Sedgwick Daniels, pastor of Holy Redeemer Institutional Church of God in Christ, in Milwaukee, called the court setback an "emotional lift" for the program. "I say this to the civil liberties union and the teachers union: 'You're picking on a giant that's bigger than you are.' My advice to them is to quit while they're behind."[15]

Several months later, in January 1996, the teachers' unions and a coalition of parents sued in two separate lawsuits to stop Cleveland's new voucher program. Ron Marec, president of the Ohio Federation of Teachers, charged the program with violating both the US Constitution and Ohio's state constitution. Barry Lynn, executive director of Americans United for Separation of Church and State, noted the coordinated effort of conservative advocates to spread private school choice programs. "There is a national campaign under way to use tax dollars to pay for religious schools. If we do not strike down the Cleveland program a dangerous precedent will be set that could affect taxpayers all over America," he said. Governor Voinovich called the suit a "slap in the face" to parents, and he promised to "vigorously defend" the program.[16]

Despite the legal challenge, state officials pushed ahead with plans to start in the fall of 1996. Thousands of parents already had applied, and about fifty private schools agreed to participate; most were religious. Out of 6,277 who applied for vouchers, 1,500 received them, including 375 students who were already enrolled in private schools.[17] No suburban school district had agreed to participate, making it difficult to argue the program was "neutral." David Brennan, the Republican political donor who championed the law, soon opened two nonsectarian private schools in Cleveland, called the Hope Academies.

In his court brief, Chanin came out swinging, calling Cleveland's voucher program a "money laundering scheme." The American Federation of Teachers, too, noted that most of the private schools were religious, writing in a court brief that parents were "inconsequential conduits"—in other words, the state was sponsoring religion despite the money going to the schools through parents. Bolick seized on the language in the AFT brief, casting it as an insult to low-income parents rather than a constitutional argument.[18] With lines drawn, Bolick and Chanin prepared to meet in courtrooms in Ohio and Wisconsin.

ON FEBRUARY 27, 1996, the lawyers walked into the Wisconsin Supreme Court in Madison to argue one of the most pivotal cases in the history of American education. Six justices—one recused herself—could decide whether the state could pay for students to attend private religious schools. During the hearing, Justice William Bablitch spoke to the broader implications of the case. "This one opens it up. If we say this is OK, there's nothing to stop the legislature from going all the way."[19]

Inside the courtroom, Starr and Bolick argued in defense of Milwaukee's expansion. They emphasized the US Supreme Court's 1993 ruling in *Zobrest*, which allowed public funds to pay for an interpreter for a deaf student at a Catholic school. With the inclusion of all private schools, religious and secular, Milwaukee's expanded voucher program was "neutral," Starr asserted. The program "now treats all [private] schools in Milwaukee alike." Starr referenced the principle of indirect aid: "Once the choice is made by an individual, then the religious nature of the institution is irrelevant. It's the parents' decision that controls."

In his arguments, Chanin emphasized the US Supreme Court's 1973 ruling in *Nyquist*, in which justices ruled against three programs in New York that benefited either religious schools or private school families. In that case, Justice Lewis Powell said the court was sympathetic to the limited educational choices available to low-income children, but the programs served to advance religion. The same principles from *Nyquist* applied in Milwaukee, Chanin argued. "In order to prevail, the governor and his allies must show either that *Nyquist* is not a direct precedent or that it has been overruled," he said. "They can do neither."

Chanin largely stuck to the constitutional principles, but he also warned that the state could be heading toward funding distinct and separate systems of education. "When does it stop? When you have side-by-side systems of [government-funded] public and private education?"[20]

>‹

By the spring and summer of 1996, judges in Wisconsin and Ohio had begun to wade into the constitutional thicket surrounding the country's only two school voucher programs. As the rulings came down, neither side could claim a clear victory, and each knew the other would appeal.

In March, the Wisconsin Supreme Court deadlocked 3–3 on the expansion in Milwaukee. Without another justice to break the tie, the court sent the case back to trial court in Madison, where the arguments would start afresh in August. A spokesperson for Thompson said voucher opponents should be "scared that three justices supported religious school choice." Far from scared, Chanin was pleased. "Short of a clear declaration that the statute is unconstitutional, we are delighted with this result," he said.[21]

That summer, in a courtroom in Columbus, Ohio, Chanin and Bolick employed many of the same arguments they'd used while dueling over Milwaukee's program earlier in the year. Chanin focused on the strong precedent set by *Nyquist* and the fact that the majority of the private schools benefiting from Cleveland's program were religious institutions. Bolick enlisted supporters to charter buses for parents and students to fill the courtroom and rally on the steps outside. He also seized on the language used in the brief from the American Federation of Teachers—calling parents "inconsequential conduits," a legal concept—to profess outrage in front of Judge Lisa Sadler. "How dare they! With this program, for the first time, the parents are not inconsequential." It was not a constitutional argument, but he hoped the emotion would resonate.

In late July, Sadler delivered her ruling: Cleveland's program did not violate either the US Constitution or the Ohio Constitution. "In a dry 39-page summary ruling, Judge Sadler held that the scholarship program fell 'within the narrow channel through which state funds can permissibly flow to sectarian institutions,'" *Education Week* wrote. Bolick would later declare Sadler's decision "thorough and well-reasoned," while Chanin called it "wrong and not particularly well-reasoned."[22]

In August, an appeals court in Ohio rejected the teachers' unions' request to prevent Cleveland's program from starting until the case was decided. With a new school year commencing, Milwaukee's voucher expansion was on hold, while Cleveland was the first school system to use public tax dollars to pay tuition for students attending religious schools.[23] The lawyers prepared for the long road ahead.

15

The Unholy Alliance Fractures

B Y THE FALL OF 1996, THE COUNTRY'S ONLY TWO VOUCHER programs were tied up in court and the splintering of the original "unholy alliance" at the heart of Milwaukee's program had become too fractious and controversial to ignore. State Representative Polly Williams, who had championed the program and made its passage possible six years earlier, had begun to publicly question the motives of conservative supporters.

Unlike most other Black politicians in Wisconsin, Williams supported Governor Tommy Thompson's 1995 expansion to include religious schools in Milwaukee's voucher program, even pushing an amendment to increase the number of students allowed to participate. She had never believed that her goals were the same as those of her conservative allies, but she had been willing to ignore their differences to advance her cause—uplifting Black children in poverty and putting pressure on the public schools to improve. Universal vouchers, or what Milton Friedman proposed in 1955, were not her goal. The latest expansion, however, could dramatically alter who Milwaukee's program served. The current program enrolled predominantly Black students, as did the city's public schools, while Milwaukee's religious school enrollment was largely white. Williams hoped the expansion might mean more private schools opening to serve disadvantaged Black children. She had no interest in simply subsidizing tuition for families who preferred private religious education.

Other Black politicians had raised concerns during the legislative process in 1995 before voting against the expansion. State Representative Spencer Coggs talked about the concerns of a church elder who told him the expansion in Milwaukee was potentially a step toward "nationwide religious school choice that would harken back to segregated academies in the South."[1]

As her concerns grew, Williams distanced herself from her conservative supporters. She didn't attend Thompson's celebration for the bill signing in 1995 or a rally at a Black church after the court approved an injunction on the expansion. Asked about her absences by the *Milwaukee Journal Sentinel*, she put it plainly: "Everything we have done has been to empower our community. We have our black agenda and they have got (their own) agenda. I didn't see where their resources really were being used to empower us as much as it was to co-opt us." The headline read, "Rift Seen in Support of Choice."

Conservatives, who had lionized Williams and promoted her nationwide as the public face of vouchers, found themselves in the awkward position of defending their intentions. Thompson and others denied that their long-term aim was to offer vouchers to all students, and they tried to downplay the conflict. Timothy Sheehy, president of the Metropolitan Milwaukee Association of Commerce, insisted the conflict was one-sided. The newspaper highlighted the awkward timing, however: "The rift comes at a critical time when choice backers are trying to rally support nationwide for an issue that is likely to go before the U.S. Supreme Court. The state Supreme Court is considering whether expanding choice to include religious schools violates the state and federal constitutions." When a reporter asked Sheehy if Williams's comments could hurt the case, he replied, "I guess it can't help."[2]

Williams worried white conservatives were taking power away from her Black and low-income constituents. She also saw some of the problems stemming from the lack of public accountability in the existing program. In the first six years, four private schools closed suddenly, leaving students without a school midyear and wasting tax dollars. When Juanita Virgil Academy shut down in the program's first year, supporters touted the closure as evidence that market forces were working, but subsequent closures were harder to explain to the public. When two schools, Exito Education Center and Milwaukee Preparatory, closed during the 1995–1996 school year, their principals were under criminal indictment—one for embezzlement and drug charges, the other for fraud and mishandling of public funds—and about 350 students were stranded. (The principal of the second school was not convicted.) With those two closures, the state of Wisconsin lost nearly $400,000 in tax dollars. Another school closed in the summer of 1996 amid a dispute between staff and parents. Williams thought her allies needed to be honest and realistic about the issues. She said, "I'm not going to be an ostrich with my head in the sand pretending we don't have a problem."[3]

AFTER SIX YEARS, no proof existed that Milwaukee's voucher experiment had lived up to its original promise: to provide low-income students with a better education. The program's primary researcher, John Witte, a professor at the University of Wisconsin–Madison, found no significant differences in achievement between voucher students and students in the city's public schools. That inconvenient fact dogged every effort to expand or to promote Milwaukee as a model nationwide.

Then, in the summer of 1996, the narrative changed on Milwaukee's vouchers. Paul Peterson of Harvard University, Jay Greene from the

University of Houston, and Jiangtao Du, also at Harvard, announced the results of their own study of the Milwaukee program. Peterson, Greene, and Du found that students who had been in Milwaukee's voucher program for three to four years scored higher on reading and math tests than public school students—and the difference was high enough to significantly close the test-score gap between white students and students of color. Peterson went so far as to predict that creating voucher programs in more cities across the country would create "gains in test scores that could close the gap between whites and minorities, by one-half."[4]

In the media flurry that followed, Witte and Peterson attacked each other's work, each accusing the other of bias. The researchers reached such different conclusions because of which students they chose to evaluate. Peterson, Greene, and Du compared the test scores of current voucher students to those of low-income students who had applied but had not been admitted to the program—in theory, a rigorous approach. But Witte noted that many students who hadn't received a voucher ended up leaving the public schools anyway, skewing the comparison. Witte compared students using vouchers against a large random sample of students in the Milwaukee Public Schools, which Peterson, Greene, and Du charged created its own issues when comparing students. Those details, however, were largely lost as the media focused on the personal and heated conflict between the professors. The *Wall Street Journal* ran a story about the disagreement on its front page under the headline "Class Warfare: Dueling Professors Have Milwaukee Dazed over School Vouchers." Peterson and Greene wrote an op-ed in the *Journal* with the headline "School Choice Data Rescued from Bad Science." In it, they called Witte's study "so methodologically flawed as to be worthless."[5]

The new study came at a critical time: during the latest court battle over Milwaukee's program and in the middle of a presidential election that, similar to 1992's contest, pitted public and private school choice in education. Voucher advocates seized on the results as proof that vouchers were a meaningful education reform worthy of replication. George Mitchell, an educational consultant and longtime supporter in Milwaukee, said, "This is going to redefine the debate."[6]

Clint Bolick called Peterson in to testify at the last minute. Peterson joined a list of witnesses that included two parents, an administrator at one of the private schools, and Howard Fuller, an early supporter of vouchers and now former superintendent of Milwaukee Public Schools. Bolick asked the administrator, Zakiyah Courtney, if she knew about the new study. She said it resonated with what people in the schools had witnessed: students improved academically after an adjustment period.[7] Robert Chanin countered Peterson's testimony with that of another professor, Alex Molnar of the University of Wisconsin–Milwaukee, who dismissed vouchers as a method of reform.

Months later, Molnar was among a group of researchers to respond to the Peterson, Greene, and Du study. Under the headline "A Flawed Design," the authors wrote that one of the problems with the study was it failed to account for selection bias in the student groups. Families motivated enough to find and apply to a voucher program could have characteristics unlike others who had not applied. They also accused the professors of deliberately releasing their results during the trial. They concluded, "School choice needs to be subjected to additional and more methodologically rigorous assessment in carefully controlled research settings before it is declared to be the educational salvation of the urban poor."[8]

⤜⤛

IN THE MONTHS leading up to the 1996 presidential election, the two nominees of the major parties, President Bill Clinton and Senator Bob Dole, attacked each other over the issue of educational choice. Dole had come out strong for school vouchers. In his speech at the Republican National Convention in August, he hailed "school choice and competition and opportunity scholarships." (The latter was a reference to his proposal for a national voucher program for low-income and middle-class students.) Dole also attacked Clinton for sending his daughter, Chelsea, to an expensive private school while refusing to support school vouchers for less affluent families: "There is no reason why those who live on any street in America should not have the same right as the person who lives at 1600 Pennsylvania Avenue—the right to send your child to the school of your choice."[9]

Dole also sought to mollify concerns that school vouchers would drain money out of the public school system. At a campaign stop in Dayton, Ohio, in the fall, he described himself as a "creature of the public schools" and said his plan for school vouchers was not an "effort to undermine the public schools." As he had in 1992, Clinton emphasized his support for greater choices within the public school system, which now included charter schools as a new public option on the books in twenty-five states and the District of Columbia. During his convention speech Clinton said, "We must give parents, all parents, the right to choose which public school their children will attend and to let teachers form new charter schools with a charter they can keep only if they do a good job."[10]

Despite the national rhetoric, however, America in 1996 had only two small, embattled voucher programs—in Milwaukee and Cleveland—and about a few hundred charter schools. Most of the country's students attended traditional public schools, and the debate about choice had little to do with what happened in their classrooms every day. In the *New York Times*, education reporter and former teacher Sara Mosle described teaching in a crowded New York City public school and how a hands-on science experiment, making boats out of clay, went awry in the cramped classroom. Her students, most from the surrounding low-income immigrant community, came to school with less background knowledge than their middle-class peers. Choice was unlikely to fix the problems she encountered in her classroom, she wrote.

Mosle opined that the country needed national academic standards and a core curriculum that spelled out what students should learn to move from one level of schooling to the next, a position she noted was controversial with both conservatives and liberals but had the support of Albert Shanker, president of the American Federation of Teachers, Diane Ravitch, an assistant secretary of education under President Bush, and E. D. Hirsch Jr., a well-known author and educator. Mosle wrote, "Neither political party, however, has ever really campaigned vigorously for [national standards]. Instead, both have embraced choice as a panacea to what ails our public-school system."[11]

For some conservatives, national standards and a core curriculum for all American students was the antithesis of school choice and went against the American hallmark of local control in public education. Some choice supporters believed parents should have the freedom to choose whatever education they thought appropriate for their children—and the state should pay for it—even if it meant teaching religious beliefs at odds with scientific facts. David Brennan, the businessman whose support was key to passing voucher legislation in Ohio, told a newspaper reporter in 1996 that he wanted to see private schools pop up in apartment buildings and factories. Parents would select the curriculum, and tax dollars would pay for it. Should the government intervene if a private school were to teach flat-earth theory? the reporter asked. "Absolutely not," Brennan replied.[12]

MANY OF THE parents who used vouchers in Milwaukee and Cleveland were removed from theoretical debates about the future of America's public education system. Their primary concern wasn't whether such programs violated the separation of church and state. Many were desperate to get their children out of public schools they believed were underperforming or even dangerous. In the fall of 1996, when parents in Cleveland started using vouchers to send their children to private schools, some described a sense of relief. Evelyn Dickerson, a single mother, said she sought a voucher for her son, Kevin, a third grader, because he felt threatened in his public school. To keep him safe, she had "lived" at the school and broken up fights between students. Another mother, Jennifer Kinsey, had three children in public schools and wanted to get a voucher for her fourth child. More than six thousand students applied—three times more than available spots—and when Kinsey got one of them she said, "I feel like I've won the lottery."

Opponents to school vouchers, however, said the programs were more likely to help the motivated few at the expense of improving the larger school system, particularly since voters would be unlikely to support paying for parallel school systems, one public and the other private. "The only way they are going to be able to pay for this is to either take money from the public schools, or to raise taxes—and you don't hear anyone talking about that," said Ron Marec, president of the Ohio Federation of Teachers.[13]

Most of the private schools in Cleveland that accepted vouchers in the 1996–1997 school year were, in fact, part of a separate school system: Catholic schools—long established, often supported financially by the church, and imbued with a mission to serve. At St. Francis Catholic School, nuns earned $7,000 a year and accounted for about half the faculty, keeping costs low. Principal Karen Somerville, or "Sister Karen" to her students, cautioned voucher supporters from thinking that Catholic schools' success in low-income urban areas could be copied quickly. "The rich heritage of the Catholic school system has been built up over 100 years," she said. "I think we really have to be careful with these schools popping up overnight."[14]

As the court battle dragged on in Milwaukee, Williams wasn't content to simply raise her concerns about the city's voucher program with the media. She wrote legislation in 1997 to expand the Milwaukee

Parental Choice Program—but only for secular schools. With the religious expansion tied up in litigation, Williams wanted to preserve the original intent of the program and the independent schools.

In a lengthy Q&A with a reporter for the *Capital Times* in Madison, Williams didn't mince words about what her goals were in crafting the legislation, and she didn't hesitate to call out her allies in the school choice movement. No one was spared in the interview—not Catholics, not the business community, not Governor Tommy Thompson, not Clint Bolick. She wanted to return the voucher program to its origins as a tool of empowerment for low-income Black children. She said her goal with the new bill was to "have schools in our community that are run and controlled by people that look like me."

Williams accused the business community, the Catholic archdiocese, and PAVE—all major players in the expansion to include religious schools—of trying to maintain the "dominance of white people in controlling the institutions in our community." Catholics in particular wanted financial support for their schools—and would never admit large percentages of disadvantaged Black students, she believed. If they did, white parents would flee, she said plainly. Thompson and Bolick, meanwhile, were largely in it for the glory—the chance to get a case in front of the US Supreme Court, she said, adding, "They could care less about low-income children."[15]

The message seemed clear: Williams was done with the unholy alliance. Less clear was whether conservatives still needed her.

16

Bolick vs. Chanin

IN COURTROOMS ACROSS THE COUNTRY, CLINT BOLICK AND Robert Chanin sparred over the legality of school vouchers. By the late summer of 1997, the decisions came back, with loss after loss stacking up for Bolick and his team. First they lost in Wisconsin's Dane County Circuit Court, where Judge Paul Higginbotham ruled that including private religious schools in Milwaukee's school voucher program crossed the church-state line in the state constitution. In his decision he wrote, "Millions of dollars would be directed to religious institutions that are pervasively sectarian with a clear mission to indoctrinate Wisconsin students with their religious beliefs." Then an Ohio appeals court struck down Cleveland's vouchers as unconstitutional and held that unless the program received a stay from the state supreme court, it would likely shut down at the end of its first year. In a less high-profile case, a trial court in Vermont struck down a town "tuitioning program," which allowed students in an area without a public high school to attend a nearby religious academy at public expense. Finally, the court of appeals in Wisconsin upheld Higginbotham's ruling.[1] For Chanin, the rulings were a triumph, holding the line against public support of private education. For Bolick, they were gutting.

Both men knew they were grinding it out in the lower courts until the US Supreme Court chose to review one of the cases. That all but guaranteed a long road of appeals and a roller coaster of devastating decisions. Still, after the appeals court ruling in Ohio, Bolick sat alone in his office and wondered if his quest to get a voucher case in front of the Supreme Court would end in failure. "The prospect of losing both Milwaukee and Cleveland, the twin pillars of urban school choice, now was a real possibility. The implications were overwhelming," he would write later.[2]

ONE ADVANTAGE BOLICK had over Chanin, however, was the rising power of the movement behind school choice. Seven years earlier, political scientists John Chubb and Terry Moe had described the movement as "extremely fragmented." By now, it had transformed into an influential national network working toward similar goals and supported by philanthropic funding and conservative think tanks. Friedman and his wife started the Milton and Rose D. Friedman Foundation for Educational Choice in 1996 to advocate for school vouchers. Other conservative foundations, including the Bradley Foundation, the Heritage Foundation, and the Reason Foundation, promoted private school choice options. Once a fringe notion of the far right, school vouchers were being studied as a tool of reform for urban school systems and promoted by advocates as the path out of poorly performing public schools.[3] The concept of school choice featured in two presidential elections, in 1992 and 1996, as Democratic and Republican candidates squared off over public school choice and private school choice. Both George H. W. Bush and Bob Dole made federal voucher proposals a central part of their education platforms during their presidential runs.

Conservatives, along with some progressive supporters, were increasingly making the case that education in the public interest was, in fact, public education. Chubb and Moe had argued as much in their 1990 book, *Politics, Markets, and America's Schools*, and Republican politicians had subsequently test-driven the idea on the campaign trail. Bush said in 1992, "Whether a school is organized by privately financed educators or town councils or religious orders or denominations, any school that serves the public and is held accountable by the public authority provides public education." Governor Tommy Thompson made the same argument when he announced his intention to expand Milwaukee's program. He defined school choice as "the belief that parents will choose the best school for their child. That's education serving the public."[4]

In other educational settings, Americans were accustomed to private institutions receiving federal or state subsidies to provide public services, such as preschool programs or Pell Grants for college students. Veterans using the GI Bill to attend college could choose private religious institutions. But Jeffrey Henig, a professor of political science at George Washington University, called the concept of education in the public interest—instead of public education—a "rhetorical sleight-of-hand" made possible by a shift in the 1980s toward privatization. He wrote, "Proposing that we stretch the label 'public' to cover largely deregulated, market-based systems of educational choice is possible only because the term *public* has been so devalued."

Many voters also remained unconvinced by conservatives' reframing of public education: voucher referendums were shot down by large margins. Legislative efforts, too, stalled in multiple states, including Arizona, Texas, and Pennsylvania, where lawmakers instead turned to charter schools as a form of school choice more readily accepted by the public. Efforts to create voucher programs failed in cities that appeared, at least from the outside, to have the makings of a Milwaukee-style coalition, with key Republican leaders, a large Black population, and underresourced and underperforming public schools. In Jersey City, New

Jersey, for instance, a plan for a five-year voucher pilot for low-income students never got off the ground despite the stated support of a Republican mayor and Republican governor. Some communities were not ready to give up on their public schools.[5]

Conservatives pressed on, however, honing their legal strategies and looking for places that seemed like fertile ground for even a small program. In Washington, DC, Republican congressmen, including House Speaker Newt Gingrich and Indiana senator Dan Coats, pushed for a voucher pilot in the summer and fall of 1997, despite the threat of a veto from President Clinton. The pitch was for two thousand low-income students to attend private or public schools in DC or in nearby suburban school districts in Virginia and Maryland with vouchers of $3,200 each. Republicans renewed Bob Dole's campaign-trail charges of hypocrisy, calling out Clinton for sending his daughter to an elite private school while opposing private school choice for low-income students. The initial voucher proposal, however, appeared to be more about elevating the issue politically than providing meaningful options for children. As the *Washington Post* wrote, a $3,200 voucher wouldn't cover tuition at most private schools in Washington, DC— certainly not at the elite Sidwell Friends School, from which Chelsea Clinton graduated that year—and not at any of the eighty schools belonging to the Association of Independent Schools of Greater Washington, where "the median price is $10,075 for elementary and $12,800 for secondary schools." The association's executive director, Ritalou Harris, told the *Post*, "Lots of money needs to be provided before the voucher is meaningful."[6]

At parochial schools, some of which were more affordable, overcrowding was an issue, which meant there likely wouldn't be enough seats for students who received a voucher. Lawrence Callahan, superintendent of schools for the Catholic Archdiocese of Washington, told the newspaper, "Trying to accommodate more kids is a real concern this year." Democrats were quick to point out what they viewed as the

Republicans' hypocrisy. Representative John Lewis, a Georgia Democrat, suggested if Republicans were truly interested in helping low-income students in the "inner city," they should invest more resources in the city's public schools. He led a protest, marching with parents and some House members to a traditional public school. Clinton's education secretary, Richard Riley, cast the debate in broader terms, saying vouchers would undermine the country's commitment to the common school, a "commitment that has helped America keep faith with our democratic ideals and become a beacon of light for people all over the world."[7]

The bipartisan coalition that sprang up around the issue, however, showed the political inroads voucher supporters had made since 1990. Though primarily favored by Republicans, vouchers also received support from some prominent Democrats, including Senator Joseph Lieberman of Connecticut, Senator Mary Landrieu of Louisiana, Senator Daniel Patrick Moynihan of New York, and Representative Floyd Flake, a Black minister from Queens. Flake, who was known for working with Republicans when it would benefit his constituents, said he supported vouchers to expand options for low-income children.

Many Black parents found arguments for vouchers compelling, particularly as their children were the ones most likely to be poorly served by the public school system, with more inexperienced teachers, fewer resources, and older buildings. Coats and Flake invited parents from Milwaukee and Cleveland to testify in favor of vouchers in 1997 at a Senate subcommittee hearing. Polls taken the previous year showed a greater percentage of Black Americans favored voucher programs for the urban poor than white Americans. Flake called it a "phenomenal step" that the Black Caucus debated the issue at all. "Ordinarily our posture has been: 'Public schools at all costs. Nothing else can ever be considered. We're not even going to hear it.'"[8]

In Washington, DC, Virginia Walden, a Black mother of three who as a child was among the first to integrate the public schools in Little

Rock, Arkansas, became a powerful voice for voucher legislation. (She was later known as Virginia Walden Ford.) The Center for Education Reform had been looking for parents to recruit to support voucher legislation in Washington and happened to call the Fishing School, an educational and social services nonprofit where Walden worked. Walden's first two children attended public schools in the district, but her third child, William, struggled in the public school system. He transferred to a Catholic high school with the financial assistance of a neighbor who agreed to pay half the tuition. Even with help, Walden struggled to pay her son's tuition, adding a night job to her day job to make it work. But William began doing better in school. When she asked him what made the difference, he said he felt safe at the school and that people there cared about him.

Motivated by her own experience, Walden started working with the Center for Education Reform, tapping into the conservative network that was pushing for private school choice nationwide. Much as Polly Williams had originally, Walden rejected the criticism she heard that Black parents were being used as pawns by their white, conservative allies. She wanted to make it easier for other parents to do what she had done and leave the public schools, if necessary.[9]

THE CONCEPT OF school vouchers remained politically controversial and, as Republicans had learned, a tough sell in many parts of the country. So in 1997, conservative lawmakers in Arizona created a new private school choice option: the tax-credit scholarship. Earlier efforts to pass a statewide voucher program had fallen short; legislators instead passed one of the country's least-regulated charter school laws in 1994. Trent Franks, a former state legislator who is credited with the idea of the tax-credit scholarship, wanted an alternative to school vouchers that would be easier to defend against legal challenge. He thought he'd found it with the scholarship, or what critics soon began calling the "backdoor voucher." Like a school voucher, the scholarship would pay for qualifying students' tuition at a private school but with a key difference: the money would bypass the state. Instead, Arizona's plan called for individuals to take a tax credit for donations of up to $500 to private schools and $200 toward extracurricular activities at public schools. The $500 donations would then be paid out as scholarships. The person making the donation would get a tax break but could not donate money for their own child. Franks called the concept both "simple and profound."[10]

Opponents weren't persuaded that the new option, which allowed students to attend private religious schools, differed much from school vouchers. Barbara Robey, of the Arizona School Boards Association, described the tax-credit scholarships "as just a step away from vouchers."[11] The association and the teachers' unions argued the new program still violated the state constitution's prohibition against public aid flowing to religious schools.

Could tax-credit scholarships withstand a successful legal challenge? In truth, choice advocates didn't know. This was uncharted territory. But they wouldn't have to wait long to find out. The teachers' union filed a lawsuit challenging the program. Once again, Chanin and Bolick prepared to meet in court, this time in Arizona in December 1997.

Bolick, working with the state's lawyers, settled on a "long-shot argument." He planned to argue that the money used to fund the tax-credit scholarships wasn't public because it never came under the direct control of the state. If successful—a big if—Bolick believed the case could establish an important precedent for future court challenges and possibly give the school choice movement another avenue to pursue if the US Supreme Court eventually ruled against school vouchers.[12]

❈

EVEN AS ARIZONA's legal fight was getting underway, charter schools enjoyed strong bipartisan support as a method of educational reform. President Clinton pushed for the expansion of charter schools, and by the 1997–1998 school year, about five hundred charters were open nationwide. But in some states it wasn't clear if charter schools were any more constitutional than school vouchers.

The US Constitution says nothing about establishing or maintaining a system of public education, leaving the matter to the states to figure out. In turn, each state constitution varies somewhat in how it spells out the government's duty to provide citizens with an education. Some call for the state to maintain a system of "common schools," while others require a "uniform" or "efficient" or even "high-quality" school system.[13] Some constitutions prohibit public money from going to private religious schools. In the 1990s, as state after state passed laws authorizing charter schools, that constitutional language became key to defining what it meant to offer a system of public education. Were charter schools truly public schools, as supporters argued, or were they a sort of public-private hybrid that fell outside the public school system? Were they private schools masquerading as public schools?

In Michigan, members of the state board of education and the teachers' unions filed a lawsuit to attack the state's charter school law soon after it passed in 1993. Michigan was among the early wave of states to craft charter school legislation, passing its law that year along with Wisconsin, New Mexico, Colorado, and Massachusetts. The lawsuit alleged the charter law allowed the state to fund private schools, a violation of the state constitution. "The legislature does not have the right to define public schools in any way it desires," one of the lawyers charged. Since the charter law's passage, a mix of private schools, alternative schools, and new schools in Michigan had successfully applied for a charter, entitling them to $5,500 in state aid per student. One of the schools, Noah Webster Academy, planned to enroll about thirteen hundred students spread across the state, all working independently from home. State-certified teachers would work with students over computer and telephone. The school's founder said he didn't believe the school would need the entire $7.7 million in state aid for the school's operations, so he planned to give parents a "laundry list" of things they could use the money for, including field trips and extracurriculars. Anything left over at the end of the year would then go into a college fund for each child.[14]

Such plans were alarming to supporters of public education in the state. They seemed to have little to do with educational innovation and a lot to do with using public money for homeschooling. They certainly didn't resemble anything Albert Shanker, one-time president of the American Federation of Teachers, had in mind when he had breathed life into the idea of charter schools in 1988. Shanker, who died in 1997, had long since dismissed charter schools as a reform method; in his view the notion had turned into a means of privatization. Charter supporters, however, dismissed the Michigan school as an anomaly. "It is an exotic that has little to do with the mainline issue," Ted Kolderie, one of the drivers of the charter school movement, told the *Christian Science Monitor*.

A state judge agreed in late 1994 that Michigan's new law was unconstitutional and blocked the state from giving $3.5 million in state dollars to private schools that had received charters under the new law. The new schools had to be under the direct control of the state board of education to be considered public schools, he ruled. "This court determines that a school must be under the immediate, exclusive control of the state to pass constitutional muster, as well as being open to all students that care to attend," Judge William Collette wrote in his decision.[15] The ruling was upheld in the appeals court and stood until the summer of 1997, when a divided Michigan Supreme Court reversed course, upholding the law and declaring that charter schools were indeed public schools. The question would be raised again in other states as efforts to create new educational options ran into state and federal constitutions.

><

In March 1998, Chanin and Bolick met again, this time in the Wisconsin Supreme Court, where six justices would decide the fate of Milwaukee's school voucher expansion. As had become the routine before court arguments, Bolick asked supporters to rally on the steps outside the court. This time, more than a dozen buses brought students, families, and other allies from Milwaukee to Madison. Students wore their school uniforms and carried homemade signs. A private school's choir sang "We Shall Overcome," a gospel song and anthem of the civil rights movement. To Bolick's great delight, Chanin and his team were forced to wade through the crowd to get inside.

This time, Bolick argued alongside Jay Lefkowitz, a lawyer in Ken Starr's law firm. (Starr was busy with a grand jury inquiry into President Clinton's affair with a White House intern.) The arguments hadn't changed. Bolick and Chanin knew what the other would say. (Bolick would joke later that not only could he present Chanin's argument; he could do it in Chanin's accent.) Chanin preferred to stick to the law. He rarely talked about whether school vouchers were sound public policy or if a voucher program could improve the educational problems in Milwaukee or Cleveland. Bolick often waded into emotional arguments—a strategy that irritated Chanin—and this day was no different. "This program is one part of a very large and aggressive effort to rescue children from the Milwaukee public schools," he told the justices in a courtroom packed with students. "These kids may not have a second chance."[16]

Chanin, who had argued the legal merits of vouchers in Wisconsin courts three times, knew this might be his last argument in the case. With the final few minutes of his time, he asked the court for a moment of "personal privilege" to address what he felt were unfair attacks from the program's supporters.

> Throughout this litigation, we have been portrayed as the bad guys;
> as uncaring, as insensitive to the needs and aspirations of disadvan-

taged minority children. That we are attempting, for some unstated, but surely unworthy motive, to deny to them this golden opportunity to escape from the jungle of urban education. . . . We have refrained from responding in kind because we are attorneys. We believe that our job is simply to argue the law and not to debate policy. But quite frankly, we resent the role in which petitioners have cast us.

As Bolick listened in astonishment, Chanin excoriated Bolick's courtroom strategies and denigrated school vouchers as the abandonment of public education.

We are fully aware of the educational problems that exist in cities, such as Milwaukee and Cleveland and other urban centers. Indeed, in at least some cities in this country, the term "crisis" is probably not an overstatement. But these problems cannot be resolved by schemes that skim off 5,000 or 10,000 or even 15,000 students from highly motivated families and leave behind 85,000 or 90,000 other students based on the dubious theory that competition with a relative handful of private schools, coupled with fewer resources, somehow will produce a dramatic turnaround in public education. . . . Every child, not just a chosen few thousand, is entitled to a quality education.[17]

Bolick would later call Chanin's extraordinary comments a "meltdown." But Chanin, who had committed most of his professional life to defending public school teachers and, by extension, he felt, America's public schools, had finally had enough.[18]

17

Florida Gets in the Voucher Game

I N THE WINTER OF 1999, FLORIDA'S NEW REPUBLICAN GOVER-
nor unveiled an ambitious education plan. Under the "A-Plus plan,"
Jeb Bush proposed to dramatically expand accountability measures
for the state's public schools, with standardized testing in grades three
through ten and an annual "report card" for schools. Similar to students,
each school would receive a grade from A to F. Lieutenant Governor
Frank Brogan said the plan would provide an "annual picture of student
achievement and performance, district achievement and performance,
statewide achievement and performance, so that we can let our parents
know how their child's school is faring."[1]

The most controversial part of the plan, however, was that Bush
planned to directly link the performance of public schools, measured
largely by test scores, to a statewide school voucher program, the first
of its kind nationwide. Students enrolled in a public school that received two F grades in a four-year period would be eligible for a school
voucher to attend private school. Opportunity scholarships, as Bush

called them, could be used by students regardless of their family income and could also be used at religious schools.

The son of a former president, John Ellis Bush was young, intellectually curious, and ambitious. Born in Texas, he moved to Florida in the 1980s and made his career in real estate. In his first run at the governor's office, in 1994, he lost in a bruising campaign to Democratic governor Lawton Chiles, a sixty-four-year-old heavyweight in Florida politics, in what was the narrowest margin in a governor's race in state history. The same year, his older brother, George Walker Bush, won the governor's office in their home state of Texas. Regrouping after his loss, Jeb Bush launched a public policy organization, the Foundation for Florida's Future, and cofounded the Sunshine State's first charter school in Miami with T. Willard Fair, head of the Miami Urban League. Liberty City Charter School focused on "character education" and required guardians to sign a contract pledging to oversee homework and volunteer at the school. An article in Fort Lauderdale's *Sun Sentinel* during Bush's 1998 campaign for governor said Bush and Fair wanted to show that "reform-minded prescriptions for education such as charter schools and vouchers can work for the underprivileged." The story continued, "While other politicians have a position paper on education, the 44-year-old Miami businessman and son of former President George H. W. Bush has a school—one with 138 students in one of Miami's most crime-ridden and crack-infested neighborhoods."[2]

Once in the governor's office, Bush wasted no time moving on his education agenda. In his State of the State speech in March 1999, Bush opened the session of the Florida Legislature with a call for both parties to work together, though Republicans controlled the executive and legislative branches. He described education as his first priority, saying the state's education system needed both more money and higher standards. He called attention to a recent report that put Florida's graduation rate at 52 percent. He urged legislators to pass his education plan, and he made it clear he wanted "opportunity scholarships" included.

"No student in our state should be forced to attend a school that repeatedly continues to fail," he said.[3]

It was no surprise that school vouchers played a key role in Bush's
first major education proposal. Republican governors and lawmakers
across the country had increasingly been toying with voucher legislation, though most efforts ultimately failed. (Efforts to pass school
voucher legislation in Florida had faltered the previous year.) School
choice had become an important part of the Republican political play-
book. Some polls suggested the Republican Party could use the issue
to appeal to people of color, particularly young, low-income Black and
Latino parents, demographic groups that typically voted Democratic.
School choice, as used by Republicans, had become an umbrella term,
one that could reasonably include open-enrollment plans, magnet
schools, alternative schools, charter schools, school vouchers, and tax-
credit scholarships. Such a broad definition blurred the line between
public and private options in a way that most Democrats objected to;
they spoke about "choice" only within the public sphere. What Republicans often meant when talking about choice, however, was school
vouchers. (In 1999, the Michigan-based Mackinac Center for Public
Policy, a conservative think tank, published a report that made a dis-
tinction between "limited" and "full" educational choice options, with
public options falling into the limited category. Charter schools were
good but not great based on that definition of school choice.) Bush,
like some other advocates, avoided using the politically loaded term
"voucher" altogether. Testifying later that year in front of the US House
Budget Committee, he said, "You all can call them vouchers. We call
them opportunity scholarships."[4]

Bush and his advisors might also have felt the legal winds shifting
toward school vouchers. In June 1997, the US Supreme Court ruled in
Agostini vs. Felton that public school teachers could provide remedial
instruction to eligible students in private religious schools, reversing an
earlier church-state case. A year later, the Wisconsin Supreme Court

voted 4–2 to uphold Milwaukee's expanded school voucher program, ruling that the program served a primarily secular purpose. The *New York Times* called the ruling the "most significant legal decision yet on the growing use of school vouchers." Chip Mellor, president of the Institute for Justice, the conservative law firm he cofounded with Clint Bolick, told the newspaper the court ruling would "help school choice spread like wildfire across the nation," a nod to a quote by Milton Friedman from a few years earlier. In the fall of 1998, the US Supreme Court declined to review the case, a move many advocates of school choice declared a victory of sorts. Though not the sweeping ruling they were hoping for, it did allow the Milwaukee program to stand. "This is a green light for other states to proceed with the most promising education reform on the horizon," Bolick told *USA Today*.[5] Not long before Bush announced his A-Plus plan, the Arizona Supreme Court narrowly upheld the state's new tax-credit scholarship program. Although the ruling applied only to Arizona, it put another case with church-state precedent within grasp of the US Supreme Court. Would the case that finally settled the matter come from Arizona, Cleveland—or Florida?

WITH A REPUBLICAN-CONTROLLED legislature, Bush didn't anticipate trouble getting the A-Plus plan passed in the spring of 1999. Lawmakers debated whether to give vouchers only to students who were struggling academically in the state's lowest-performing schools. They discussed tracking how students did in the years after they accepted a voucher to attend a private school. And they also talked about a requirement that private schools exist for one year before taking state money. Ultimately the plan they hammered out closely resembled the one Bush had pitched. As some constitutional bulletproofing, the legislation included a provision to allow students at an F-rated school to transfer to another public school. (The legislation also included a pilot for vouchers for students with disabilities.) A headline in the *Orlando Sentinel* read, "School Vouchers Look like a Sure Thing."[6]

In the spring and summer of 1999, Florida wasn't the only state with vouchers in play. School voucher legislation sprang up across the country that year, including Texas, Pennsylvania, and New Mexico. In California and Michigan, voucher advocates were pushing for statewide referendums for the 2000 election. In Washington, DC, where President Clinton had vetoed voucher legislation in 1998, as promised, the coalition in favor of vouchers had grown stronger and still was pursuing the issue. And in New York City, Mayor Rudy Giuliani, a Republican, created a firestorm of opposition by proposing a voucher pilot in one of the city's educational districts. His schools chancellor, Rudy Crew, threatened to resign, and a coalition of more than seventy organizations, including labor, religious, and community groups, quickly formed in opposition, calling itself the Emergency Campaign Against Vouchers. After backing off briefly, Giuliani doubled down on his proposal and unleashed hyperbolic criticism of the city's public schools, saying, "The whole system should be blown up and a new one should be put in its place." In its newsletter, the People for the American Way, a liberal advocacy group opposing voucher legislation across the country, referred to the movement nationwide as "this year's gathering storm."[7]

Republican politicians were the ones largely pushing legislation, and they crafted myriad proposals. Some resembled Milwaukee- or Cleveland-style programs, while others were broader. In Pennsylvania, Republican governor Tom Ridge, who had failed to secure a voucher plan in previous years, came back in 1999 with a pitch for a five-year pilot for low-income students in more than a dozen communities. In Michigan, a ballot item proposed to give vouchers to any student attending a school district with a four-year graduation rate below roughly 66 percent. The Associated Press reported that many of the school districts that qualified had suddenly improved their graduation rates after plans for the referendum became known.[8]

And in New Mexico, Republican governor Gary Johnson proposed the most far-reaching plan, one that invited instant controversy. Johnson wanted to start with a voucher program for a hundred thousand students from low-income families—or about one-third of the state's school population—and then slowly raise income requirements until, after a period of four years, all children in New Mexico would be eligible.[9]

In Texas, where voucher proposals had stalled in prior years, Governor George W. Bush made it clear that he supported the idea, both at home and nationally. Considered the front-runner for the Republican Party's nomination for president in 2000, Bush proposed a plan similar to what his brother had done in Florida. He said if he were elected president he would force public schools to improve or give some of their federal funds to parents to spend on educational alternatives. "The governor carefully avoided using the politically sensitive term school vouchers, but he clearly embraced the concept," a story in the *New York Times* said.[10] Vice President Al Gore, who sought the Democratic Party's nomination for president, emphasized that he opposed vouchers.

In most places, the push for vouchers came from Republicans, but they couldn't always count on support from members of their own party. Many Republican voters in suburban communities were reluctant to support school vouchers; often they had moved to the suburbs for the perceived quality of the public schools. Afraid of losing voters' support, many elected representatives backed off the issue. In New Mexico, Johnson took a different approach when faced with political resistance. He threatened to veto the education budget, a move that would shut down the state's public schools, unless lawmakers passed his voucher plan. Still, a bipartisan group voted it down after a coalition of teachers, school administrators, and others fought the proposal and ran negative radio spots in conservative-leaning areas.[11] In Pennsylvania, Ridge rallied with supporters at the capitol in Harrisburg, but his proposal was dogged by criticism that it would do more to help the wealthy than the poor.

By the fall of 1999, only Florida had succeeded in passing a new voucher plan. For the first time, a state would link a public school accountability measure with a statewide voucher plan. Bush, who had signed the bill into law in June, framed the groundbreaking and controversial law this way: "This is vital for our long-term competitiveness as a state, vital for restoring our civil society. It pushes the resources and attention where it needs to be. It will improve the public schools."[12]

In the first year, only two elementary schools in Pensacola qualified. Clint Bolick, who seemed to have a preternatural ability to be anywhere a new voucher plan was being drafted, helped to get the word out to parents. Never one to miss a good public relations opportunity, he referred to Florida's plan as the "first money-back guarantee in the history of public education." He told a reporter at *USA Today*, "One of the delicious ironies, from our perspective, is that if the teachers unions want to keep vouchers from occurring in Florida, what they have to do is offer a quality product. If no public schools fail, there are no vouchers."[13]

The teachers' unions had a different idea. They sued.

IN MILWAUKEE, STATE Representative Polly Williams failed to cut religious schools out of the city's voucher program and now found herself increasingly at odds with her conservative allies in the school choice movement. She loudly and frequently accused conservatives, including Governor Tommy Thompson, of using poor children to start a voucher program with the long-term goal of giving vouchers to the wealthy. "They got the door open, and that's all they needed," she said. A spokesperson for the governor called her accusations "outrageous." Feeling isolated, Williams told reporters how she had been excluded from the movement she had started. A 1998 headline in the *Milwaukee Journal Sentinel* read, "School Choice Pioneer Chafes at Her Status." One in the *National Catholic Reporter* in 1999 read, "Voucher Godmother Skeptical of Allies." In *USA Today*, another headline read, "'Rosa Parks' of Choice Sits Out Voucher Fight."[14]

As usual, the sixty-two-year-old Democrat didn't hold back in her criticism of either provoucher conservatives or antivoucher liberals, saying for Black and low-income people it was a "fight over a change in slave masters." Poor parents, particularly Black ones, needed to fight for their own agenda, she said. She reserved her fiercest barbs for her former allies, white conservatives who had championed school vouchers and made her the face of school choice. "The conservatives made me their poster girl as long as it appeared I was supporting their cause," she said. "And now I am the odd person out. . . . Blacks and poor are being used to help legitimize them as the power group."

Williams reached out to some of her former opponents on the issue, including the NAACP, with mixed success. Black school board members held a fundraiser for her. But in some cases she didn't find much sympathy for her position as the nonconformist in what had become a protracted and often bitter fight. One opponent said simply, "She got paid," a reference to the fees Williams had collected when she'd traveled around the country speaking at Republican events after the 1990 passage of Milwaukee's voucher program.

If Williams didn't want to be the face of the school choice movement, conservative allies had another supporter who would step in: Howard Fuller. Personable and charismatic, Fuller had credibility as an early backer of school vouchers and a former school superintendent. After leaving the Milwaukee school district, he took a job at Marquette University as the head of the new Institute for the Transformation of Learning, which was funded in part by the Bradley Foundation, among other organizations. Fuller also founded the Black Alliance for Educational Options (BAEO), a group intended to spotlight Black support for school choice. Fuller, who described himself as a "full-time advocate for the parental choice movement," had no illusions about why conservatives were calling him. "I was a novelty, an outspoken Black man and former schools superintendent who supported a growing movement that was largely championed by conservative white people," he wrote later. But Fuller believed, as Williams had, that school choice "offered the best hope for Black children from poor and working-class families."[15]

Williams, who had known Fuller since high school, didn't appreciate being replaced by him. In 1998, she called him "the person that the white people have selected to lead the choice movement now because I don't cooperate." She added, "he cannot replace me. . . . He cannot fill Polly Williams' shoes." Fuller refused to be pulled into a battle with Williams, a longtime friend and political ally. "If it's a war, I'm not in it," he said.[16] The truth was the school choice movement had eclipsed Williams, and whether she liked it or not she was no longer necessary to its forward march.

>‹

IN LATE MAY 1999, about a month before Florida's voucher bill became law, the Ohio Supreme Court issued an unusual split ruling. The court ruled 4–3 that Cleveland's program was invalid because it had been buried in the state budget rather than considered as a stand-alone bill. But the justices also ruled 4–3 that the program didn't violate the First Amendment's establishment clause. Newspapers across the country carried the news, though they struggled with how to frame it. The *Detroit News* declared, "Vouchers Are Constitutional," while the *Orlando Sentinel* ran "Ohio's Supreme Court Strikes Down Vouchers." The *Cleveland Jewish News* spelled it all out for its readers with "Ohio Supreme Court Rules Vouchers Unconstitutional: Opponents of Vouchers Score Technical Victory as Cleveland Pilot Program Struck Down."[17]

The split ruling left both sides scrambling. To preserve the voucher program, now entering its fourth school year, advocates had to quickly get the Ohio legislature to pass a stand-alone bill, even as the legislative session approached its end. With Republican businessman David

Brennan pressing the issue—and Republicans in control of both the governor's mansion and the statehouse—they quickly succeeded. Bolick expected his longtime opponent, Robert Chanin, to petition the US Supreme Court for review, potentially triggering the showdown they had been building toward for years. But Chanin had a surprise for Bolick. Instead of pressing the Supreme Court to take up the case, Chanin filed a new lawsuit, again on First Amendment grounds, in the federal district court in Cleveland. He also asked for an injunction to stop the program during the legal challenge.

It was an unexpected curveball from Chanin, and it worked. One day before the 1999–2000 school year started, Judge Solomon Oliver Jr. granted the injunction, which meant nearly four thousand students no longer had vouchers to cover their tuition at fifty-six private schools in Cleveland. Bolick blasted the ruling as an "outrageous abuse of judicial power." A spokesperson for Americans United for Separation of Church and State declared the ruling a "tremendous victory."[18] Even as he approved the injunction, Oliver suggested that regardless of what he heard in court in the months to come, he was likely to strike down Cleveland's program on the grounds that it violated the US Constitution.

His injunction caused a swift backlash, however, as newspapers ran stories about students being shut out of their schools a day before the school year was to start. Under pressure, Oliver largely reversed his decision within days, allowing students to continue attending private schools during the court proceedings. "This timing caused disruption to the children previously enrolled in the program beyond that normally associated with a student's transferring from one school to another," he conceded.[19] He did not, however, allow students new to the program to receive vouchers, which affected a much smaller number of children. The roller coaster for families continued in November when the US Supreme Court intervened at the defendants' urging, ruling that the program would remain intact throughout the court battle.

At the end of 1999, Oliver did as promised and struck down the program. In his ruling, he wrote that it had the effect "of advancing religion through government-sponsored religious indoctrination." Most of the participating private schools were religious, and he gave examples of their inherently religious nature: the student handbook for one Catholic school said the main objective of education was "to communicate the gospel message of Jesus," while a Lutheran school promised students a "Christ-centered approach."[20]

The decision pushed the case to the Sixth Circuit Court of Appeals, where, a year later, the court ruled 2–1 against Cleveland's program. The ruling was unusually vitriolic, with the judges trading angry barbs back and forth. In a fiery dissent, Judge James L. Ryan accused the other two of "nativist bigotry." In turn, Judges Eugene E. Siler and Eric L. Clay accused Ryan of making "gratuitous insults." With the win, Chanin told the *New York Times*, "We certainly hope everyone will get the message. The message is, let's focus on improving the public schools and stop playing around with vouchers as a panacea." Bolick called the ruling a "disaster" but predicted it wouldn't stand for long: "The day of reckoning is drawing closer."[21]

It seemed more likely than ever that the US Supreme Court would have to wade into the decidedly murky church-state waters. The court declined to review the decision of the Wisconsin Supreme Court, which upheld vouchers. It declined to review the decision of the Arizona Supreme Court, which upheld tax-credit scholarships. It declined to review two cases from Maine, one from the state's supreme court and another from federal court, in which the courts upheld the exclusion of religious schools from a long-standing tuition program.[22] Now two courts in Ohio had reached drastically different conclusions about the constitutionality of school vouchers. And in Florida a judge had struck down the new statewide program in its first year—a ruling reversed on appeal within months. With such a confusing and contradictory legal landscape taking shape across the country, only the US Supreme Court could step in and say where the church-state line should be drawn—a ruling that would shape American education for decades to come. The *New York Times* zeroed in on what was at stake outside the courtroom: "Apart from the constitutional disputes, the political battle over vouchers concerns the very definition of the public-school system."[23]

18

A Chartered Future?

DESPITE HIGH-PROFILE EFFORTS BY REPUBLICAN GOVERNORS to start school voucher programs, the charter school had become the ascendent school choice reform. Charter schools were popular with parents and politicians in both parties, and media coverage often was favorable too. Many Democrats pushed charter schools as an alternative to school vouchers and tax-credit scholarships that allowed students to attend private schools. Charter schools offered families more choices outside the traditional school system but without raising difficult questions about church-state separation. Some supporters referred to a distinctive "charter school movement," separate from the larger school choice movement.

At City Academy in St. Paul, Minnesota, the nation's first charter school, it had not been easy to keep the lights on and the place running. To open on time in 1992, the school's founders used a $30,000 loan. Milo Cutter and Terry Kraabel went six months without receiving the state funding they were promised. In their first year of operation, the 1992–1993 school year, their budget was under $200,000.

City Academy didn't receive federal money for students with disabilities or students living in poverty until 1996, four years after opening in a recreation center. Most of their students were considered "at-risk," teenagers who had struggled in school or dropped out. City Academy was likely their last shot to graduate. Many, if they committed to the highly personalized program, would need only one or two years before graduating high school. Cutter collected and framed pictures of each graduating class, evidence of an annual miracle for the tiny experimental school and its students.[1]

State officials often didn't know how to handle the unusual program at City Academy, where students weren't assigned to formal grade levels and the course of study was tailored to the individual. As the school leaders tried to innovate, as intended under Minnesota's chartering legislation, they ran into state accountability requirements based on a traditional system of public education. Simply calculating graduation rates could be difficult for a school where students were often considered seniors or "post–twelfth graders," if they were labeled anything at all.

In May 2000, nearly eight years after it opened, City Academy hosted President Clinton for a visit in the final year of his presidency, part of a two-day educational tour he had scheduled, with other stops in Kentucky, Minnesota, and Iowa. Since Minnesota had passed the first law authorizing charter schools in 1991, more than two dozen other states and the District of Columbia had followed with charter laws of their own. The country's charter sector had exploded, with more than fifteen hundred schools open nationwide in the 1999–2000 school year. Clinton, in his speech at City Academy, recalled that when he had been elected eight years earlier, he'd believed the concept had "enormous promise," but it was still relatively unknown. "I wanted to come here today because of what you've done, because you've proved that charter schools were a good idea," he said. "As I said, when I started running for president, there was a grand total of one charter school. You. You were it."[2]

Clinton acknowledged that some charter schools had closed. Some states had enacted laws that left the charter sector largely unregulated. He praised Minnesota for striking the right balance with its law, which he deemed neither too restrictive nor too permissive. He also responded to critics who said charter schools drained money away from traditional public schools. "That's just not true," he said. "You would be in school somewhere. And if you were, whether your school was doing an effective job or not, the tax money would be going there." Clinton then went a step further and said charter schools had the potential to save America's public school system. "The charter school movement, if it works, can help to save public education in this country by proving that excellence can be provided to all children from all backgrounds no matter what experiences they bring to school in the first place," he said. "That's what this whole thing is about."

Coming into the presidency, Clinton had hoped to see three thousand or more charter schools open across the country by the time he left office. He fell short of that goal when he welcomed a new president to the Oval Office in early 2001, but with his support charter schools had become an indelible part of the landscape of American education. A headline in the *New York Times* proclaimed, "Staking Claims to New Frontiers in Education: Plenty of Pioneers but Few Detailed Maps in Flourishing Charter School Movement." The *Daily Press* in Newport News, Virginia, asked simply, "A Chartered Future?"[3]

PRESIDENT GEORGE W. Bush made it clear that education was a top priority for the new administration. Three days after his inauguration, he unveiled the blueprint for No Child Left Behind, or NCLB, a major policy initiative that, if passed by Congress, would require annual standardized testing in reading and math for students in third to eighth grades and one time in high school, assistance to "failing" schools, and school vouchers that would allow students to leave public schools that didn't improve. Under his proposal, students who attended low-performing schools for three consecutive years would get federal funds—about $750—plus matching state funds to spend on educational options, including private school tuition, tutoring, or after-school programs. In a ceremony at the White House, Bush said, "American children must not be left in persistently dangerous or failing schools. When schools do not teach and will not change, parents and students must have other meaningful options. Both parties have been talking about education reform for quite a while. It's time to come together to get it done, so that we can truthfully say in America: No child will be left behind, not one single child."[4]

President Bush wasn't new to education reform. As governor of Texas, he had added to the state's existing standardized testing plan, connecting results to grade-level promotion and high school graduation.[5] On the campaign trail, Bush touted an increase in test scores in Texas and a decreasing gap between white children and Black and Latino children. Skeptics of the "Texas miracle," however, said the schools' emphasis on test prep narrowed the curriculum, particularly for Black and Latino students. Bush also supported charter schools and school vouchers, though Texas didn't pass a voucher law while he was governor.

Bush wasn't willing to let the divisive issue of vouchers threaten his first major piece of legislation, however, wrote Christopher T. Cross, a former assistant secretary of education in the US Department of Education. Almost immediately Bush downplayed that aspect of NCLB. In a radio address, he said, "I have my own plan, which would help children in persistently failing schools to go to another public, private, or charter school. Others suggest different approaches, and I am willing to listen." He made it clear in private meetings with governors and members of Congress that he would fight hardest for the testing piece of the plan. Senator Ted Kennedy, a Democrat from Massachusetts, who strongly opposed school vouchers, seemed hopeful the two parties could find a compromise. "There are some areas of difference, but the overwhelming areas of agreement and of support are very, very powerful," he said.[6]

Much like his father had a decade earlier, President Bush ran into opposition from the most conservative members of his party. NCLB would greatly expand the federal role in education, and Bush made it clear that he would let go of private choice options to win bipartisan approval. Conservatives generally favored a limited federal role, and the concept of school choice had become an important and highly visible aspect of their educational platform, with voucher or tax-credit scholarship programs now up and running in Milwaukee, Cleveland, Florida, and Arizona. Although legal questions loomed over voucher policies, it seemed there was momentum to pass one at the federal level; Republicans controlled both the legislative and executive branches. But Bush wanted a bipartisan win, not a bitter or prolonged partisan fight. One of his top advisors would say later that they simply could not pass the bill without some Democratic support. Still, when vouchers were subsequently removed from the House version of the bill, several Republican lawmakers were outraged. Representative Peter Hoekstra of Michigan said, "This is no longer a George Bush education bill. This is a Ted Kennedy education bill."[7]

Bush had wiggle room, though, to win over enough Republicans and Democrats with NCLB. Both parties were interested in education reform, particularly increased accountability for public schools, and an increased push for standards had been underway in states since the publication of the Reagan administration's *A Nation at Risk* in 1983. By 2001, the vast majority of states had testing programs and subject-area standards, though the two were not always aligned, Cross wrote. Some states, including Texas, already administered high-stakes tests in which the results were linked to graduation or grade-level promotion. In many ways, a line could be drawn from the rapid growth of public school accountability measures that followed *A Nation at Risk* to the 2001 blueprint for NCLB; the natural outcome of a push for "excellence" was to measure whether schools were living up to their promises. Bush's proposal also zeroed in on racial and socioeconomic test-score gaps, highlighting inequities in the public schools. And Bush's plan featured something Democrats favored: more money for struggling students and public schools. Faced with a potential revolt from some of the more conservative members of his party, Bush could court a lot of Democrats. Even Kennedy, a liberal stalwart, said he found Bush to be both knowledgeable and passionate about education reform.

In the summer of 2001, both the House and the Senate passed versions of NCLB, a bold and far-reaching reauthorization of the Elementary and Secondary Education Act. The House vote was 384 to 45, while the Senate passed it 91 to 8—a solid bipartisan victory for Bush. As expected, he lost some Republican lawmakers, including Senator George Voinovich, Ohio's former governor and a champion of vouchers, and Representative Mike Pence, a Republican from Indiana, who thought NCLB amounted to a huge federal overreach in education. Bush signed the act into law on January 8, 2002, calling it the start of "a new era, a new time in public education in our country."[8] Instead of committing himself to a partisan fight over school vouchers, he had steered the country onto a path toward a far greater role for standardized testing in public schools. In doing so, he effectively left the issue of school choice to the jurisdiction of the states.

A DECADE AFTER America started its experiment with charter schools, it was still difficult to assess what had been accomplished by the rise of this new brand of public education. Charter schools provided new options—some, like City Academy, targeted "at-risk" students, while others offered an extended school day, instruction in second languages, or a focus on "back-to-basics" education—and parents, particularly Black and Latino parents, were flocking to them. In Massachusetts, where only twenty-five charters were initially allowed to open statewide, waitlists numbered into the thousands.[9] But it was hard to judge a sector of schools intended to operate as laboratories of innovation—particularly when considered through the lens of charter schools versus traditional public schools—since by virtue of their design the schools varied widely in programming, hours, curriculum, and even student population. City Academy was the perfect example of that.

"No excuses" charter schools had emerged as an early success story, one highlighted in the media. The schools were lauded for raising the test scores of low-income students, who were often predominantly Black or Latino, by increasing the amount of time spent in school and emphasizing parental involvement and student discipline. A core part of the idea was that adults in the schools couldn't make excuses for failure. The model required teachers to work extremely long hours. Often operating without the protection of a union, teachers could be fired more easily. Still, some teachers were drawn to the academic results, team spirit, and mission.

One program, called the Knowledge Is Power Program, or KIPP, became a model for others and was featured on *60 Minutes* and in national newspapers. Education writer Jay Mathews wrote that Mike Feinberg and David Levin piloted KIPP in a classroom at a public elementary school in Houston in 1994 before splitting up to open two middle schools, one in Houston and one in New York City, the following year. The pair were young alumni of Teach for America, a nonprofit organization that trained new college graduates to work for two years in public schools in low-income communities. At first, Feinberg and Levin's schools were part of the public school districts; neither Texas nor New York had charter laws when KIPP began. Feinberg and Levin asked for space in school buildings for their pilot programs. The KIPP model required students to attend school for nine and a half hours a day, go to Saturday classes, and enroll in summer school.

Levin and Feinberg were inspired by the teaching practices of two veteran educators, Harriet Ball and Rafe Esquith, and built some of their techniques and ideas into KIPP. Ball had been a teacher in Levin's school when Levin was part of Teach for America. Charismatic and effective, Ball was known for using mnemonic chants in her classroom, Mathews wrote. (One of them became the inspiration for KIPP's name.) Esquith was an elementary school teacher in Los Angeles whose students—many of them low income and immigrants—learned and performed a Shakespeare play every year. He asked his fifth and sixth graders to spend about ten hours a day at school. Nominated for a national teaching award in 1992, Esquith told a reporter at the *Los Angeles Times* there was no secret to his success. It was just hard work. "There are no shortcuts," he said.[10]

KIPP emphasized hard work and discipline for students, teachers, and parents alike. Teachers were "on call" twenty-four hours a day for phone calls from families. The intense formula appeared to dramatically boost test scores. At the Houston middle school, which enrolled predominantly low-income Latino students, the incoming fifth graders' pass rate on the state's reading exam was 33 percent in 1998. The following year, after the same students attended KIPP as sixth graders, it was 92 percent. A story in the *New York Times* about Levin's school in the South Bronx ran with the headline "Structure and Basics Bring South Bronx School Acclaim." The *Christian Science Monitor* featured KIPP's Houston program in a series called "Reinventing Our Public Schools."[11]

After Texas passed its chartering law in 1995 and New York passed its law in 1998, both KIPP programs officially became charter schools. In the fall of 1999, after the *60 Minutes* story about the program, Feinberg and Levin started getting phone calls from politicians asking if they would consider expanding to new locations. They were interested but unsure how to go about it. Mathews described how a personal connection led Feinberg and Levin to Donald and Doris Fisher, cofounders of the Gap clothing stores. The Fishers approved a $15 million business plan to take KIPP national. In a private meeting, Don Fisher asked the two if they thought they could pull off the plan. According to Mathews, Levin said, "Well, Mr. Fisher, I don't know, but we'd be more than happy to use your money to find out."[12]

KIPP seemed like a promising model, but other charter schools didn't live up to the hype. There were problems, just as critics had predicted: Schools that closed abruptly. Schools with financial woes. Schools that failed to deliver on academic promises. In Waco, Texas, a Democratic lawmaker claimed that "close to 200 kids had to repeat a grade" after a charter school suddenly closed. Some charter applicants were accused of trying to create white enclaves in predominantly Black school districts, deepening segregation and bleeding the larger school system of resources. In the fall of 2000, a superintendent in Mount Vernon, New York, just north of New York City, claimed that competition from charter schools had hurt his efforts to reform the school district. Efforts to open one charter school, in particular, were being pushed primarily by wealthy white parents, he said, an accusation strongly refuted by the charter applicants. "The bigotry of parents ought not be funded at taxpayer expense," he said.[13]

Some charter schools seemed to operate as profit-making ventures. In one case in St. Paul, Minnesota, an audit found that charter leaders used state funding to lease cars and buy a condo for a school director. An Arizona lawmaker who supported both school vouchers and charter schools noted that some charter schools were staggering students in two or three shifts per day to make money off per-pupil funding. "Not all innovations are great innovations," she conceded. One study in Arizona found that some charter schools in the state offered religious instruction, discriminated against students with disabilities, and mismanaged their finances. Charter supporters worried that Arizona, one of the least regulated states, was giving the entire movement a bad name.[14]

In Ohio, charter schools were required to be nonprofit, yet many hired for-profit firms to handle managerial duties, an arrangement that didn't violate the state's charter law. David Brennan, the Republican businessman who championed school vouchers, converted his private schools into charter schools after Ohio's law passed in 1997. He said it simply made better business sense: school vouchers were worth less per student than the amount of per-pupil aid given for each student in a charter school. He opened White Hat Management Company, which by 2001 had contracted with about twelve charter schools. Brennan saw no problem with charter operators making a profit. "If we are able to make a profit out of an enterprise where everybody else is losing money, is that bad?" he asked.[15]

The Ohio Federation of Teachers viewed the use of public dollars to turn a profit as not only bad but unconstitutional. The union announced in 2001 they planned to file a lawsuit alleging that charters, called "community schools" in Ohio, were a violation of the state's constitution, which called for a "thorough and efficient system of common schools." Tom Mooney, union president, said the state's charter schools weren't living up to their ideals. "Charter schools were supposed to be small, autonomous public schools with a unique or innovative instructional program," he said. "Instead, they have become a vehicle for privatizing education for the sake of privatizing, at least in this state. . . . The system here is a complete perversion of the concept of charter schools."[16]

Even as new states, such as Indiana, approved charter laws in 2001, legislators in states with existing charter schools debated whether to tighten regulations or limit the number of new schools that could open. In Pennsylvania, a Republican lawmaker suggested a moratorium to give the state time to study the results of the new schools; Republican governor Tom Ridge opposed the move. In Texas, a Democratic lawmaker proposed a cap to limit growth; similarly, Republican governor Rick Perry opposed it.

In Massachusetts, state leaders allowed for just 25 schools to open statewide, part of a sweeping education reform law passed in 1993. As parents advocated for more charters in the state, lawmakers increased the cap to 50 schools in 1997 and to 120 schools in 2000. But they added an unusual provision to the law, agreeing to reimburse the traditional public schools for a period of time after any student left for a charter school, an acknowledgment that losing students hurt the traditional public schools' budgets. They also agreed in 1997 that 13 of the 25 new schools would be "in-district" charters, which were subject to approval by the teachers' union and a local school committee rather than by state officials.[17]

With the bipartisan alliance behind the new schools, Democratic charter supporters sometimes found themselves uncomfortably associated with advocates for private school choice. At a charter school conference sponsored by the US Department of Education in 2002, Joe Nathan, a prominent charter supporter, complained about sessions focused on school vouchers. "If the U.S. Department of Education wants to promote vouchers, which I think it has at this conference, we need to have a complex discussion of it," he said. But Lawrence Patrick, president of the Black Alliance for Educational Options, or BAEO, said, "I think that the reality is that we're part of the same movement."[18] Choice was choice, some said, but tensions were obvious. Some charter supporters took a market-based approach to school closings and low-quality schools, while others advocated for more restrictions and accountability and a greater emphasis on quality.

Howard Fuller, a longtime voucher supporter who founded the BAEO and supported charters, suggested charter schools were not yet living up to their promise as a tool of educational innovation. He said some operators were making the same excuses about their poor results as the traditional public schools had—that they could only do so much to overcome poverty and other disadvantages affecting students. "After 10 years of the charter school movement, we've got to ask ourselves: 'Is this a revolution or a timid reform masking as a revolution?'"[19]

→←

WITH THE LEGALITY of school vouchers still in question, Republican lawmakers in some states pressed ahead with tax-credit scholarships. After Arizona pioneered its tax-credit scholarship program, Florida and Pennsylvania became the next two states to pass new laws authorizing similar programs. Governor Jeb Bush backed the idea, though Florida had two existing voucher programs, one for students with disabilities and another for students at low-performing public schools. Legislators agreed in the spring of 2001 to create a tax-credit scholarship for low-income children, offering tax breaks to businesses that donated to the program. The measure passed on largely partisan lines, with Republicans in favor and Democrats opposed.

In Pennsylvania, Governor Tom Ridge unsuccessfully pushed for school vouchers three times before he embraced the tax-credit concept in 2001. The editorial board of the *Wall Street Journal* noted with approval the use of the tax code to advance private school choice: "If opponents of school choice continue to block vouchers at every turn, they shouldn't be surprised if the pent-up demand for reform comes in through the back door of tax credits."[20]

Then, in the fall of 2001, the US Supreme Court announced it would review a school voucher case. The wait and speculation were at an end. The court chose Cleveland. In Ohio, a Republican lawmaker had drafted a tax-credit scholarship bill—just in case. "I would be hopeful that the Supreme Court wouldn't find that the Cleveland program has a constitutional problem, but if they do, [the tax-credit bill] is ready to go," he said.[21] The tax-credit scholarship, still a new idea, already seemed fixed in the minds of conservatives as a means to achieve the same end as the school voucher: public support for private education. But would other concepts even be necessary if vouchers survived this legal challenge?

After a decade of courtroom battles across the country, Clint Bolick and Robert Chanin would meet at the Supreme Court—and the justices would finally determine whether school vouchers were constitutional.

19

Finally, the US Supreme Court

HUNDREDS OF PEOPLE LINED UP OUTSIDE THE US SUPREME Court on February 19, 2002, braving the winter cold a day early to get a seat inside the courtroom for the long-awaited legal showdown over school vouchers. *Zelman vs. Simmons-Harris* would determine whether Cleveland's six-year-old school voucher program violated the wall separating church and state—and it had the potential to redefine the parameters of America's system of public education. Opponents and supporters held dueling rallies on the white plaza in front of the courthouse. They sang, chanted, waved signs, and occasionally traded insults. Many voucher supporters wore hats in the bright orange of the Cleveland Browns. Their signs read, "Choice Is the American Way" and "School Vouchers Are Constitutional," or simply "Cleveland Parents." Opponents chanted, "Public funds for public schools!" One public school parent waspishly noted that his children were in school that day, while many voucher students had skipped classes to wave signs in front of the US Supreme Court. Former state representative Mike Fox, a Republican who had been instrumental in passing Cleveland's voucher program in 1995, dragged the pillows and blankets from his hotel room to make the long wait in line slightly less miserable. "The last time I camped out was in 1969, after a Peter, Paul and Mary concert in Cincinnati," he joked to a reporter.[1]

The Supreme Court had agreed in the fall of 2001 to review the case, after declining to take up other church-state cases in Milwaukee, Arizona, and Maine. Robert Chanin had filed the suit in federal court on behalf of a group of citizens in Ohio after losing on church-state grounds in the Ohio Supreme Court. The federal court had ruled that the voucher program was a church-state violation, and the appeals court had agreed. Now the US Supreme Court would decide the matter. In asking the justices to review the case, US Solicitor General Theodore Olson of the Bush administration argued that the previous, conflicting rulings in the lower courts had resulted in a "clear conflict" that needed to be resolved "so that policymakers may know, without further delay, whether such programs are a constitutionally permissible option for expanding educational opportunity for children enrolled in failing public schools across America, or whether other solutions must be sought for this critical national problem."[2]

Both sides in the case agreed that the Cleveland school district had serious, deeply entrenched problems. When a federal judge ordered the state to take over the school system in 1995, he cited severe financial mismanagement, crumbling school buildings, and a leadership vacuum; prior to the ruling, the city schools had churned through eight superintendents in ten years. City residents passed a referendum in 1996 to help pay for repairs to schools; more than half needed renovations. Three years after the state takeover, the mayor assumed control of the school system; in the 1996–1997 school year, fewer than half of eighth graders met the state standard for reading, and just 16 percent met the math standard.[3]

Where the two sides in *Zelman* disagreed sharply was in the solution to Cleveland's educational problems. In a brief submitted to the court, the Ohio School Boards Association, Ohio Association of School Business Officials, Buckeye Association of School Administrators, and Ohio Coalition for Equity and Adequacy of School Funding, among other entities, wrote, "We agree that Cleveland's children are entitled to something better . . . [but] where we part company . . . is in their advancement of publicly funded religious education as a remedy for this crisis."[4]

They pointed to the Ohio Supreme Court's landmark ruling in 1997, which found that the state fell short of its constitutional mandate to provide a "thorough and efficient" system of education, with funding gaps that put students in poorer school districts at a disadvantage. "Yet, rather than remedy its failing schools, the state here flaunts the crisis in public education for which it is responsible, seeking to advance that crisis as justification for a voucher program dominated by religious institutions," they wrote.

AFTER YEARS OF arguing in courtrooms across the country that school vouchers were unconstitutional, Chanin, the grizzled veteran lawyer for the National Education Association, would make his case in the US Supreme Court, along with his sometime partner, retired federal judge Marvin Frankel. Chanin's frequent opponent, Clint Bolick, however, would sit this one out. It was a severe disappointment for Bolick after roughly a decade of courtroom arguments but not completely unexpected: he often intervened in cases as a third party, and the Supreme Court doesn't usually hear from intervenors. The state of Ohio wanted to take the lead in one of the most prominent church-state cases in years, one that would answer a long-standing question about school voucher programs. The state superintendent of public instruction, Susan Tave Zelman, who was named on the lawsuit, was represented by Judith French, Ohio's assistant attorney general, with support from US Solicitor General Olson. Ken Starr, who had become a household name for investigating President Clinton's affair, had his name on the court brief but didn't plan to argue in the courtroom.

While Bolick didn't get to realize his dream of arguing in front of the US Supreme Court, he played a key role behind the scenes in crafting media and courtroom strategies in the months leading up to the oral arguments. In a brief to the court, Bolick and his colleagues at the Institute for Justice began with "background principles" rather than arguments about the establishment clause. They emphasized the rights of parents, as recognized in *Pierce vs. Society of Sisters*, which declared that a child is not "the mere creature of the state." They said the fifty states were meant to serve as laboratories for the development of new public policy ideas, and the "proliferation of parental choice programs reflects federalism at its best." And they drew a clear line from *Brown vs. Board of Education*, which had prohibited racial segregation in the nation's schools nearly fifty years earlier, to *Zelman vs. Simmons-Harris*: "Many of the themes in this case reflect those raised 47 years ago in Brown v. Board of Education. There, children were forced to travel past good neighborhood schools to attend inferior schools because the children happened to be black; today, many poor children are forced to travel past good schools to attend inferior schools because the schools happen to be private."[5]

Bolick deliberately linked the school choice movement to the civil rights movement. At his law firm, every case required a clear overarching message for the judge, the jury, the media. For *Zelman*, Bolick wanted the message to be "This is the most important education case since *Brown v. Board of Education*." Not everyone embraced the idea. Howard Fuller, who had been a civil rights activist, found it offensive. He argued that school choice had to win on its own merits. He also thought the strategy could backfire—indeed, the NAACP wrote in its brief to the court that linking the two cases was "manipulative" and "insulting"—but Fuller lost the argument. In the months before the hearing, major media outlets such as the *Washington Post* quoted Bolick as he repeated some variation of the message.[6]

Chanin's strategy wasn't based on providing an overarching message to the court, the press, or the public. Throughout the years of voucher litigation across the country, he had focused on the constitutional issues in play, not whether he believed school vouchers were good public policy. He rarely deviated from that path. In *Zelman*, he noted that 96 percent of students in the Cleveland program were using vouchers at religious schools, and in fact, most of the private schools participating were religious, effectively limiting parents' choices. In his brief to the court, Chanin wrote, "The Ohio voucher program is so 'heavily skewed towards religion' as to make it inevitable that, no matter what 'private choice' individual Voucher Program parents make, a 'significant portion of the aid expended under the program as a whole will end up flowing to religious education.'"[7]

BOTH SIDES BELIEVED that Justice Sandra Day O'Connor would be the swing vote. The first woman on the court, O'Connor had been appointed by Ronald Reagan in 1981 when she was fifty-one years old and had enjoyed a distinguished political and legal career in Arizona. Now seventy-one, O'Connor had been rumored by some to be a potential successor to Chief Justice William Rehnquist, six years her senior. She often was the deciding vote on matters ranging from abortion rights to affirmative action to church-state issues. O'Connor, like some of the other conservative-leaning justices, favored a limited federal role, but unlike Justices Clarence Thomas and Antonin Scalia, she wasn't known for writing bold, ideologically based opinions. A 1993 profile of Scalia in *Playboy* magazine described him as the "Arnold Schwarzenegger of American jurisprudence." In contrast, O'Connor was known for taking an incremental approach to the law, and she was often criticized for it. Justice Stephen Breyer said, "She does not believe you should go further than you have to go."[8]

As the court's frequent swing vote, O'Connor was powerful, but with a pragmatic and narrow approach, she also could be unpredictable. In a 2001 cover story in the *New York Times Magazine*, writer and law professor Jeffrey Rosen called her "the most powerful woman in America."

> We are all now living in Sandra Day O'Connor's America. Take almost any of the most divisive questions of American life, and Justice O'Connor either has decided it or is about to decide it on our behalf. The Supreme Court may tell us soon whether affirmative action in public universities is permissible, and if it does, O'Connor is likely to cast the deciding vote. The court is divided about school vouchers too; O'Connor's views will probably tip the scales.

Rosen's piece was titled "A Majority of One."[9]

Court cases involving direct aid to religious schools weren't straightforward, simple, or predictable. Since 1971's *Lemon vs. Kurtzman*, in which the court ruled that it was unconstitutional for a state to supplement the salaries of religious school teachers, the court had used the "*Lemon* test" to consider where the church-state line fell. The three-pronged test said a program must have a secular purpose, must not have the "primary effect" of inhibiting or advancing religion, and could not create excessive government entanglement with religion.

Applying the *Lemon* test, however, often resulted in varied and seemingly inconsistent rulings. Jesse Choper, a constitutional scholar and professor at the University of California, Berkeley, wrote with exasperation in 1999 that the *Lemon* test had "produced a conceptual disaster area, generating ad hoc judgments that are incapable of being reconciled on any principled basis." He noted that the court, applying the *Lemon* test, had ruled that government could provide parochial schools with textbooks but not "tape recorders, films, movie projectors, laboratory equipment and maps." Tax dollars could pay for buses to parochial schools, but not for "field trips *from* these schools." (Italics are his.) Leonard Levy, a constitutional historian at the Claremont Graduate School, wrote in 1994 that the test hadn't proved all that useful either, as justices "frequently disagree on the test's application in particular cases." The third prong of the *Lemon* test—excessive entanglement—"seems to carry the seeds of its own misconstruction. 'Excessive,' after all, is a relative term that cannot possibly have a fixed or objectively ascertainable meaning." Regardless of the *Lemon* test, Levy observed that certain judges tended to vote in favor of religion, while others did not.[10] Observers of the court rarely had trouble figuring out which way most of the justices would go.

In the two decades leading up to *Zelman*, the court, largely under Rehnquist's leadership, had hinted at a path for more government aid to religious schools. In 1983, the court ruled 5–4 in *Mueller vs. Allen* that tax deductions for religious school expenses didn't violate the establishment clause—a case Levy said "radically altered the constitutional matter of the law." In 1984, O'Connor contributed to modifying the *Lemon* test by asking whether a "reasonable observer" would believe the government was endorsing religion in a case concerning religious displays.[11] Two years later, the court ruled unanimously in *Witters vs. Washington Department of Services for the Blind* that a visually impaired student could use a state program, funded primarily with federal dollars, to attend a religious college with the objective of becoming a pastor. The court found that the program had a secular purpose—to assist blind students—and money flowed to religious organizations only through a private individual's choice. In the case, O'Connor again mentioned the idea of a "reasonable observer."

Similarly, in 1993's *Zobrest vs. Catalina Foothills School District*, justices ruled 5–4 that a school district should pay for an interpreter for a deaf student who chose to attend a Catholic school. Then in 1995, in *Rosenberger vs. Rector and Visitors of the University of Virginia*, the majority found that a university had to offer the same financial support to a religious magazine that it gave to other publications. Finally, in 1997, in *Agostini vs. Felton*, the court combined two of the prongs in the *Lemon* test—the primary effects of a program and whether it created church-state entanglement—and reversed an earlier ruling that prohibited some public school teachers from teaching remedial classes to low-income children in Catholic schools as part of a federal antipoverty program.[12] In only one of the cases had O'Connor dissented.

Going into *Zelman*, the justices who were considered to be solidly in the provoucher column were Antonin Scalia, Clarence Thomas, Anthony Kennedy, and William Rehnquist. On the other side were thought to be Ruth Bader Ginsburg, John Paul Stevens, David Souter, and Breyer. If this case went like many of the prior school choice cases, the outcome would be a 5–4 ruling. O'Connor would likely decide the case, but court observers couldn't say with any certainty which way she would go. Both sides tailored their arguments to O'Connor, hoping to pull her to their side. Choper, the constitutional scholar, wrote, "Justice O'Connor's posture in several recent decisions suggests real uncertainty on her part."[13]

≫≪

ON FEBRUARY 20, 2002, at about nine thirty a.m., the line of people waiting outside the US Supreme Court was allowed inside for the oral arguments. The court agreed to an eighty-minute hearing, in what *New York Times* court reporter Linda Greenhouse called a "rare departure from the court's one-hour standard."[14] Among those sitting in the audience were former Wisconsin governor Tommy Thompson, now health and human services secretary in the Bush administration, Fannie Lewis, the Cleveland city council member who had championed the city's voucher program, and Paul Peterson, the Harvard professor who had sparred over studies of Milwaukee's program.

The oral arguments moved quickly as each attorney emphasized the previous cases they believed justices should rely on to issue a ruling. For Judith French, who was defending Cleveland's program, that meant highlighting *Mueller, Witters,* and *Zobrest*—cases that suggested a state voucher program could be found constitutional if it offered benefits to both private and public school families, and if state dollars flowed to religious schools only through the private choices of parents. For Robert Chanin, the most important precedent was *Nyquist,* the 1973 case from New York in which the court, under Chief Justice Warren Burger, had ruled 6–3 that reimbursing low-income families for private school tuition was unconstitutional. Justice Lewis Powell, now retired from the court, had written, "In its attempt to enhance the opportunities of the poor to choose between public and nonpublic education, the State has taken a step which can only be regarded as one 'advancing' religion." Chanin believed justices should reach the same conclusion about *Zelman.*

French opened by describing the Cleveland Scholarship and Tutoring Program as the state's response to an "unprecedented educational crisis" in Cleveland. She had been speaking for less than two minutes when the first question was fired at her from Justice Souter. It was quickly followed by one from Justice Scalia, then Justices Kennedy, Stevens, Ginsburg, and Day O'Connor—all in about five minutes. French remained calm under pressure. She responded to the implication by Souter that religious schools were proselytizing by merely saying, "We, of course, your honor, do not agree that they're proselytizing." When O'Connor asked why the court wasn't considering the educational options available to families beyond the voucher program—including magnet schools and charter schools, or "community schools" as they were called in Ohio—French offered, "We would like the court to take very much account of the community schools, your honor."

O'Connor, known for her courtroom decorum, asked French politely about *Nyquist,* the case that underpinned Chanin's argument, saying,

"May I ask you if this court would have to overrule the *Nyquist* case to support your position? It certainly points the other way, doesn't it?" Treading lightly with her answer, French said, "It does point the other way, your honor, but we think there are a number of distinctions which this court has drawn between the programs at issue, say, in *Mueller* and *Witters* that distinguish it from the New York program at issue in *Nyquist*." French outlined that in *Nyquist*, tuition reimbursement was offered only to private school families. In Cleveland, all students could benefit, either by taking a voucher to a private school or by using a grant for tutoring in a traditional public or charter school. Only income limits determined the amount of the voucher available to students to use in private schools. French said those differences rendered Cleveland's program neutral, which meant it didn't advance or inhibit religion.

Souter pressed her on that point, however. "At the end of the day, I think what's bothering me about *Nyquist*, and I suspect Justice O'Connor too, is that *Nyquist* depended not merely on a question of neutrality but on the effect. And at the end of the day the effect is a massive amount of money into religious schools in *Nyquist*, a massive amount of money into religious schools here. That I think is the sticking point," he said.

French, who seemed unflappable, politely deflected. "We, of course, disagree, your honor, that there is a massive amount going to religious schools as a result of something that the government is doing."

Rehnquist interjected in the exchange and said *Mueller* "made the point, I think, that where the parents do the choosing, as they did not do in *Nyquist*, it was a different ball game."

"Absolutely, your honor," French replied.

O'Connor then asked French another direct question about the precedents at play in the *Zelman* case: "What is the closest of our cases, do you think, to the Ohio program? Is it *Witters*?"

French immediately agreed. "I would suggest *Witters*, your honor, because it's a financial aid going to, there it was a college student, but an adult, to make a decision about where to send the money. Here it's an adult parent making the decision about where to send the money on behalf of the child."

O'Connor: "The difference would be, however, that according to respondents, the choices are much more limited here . . ."

French: "That's true."

O'Connor: "Than in *Witters*."

French: "That's true, your honor, but in *Mueller* the court did address that concern, as Justice Powell said in his concurrence in *Witters*, that it didn't matter that there was only one person, uh, Mr. Witters, using the money for seminary, for the Inland Empire School of the Bible, nor did it matter in *Zobrest* that there was only one child or one parent, set of parents, for a child looking for an interpreter for a religious school."

In a fast-moving sixteen minutes, French ably argued that Cleveland's program was neutral, that state aid went to religious schools only indirectly through the private choices of adults, and that the percentage of religious schools in the program in any given year didn't matter. She also argued that it didn't matter if the policy ultimately affected one student or one school, though it spoke to the neutrality of Cleveland's program that it was open to "all comers" and was part of a larger ecosystem of "choices" in the city in which students could select from traditional public schools, magnet schools, and charter schools. She hit all the right notes.

Two more lawyers, David Young and Olson, argued for the pro-voucher side before Chanin rose to address the court. Where French seemed calm, polite, and self-possessed, Chanin at times sounded condescending and combative.

He began, "Under the Cleveland voucher program millions of dollars of unrestricted public funds are transferred each year from the state treasury into the general coffers of sectarian private schools and that money is used by those schools to provide an educational program in which the sectarian and the secular are interwoven." He called it a "mathematical certainty that almost all of the students will end up going to religious schools that provide a religious education."

O'Connor immediately challenged Chanin.

"Well, Mr. Chanin. Wait, wait, wait, just a minute. Couple of things. Do we not have to look at all of the choices open to the students—the community schools, the magnet schools, etc. How is it that we can look only at the ones looking, uh, to the religious schools?"

Chanin replied, "The limitation to looking at the voucher program as a free-standing program is consistent both with the precedents of this court and with absolute logic, your honor."

O'Connor: "I don't understand either point, to tell you the truth. I mean, if you want to look at what parents' choices are, do you not have to look at the reality of the whole program? Then it isn't a 96 percent."

Chanin: "Your honor, this court has always been program specific in its financial aid cases. In *Nyquist*, the court looked at three separate programs under the one statute, viewed them all in independent terms, and viewed them all independently of whatever else was going on in the New York City public schools."

O'Connor interrupted Chanin and said, "But I'm not sure that's proper. That's what I'm asking you. Why should we not look at all of the options open to the parents in having their children educated?"

Chanin: "Because what that does, your honor, is it mixes together programs that are quite qualitatively different in both function and purpose . . ."

Justice Kennedy interrupted and suggested Chanin was asking the justices to "put on blinders" and to "make a decision based on a fictional premise." Chanin responded that he was asking the court to "look at the reality," to which Kennedy replied, "You're asking us to look at part of a reality."

As the justices pressed Chanin, his voice rose higher.

Justice Scalia pushed Chanin to commit to whether the money could go to nonreligious schools. Chanin first said no and then reversed himself under further questioning. Rehnquist then reminded Chanin that in the *Mueller* case the percentage of religious schools was 96 percent. Chanin countered that he didn't believe the case was controlled by *Mueller*.

O'Connor said the program seemed almost "skewed against the religious schools" because the amount of the voucher was lower than the per-pupil funding for public and charter schools. As Chanin struggled to answer her line of questioning, Kennedy quipped, "So far you are doing a very good job of not answering Justice O'Connor's question." Laughter broke out in the courtroom.

At one point, it seemed as though Justice Breyer could be in play, that he might join the justices thought to be in the provoucher column. After Chanin made the point that parents weren't truly able to make an independent choice because most of the private schools were religious, Breyer interjected. "Well, suppose it weren't that number." He asked if it would be constitutional in a hypothetical case if half the parents chose nonsectarian schools and half chose religious schools. "Not in my mind, your honor," Chanin said.

Justice Stevens then tried to get Chanin to say at what point a program would run afoul of the establishment clause based purely on the number of religious schools participating.

"Let me just be sure I understand your position," he said. "Suppose there are 10 schools out there, 10 private schools, nine of which are nonreligious and one of which is religious. But the government money will pay the tuition for the parents who choose the religious school. Is that in your view consistent with the establishment clause or not?"

Chanin: "Well, that's clearly unconstitutional, your honor."

Stevens: "So even if it's 10 percent?"

Chanin: "Oh no, that, I, I'm only, I'm responding to what I think Justice Breyer put to me . . ."

Stevens: "The interesting thing is, if I understand the case correctly, your view is if any one school gets the money it's unconstitutional."

Chanin: "No, your honor."

Stevens: "Well, I thought you said yes."

Chanin: "No, I'm sorry if you thought I did. I did not. Or I may have, but I didn't mean to."

Observers again laughed. Stevens continued to present different numbers—"Well, say there are 100, and 99 nonsectarian and one"—until again, the courtroom broke into laughter. Chanin tried again to make his case, even interrupting Stevens.

O'Connor pressed Chanin on the other choices available in Cleveland, and then Scalia interjected, with both O'Connor and Scalia suggesting charter schools were not actually public schools. Rehnquist also pressed the point, asking why Chanin was drawing a "bright line" between private schools and charter schools. "Here, the community schools, as I understand it, are set up because they wanted to get away from the kind of failing system that so many public schools are and do something different," he said. Chanin responded that the "only rational line to draw is between public education and private education."

As they went back and forth, Chanin interrupted Rehnquist. Recognizing his mistake, Chanin quickly apologized. "I didn't mean to interrupt you, your honor."

"You'd better not," Rehnquist responded to laughter.

Rehnquist told Chanin a "number of members of the court are really not satisfied with that explanation." Kennedy then pressed him on what remedies the state of Ohio could pursue as a corrective to Cleveland's troubled school system. State officials were trying to create a system in which "different school systems . . . can begin to flourish, and the question is, how can they do that in the long term, and you say they cannot do it."

Chanin responded, "No, I say this, your honor. I say that the Ohio Legislature has the right to make an educationally unsound judgment.

It does not have the right to make an unconstitutional judgment. It must solve the problems in Cleveland within the parameters of the establishment clause."

Chanin also told the justices the Ohio Supreme Court had ruled that the state wasn't funding its public school system fairly, which disadvantaged students living in poorer school districts. He suggested that the state could look at funding as a solution for Cleveland. In her rebuttal, French fired back that the Ohio Supreme Court had also upheld the Cleveland voucher program as constitutional under the establishment clause. Then she said it appeared that "respondents have either ignored or do not accept the last 20 years or so of this court's jurisprudence. Each of the legal principles they have raised here today and in their briefs have been expressly rejected by the court."[15]

Neither side would know for several months who had won, but supporters of Cleveland's voucher program suspected they had convinced O'Connor and perhaps one other justice. Walking outside the courthouse to the dueling rallies of supporters and opponents in the plaza, Fannie Lewis put her arms in the air and shouted, "We won!"[16]

20

A Decisive Step

FOUR MONTHS LATER, THE US SUPREME COURT RULED 5–4 that Cleveland's school voucher program was constitutional, clearing the legal clouds from an educational reform that allowed religious school tuition to be paid for with public dollars. In his opinion for the majority, Chief Justice William Rehnquist wrote that the program had been "enacted for the valid secular purpose of providing educational assistance to poor children in a demonstrably failing public school system." The next question, then, was whether it had the "forbidden 'effect' of advancing or inhibiting religion." The majority found that it did not because the money flowed to private religious institutions only through the "genuine and independent choices of private individuals." As expected, Justice Sandra Day O'Connor made the decisive vote. In a concurring opinion, she wrote, "Although the court takes an important step, I do not believe that today's decision, when considered in light of other longstanding government programs that impact religious organizations and our prior Establishment Clause jurisprudence, makes a dramatic break from the past."[1]

The four dissenting justices strongly disagreed with her assessment. Justice David Souter wrote that the majority had "misapplied its own law" and expressed hope that a future court would "reconsider today's dramatic departure from basic Establishment Clause principle." Souter noted the troubling state of Cleveland's public schools, but much as Robert Chanin had argued in court, he said that wasn't a reason to abandon the Constitution. "If there were an excuse for giving short shrift to the Establishment Clause, it would probably apply here. But there is no excuse. Constitutional limitations are placed on government to preserve constitutional values in hard cases, like these," he wrote in a dissent joined by Justices John Paul Stevens, Ruth Bader Ginsburg, and Stephen Breyer.

In a separate dissent, Breyer also wrote that school vouchers posed a risk to the "Nation's social fabric" by inviting religious conflict. The clauses in the First Amendment "reflect the Framers' vision of an American Nation free of the religious strife that had long plagued the nations of Europe," he wrote. The answer wasn't to provide every religion with an "equal opportunity," but to draw "fairly clear lines of separation between church and state—at least where the heartland of religious belief, such as primary religious education, is at issue."

As the reactions to the decision in *Zelman vs. Simmons-Harris* rolled in, a familiar theme began to emerge. In a speech in Cleveland shortly after the decision, President George W. Bush called the case "just as historic" as *Brown vs. Board of Education*. In an op-ed for the *Washington Post*, US Secretary of Education Rod Paige wrote that *Zelman* "holds the same potential" as *Brown* and "recasts the education debates in this country, encouraging a new civil rights revolution and ushering in a 'new birth of freedom' for parents and their children everywhere in America." And the *Wall Street Journal*'s editorial board opined, "The U.S. Supreme Court yesterday struck the greatest blow for equal public education since *Brown v. Board of Education* in 1954. In the process, it also stripped away the last Constitutional and moral fig leaf from those who want to keep minority kids trapped in failing public schools."[2]

The overarching message Clint Bolick and his colleagues at the Institute for Justice had crafted for the case worked: in the days and weeks following the decision, *Zelman vs. Simmons-Harris* was compared repeatedly to *Brown vs. Board of Education*. Linda Greenhouse, courts reporter for the *New York Times*, wrote about the effectiveness of the strategy in a piece titled "Win the Debate, Not Just the Case": "Equating the voucher ruling to the watershed constitutional moment in the struggle for racial equality was political rhetoric at its most powerful. . . . Such strategic use of language rarely occurs by chance." Bolick told Greenhouse the message had been a key part of their approach, not only in the Supreme Court but in the court of public opinion. "We wanted to make sure this was seen not as a case about religion but about education," he said. "If the court perceived it as a religion case, then we would be in serious trouble. If they saw it as an education case, then we would win."[3]

The message also resonated with the court's only Black member, Justice Clarence Thomas, who echoed the theme in his concurring opinion, writing, "Today many of our inner-city public schools deny emancipation to urban minority students. Despite this Court's observation nearly 50 years ago in *Brown v. Board of Education*, that 'it is doubtful that any child may reasonably be expected to succeed in life if he is denied the opportunity of an education,' . . . urban children have been forced into a system that continually fails them."

Others told Greenhouse they were offended by the comparison. Theodore Shaw, associate director-counselor of the NAACP Legal Defense and Educational Fund, called it "extraordinary" to link the two cases. He said vouchers weren't "the answer for the vast majority of black students, who will remain in the public schools with no systemic reform and no systemic commitment of resources." Republicans wanted to be "color-blind" in all other areas of public policy—but not this one, he said pointedly. Howard Fuller, who disagreed with Bolick's strategy, maintained his distance even after the victory. "I'm not criticizing anyone, but I tend to be very careful about equating anything we do to the historic civil rights movement," he said. He called *Zelman* "revolutionary in its own way." Chanin viewed the loss in *Zelman* in straightforward terms. It simply came down to who had convinced O'Connor: "We aimed at her, and we never got her," he said later.[4]

In the five decades since Milton Friedman's seminal essay, the concept of the voucher had traveled a long and circuitous journey to reach the decision by the US Supreme Court in 2002. It had been supported by white segregationists in the South looking to skirt *Brown*, by Catholics who viewed their schools as providing a public service, by some Black and Latino parents searching for an escape from troubled urban school systems, and by conservatives who wanted to disrupt and possibly destroy America's public school system. Now some supporters had found the sweet spot in their messaging by promoting school vouchers as a tool for racial justice. Greenhouse wrote, "The fact is that the public debate is now taking place on the [Institute for Justice's] terms: *Brown v. Board* and not church v. state."

For Friedman, who was about to turn ninety, the outcome of the court case was not the end but "a great step forward" in his quest for universal school vouchers. "We are more and more approaching the tipping point," he said.[5]

IN THE AFTERMATH of *Zelman*, it seemed clear the legal fight over private school choice would move to the state courts. What the Supreme Court had done was to remove the establishment clause from future lawsuits; lawmakers now had a clear blueprint for legislation. But opponents could still pursue litigation based on state constitutions, many of which explicitly forbade the use of tax dollars to support religious schools. Even before the *Zelman* decision, Chanin said that

would be the strategy if the ruling went against voucher opponents—
an approach that Bolick termed a "war of attrition." Chanin said, too,
that the most effective strategy was to prevent new programs from being created: "The first line of defense has always been political." Bolick
believed supporters of school vouchers now had the green light to go on
the legal and political offensive. Within months of the *Zelman* ruling,
he and his colleagues at the Institute for Justice held a press briefing to
outline a new legal strategy: they planned to sue states with constitutions that prohibited direct aid to religious schools. They also wanted
to get a case in front of the Supreme Court again—only this time they
planned to argue that a state can't discriminate against religious school
options under the First Amendment's right to free exercise of religion.
The strategy was similar to what the Reverend Virgil Blum had advocated for decades earlier. Bolick also said he wanted to revisit the case
he had lost in Maine in which religious schools were prohibited from
participating in the state's voucher program.[6]

Opponents were skeptical that the Institute for Justice's tactics
would amount to much. A strategist for the National School Boards
Association said the plan would likely be a "footnote" in the history
of school vouchers. "The constitutional issue is not the big issue anymore when it comes to vouchers. Ultimately, it is up to the voters
and elected officials to decide whether voucher programs are going
to be enacted," he told *Education Week*. On that front, opponents of
private school choice could be confident: voters consistently turned
down voucher referendums by large margins, with the two most recent losses having occurred in Michigan and California in 2000, and
voucher legislative proposals had repeatedly failed in states across the
country. *Zelman* wouldn't change that. In *Education Week*, James W.
Fraser, a professor of history and education at Northeastern University, said it would take years to see the results of *Zelman*. "This ruling
is the single largest move away from the concept of common schools
in our history," he said. "And it remains to be seen whether it will actu-

ally result in a real movement away from common schools. The future is really up for grabs."

✣

IN THE YEAR after the *Zelman* ruling, voucher supporters made little progress in advancing their cause nationwide, with one new program passing in Colorado. One of the ugliest political battles over school vouchers played out in the nation's capital, where efforts to create a federal program for students in Washington, DC, had failed three times before. The editorial board of the *Wall Street Journal* urged President Bush to support a program for the district, saying he had given up vouchers "without a fight" while trying to get bipartisan support for the No Child Left Behind Act. The board asked, "What better place to start leaving no child behind than in the shadow of the White House?"[7]

Still, a voucher program wasn't going to be an easy sell in Washington, DC, where many of the city's officials, including Democratic mayor Anthony Williams, were against the idea. The growth of charter schools, introduced in 1995, also prompted some local leaders to question the need for another type of school choice. In an op-ed in the *Washington Post* in the summer of 2002, Kevin Chavous, a Democrat on the Council of the District of Columbia, urged congressional leaders to let the district "choose for itself." A charter school supporter, Chavous wrote, "We are accomplishing the same goals that vouchers would accomplish through the charter school movement." The district enrolled about sixty-five thousand public school students and about fourteen thousand charter school students. The city should pursue vouchers only "if that is the people's choice."[8]

Parents lined up on both sides of the issue. Virginia Walden Ford, a mother of three who became interested in school vouchers after her son transferred to a Catholic high school, had formed DC Parents for School Choice, a nonprofit organization. Ford testified before congressional subcommittees to support vouchers, invoking her son's story. She had been able to pay his tuition only by taking a second job and getting financial help from a neighbor. After switching to a charter school his senior year, William Walden had graduated and joined the military, serving in Iraq and Afghanistan. "I still shudder to think how very different his life would have been had he not been able to attend a school that offered a strong academic program and an environment that inspired him to succeed," she said, referring to the private school, at a hearing in 2002. As the voucher debate grew heated, Ford and other members of her group visited Capitol Hill daily, wearing shirts that read, "D.C. Parents for School Choice."[9]

Iris Toyer, a lawyer who served as a cochair for Parents United for the D.C. Public Schools, a long-standing group that had been advocating for improvements to the public school system for years, became a strong voice against school vouchers. Toyer, who had grown up in Washington and served as a school board member and PTA president, sent her four children to public schools. She believed school vouchers were an attack on the public school system by people with something to gain. "The folks who are making those arguments should put some of their energy into improving public schools," she said.[10]

As lawmakers debated whether the district needed school vouchers, Toyer and Parents United were trying to draw attention to serious deficiencies in public school buildings, which were sixty-five years old, on average, and had myriad structural problems, including leaky roofs, missing floor tiles, and malfunctioning heating and plumbing. "The situation is so dire that students often avoid the use of the bathrooms altogether," one report said. A plan to upgrade the district's nearly 150 schools in the next decade and a half was estimated to cost more than $2 billion. After the city budgeted less than the school district had requested for repairs in fiscal year 2003, Toyer accused local politicians and Congress of a "lack of will and lack of, quite frankly, desire to support public education." The *Washington Post* featured the two mothers, Ford and Toyer, in a story about school vouchers that ran with the headline, "Two Passionately Involved Parents, One Divisive Issue."[11]

As had been the case in Milwaukee and Cleveland, few were arguing that Washington's public schools were a model of academic excellence. Far from it. More than 70 percent of fourth graders were considered below proficient on reading tests given as part of the National Assessment of Educational Progress; about 90 percent of eighth graders scored below proficient in reading. The graduation rate was just below 60 percent. More than 60 percent of the students in the public schools lived in poverty—far more than in the surrounding suburbs. The District of Columbia Public Schools remained segregated by race and income and enrolled more students with disabilities than suburban schools. A report prepared for Parents United said educational programming had deteriorated in the public schools in the fifty years since *Brown vs. Board*: "Of the district's 100 elementary schools, 21 had neither a music teacher nor an art teacher; 30 have no physical education teacher; and almost none has foreign language teachers." For advocates of public education, potentially pulling funds away from an already underresourced public school system was unthinkable, and many of the people pushing for school vouchers weren't from Washington. Eleanor Holmes Norton, the district's nonvoting congressional delegate, said voucher advocates "don't care beans about D.C."[12]

Still, local leaders in Washington were under intense pressure to find solutions for the school system. Mayor Williams, in particular, faced harsh criticism about education during his bungled bid for reelection in 2002. After he was forced to run a write-in campaign—his nominating petitions were found to contain forged signatures—Courtland Milloy, a columnist for the *Washington Post*, lambasted him in a piece titled "Williams Wants Write-Ins When People Can't Read": "Residents will be called on to demonstrate those most basic of educational skills—the ability to read and write—something that the D.C. government, unfortunately, has so often failed to provide."[13] Milloy

cited US Census figures showing that 35 percent of the district's population was illiterate.

By the spring of 2003, key local leaders in Washington began to
announce they had changed their minds on school vouchers. The shift
was noticeable in part because they were influential Black Democrats in
a Democratic city, and the change of heart appeared to have come after
a full-court press by the Bush administration. Board of Education president Peggy Cooper Cafritz announced her shift in position in an editorial in the *Washington Post*, suggesting the city should get money for
vouchers and demand more funding for traditional public and charter
schools at the same time. Chavous said he would drop his opposition
to a voucher program if the public schools received additional federal
funding. Williams took a similar stance, announcing his new support
for school vouchers at an event with US Secretary of Education Paige
in May. He said vouchers could attract new residents to the city and
offer better educational options for five thousand to ten thousand students. "We're willing to try an experiment," he said. Norton and other
critics suggested Williams's change of heart was a result of behind-the-
scenes dealmaking. She accused him of "selling out."[14]

The support of local leaders, particularly the mayor, made it easier
for some lawmakers in Congress to support voucher legislation for the
district as a proposal began to take shape in the latter half of 2003. A
Republican senator from Minnesota, Norm Coleman, said he wouldn't
support a voucher plan for Minnesota or nationally, but he would
"certainly support the local mayor in his effort to provide greater opportunity for his kids." (Coleman, who said he had been "hammered"
by his support for school vouchers during a failed gubernatorial run in
Minnesota, called vouchers the "deadly v-word.") After having opposed
school vouchers for thirty years, Senator Dianne Feinstein, a prominent
Democrat from California, announced in an editorial in the *Washington Post* that she would support "Williams's effort to experiment with
this program" and called education a "local issue."[15]

Senators who opposed the voucher legislation faced heated attacks. Two senators, Mary Landrieu, a Louisiana Democrat, and Arlen Specter, a Pennsylvania Republican, drew intense backlash after they declined to support voucher legislation in 2003 despite having voted for a different proposal six years earlier. DC Parents for School Choice ran a full-page ad in a Louisiana newspaper chastising Landrieu for sending her children to private schools while voting against vouchers. The ad showed a picture of a child with a caption that read, "My mom wants you to know that Sen. Mary Landrieu doesn't want me to go to the same school where her children go." The editorial board of the *Wall Street Journal* attacked both senators, noting that Specter's children also had attended private schools. "Senator Specter's cynical bet is that denying choice to inner-city black and Latino kids won't hurt him among the Republican suburbanites in his primary battle next year . . . and will help keep Pennsylvania teachers unions off his back in the general election," the board wrote. DC Parents for School Choice also targeted Democratic senator Ted Kennedy with attack ads on television in Washington, DC, and his home state of Massachusetts. The commercial compared him to segregationist Bull Connor, the racist Birmingham city commissioner in the 1960s. "Senator Kennedy, your brothers fought for us. Why do you fight against us?" the ad said. A spokesperson for the senator called the ad "outrageous" and not worthy of a response.[16] The mayor called on the group to stop the ads, saying they were hurting efforts to get the legislation passed.

By the fall of 2003, voucher legislation in the US House of Representatives called for a five-year pilot program in Washington that would provide about thirteen hundred low-income students with vouchers worth up to $7,500—far more than had been proposed in the past—and give priority to students enrolled in low-performing public schools, as determined by their status under No Child Left

Behind. Religious schools would be allowed to participate. Another $26 million would be split evenly between the city's traditional public schools and its charter sector.

It was clear any vote on a voucher program for Washington would be breathtakingly close in both the House and Senate. A small number of Republicans in Congress were opposed to vouchers, while only a few Democrats supported them. Republican leadership in the House scheduled the vote to start after eight p.m. on the same day Democratic presidential candidates were scheduled to participate in a debate at a university in Baltimore. That meant some Democratic lawmakers would be out of town. House Majority Leader Tom DeLay, a Texas Republican, declined Democratic leaders' requests to reschedule. Even with antivoucher members absent, the vote came down to an extraordinary tie, 208 in favor and 208 opposed. Representative Ernie Fletcher, a Kentucky Republican who had previously opposed the program, had cast the vote to create the tie. The *Washington Post* described the wild scene that followed: "Republicans then held open the vote for roughly 40 minutes in a frantic effort to round up the last votes needed to overcome anti-voucher forces." Then Representative John Linder, a Republican from Georgia, finally cast the tie-breaking vote.

Democratic representatives accused Republicans of using political tricks to secure passage of the bill. They suggested that Republicans had overplayed their hand and would now face stiff opposition in the Senate. A spokesperson for Richard Gephardt, a Democrat from Missouri who had participated in the presidential debate, said Republicans "clearly" created the scheduling conflict to win the vote. "They knew the debate was tonight. They knew there would be a couple dozen members that wanted to attend. . . . This is the way this Republican House leadership operates." A spokesperson for DeLay said Democrats were giving Republicans "too much credit" for advance planning.[17]

A month later, Republicans in the Senate were forced to remove a voucher bill from the city's budget after intense opposition from Democrats. Once again, the debate was rancorous. Judd Gregg, a Republican from New Hampshire, spoke from the Senate floor with a large poster featuring a photograph of two Black schoolchildren. "They're saying to the children they're just casualties of the politics of the Senate—tough luck," he said.[18]

Republicans vowed to bring back the legislation, and they did in January 2004, when it was included in a massive $328 billion omnibus spending bill. The DC School Choice Incentive Act of 2003 could be found on page 124 of the 455-page bill. The same tactic had been used by state lawmakers to pass Milwaukee's and Cleveland's programs. The measure was nearly the same as the earlier House legislation. It would give priority to students enrolled in low-performing public schools, as determined by No Child Left Behind, and require private schools to accept students on a first-come, first-served basis or through a lottery. Religious private schools could participate. The program would be the first to use federal dollars to pay for school vouchers, and students who used vouchers would have to take the same standardized tests as their peers in the public system. The bill also noted that the program followed the *Zelman* precedent.[19]

Including the pilot in the spending package made the legislation harder to vote down, and the bill passed the Senate 65–28. Landrieu and Specter voted for it, while Kennedy voted against. President Bush signed it immediately, ending the showdown over vouchers in the nation's capital—for the moment.

NOT SIX MONTHS later, the Colorado Supreme Court ruled 4–3 that a new school voucher program was unconstitutional. The court found that the plan violated the local control provision in the state constitution by directing school districts to give "a portion of their locally raised funds to nonpublic schools over whose instruction the districts have no control." The majority wrote that the goals of the program were "laudable," but "we see no way to reconcile the structure of the program with the requirements of the Colorado Constitution."[20]

The program, which never went into effect because of the lawsuit, would have provided public school students with $4,500 vouchers to attend private schools, including religious ones. A Republican-controlled legislature passed the bill, which would have allowed up to twenty thousand students to qualify for vouchers. School districts were required to participate if at least eight of their schools were rated as low performing, another effort to tie school vouchers to public school accountability.

The Colorado law was the first to pass after the *Zelman* ruling, and its defeat in the state courts system underscored the shape of the legal fights to come. The war of attrition Chanin had promised was underway and the next big battle would be in Florida, where a legal challenge against the nation's first statewide voucher program had been winding through the court system.

21

"Parallel to and in Competition with the Free Public Schools"

IN LATE SUMMER 2005, HURRICANE KATRINA STRUCK THE
Gulf Coast with stunning force, leaving more than 80 percent of
New Orleans underwater. More than eighteen hundred people died.
Aerial footage of the city showed neat rows of submerged houses, just
their roofs visible above the floodwaters. Amid the devastation, Milton
Friedman saw an "opportunity to radically reform the educational system." The ninety-three-year-old economist said the city's public schools
had not served students well before the storm, and he laid the blame
for that failure on government control of education. He was, as always,
consistent. In an op-ed for the *Wall Street Journal*, he wrote, "New Orleans schools were failing for the same reason that schools are failing in
other large cities, because the schools are owned and operated by the
government. . . . The only recourse of dissatisfied parents is to change
their residence or give up the government subsidy and pay for their
children's schooling twice, once in taxes and once in tuition."[1]

Among the country's urban school districts, New Orleans stood out as particularly troubled, with long-neglected buildings, financial mismanagement and corruption, and a record of poor academic performance. The reasons for the school system's difficulties couldn't be as easily explained as Friedman suggested, however. New Orleans had a 250-year tradition of Catholic education with a well-attended, separate school system. White flight and disinvestment from New Orleans's public schools also predated *Brown vs. Board of Education* by about eighty years, starting with the temporary but successful desegregation of its schools in the 1870s and continuing through the violent enforcement of racial segregation during the Jim Crow era. Historian Walter C. Stern wrote, "In New Orleans, the proliferation of private schools and the steep divestments in public education were simultaneous and mutually reinforcing. As residents left the public system . . . they lost interest in supporting it financially, which further undermined the system's quality and desirability and encouraged still more residents to switch to private schools." After court-ordered integration began in November 1960, overall enrollment declined in the city's public schools, and the percentage of white students steadily decreased until low-income Black students made up the majority. Meaningful integration was no longer possible in New Orleans.[2]

Before Hurricane Katrina struck Louisiana, the Orleans Parish School Board was deeply in debt, was under federal investigation for financial irregularities, and had cycled through eight superintendents in seven years. A state auditor reported the school system's central office didn't have a single accountant—unqualified teachers and principals were promoted into those roles instead—and, incredibly, $70 million in federal dollars had been misspent or gone missing. In 2004, the superintendent said he would fire a politically connected janitorial contractor with an "extensive record" of complaints about ignoring unsanitary school conditions, including "human feces" in sinks at a high school, "countless number of bloodied sanitary napkins left for a long period of time" at a middle school, and "dead pigeons and their excrement encrusting a classroom and lab" at another middle school. Some of the school district's woes were detailed in an Associated Press story in April 2005 with the headline "New Orleans Schools a National Horror Tale." A sociologist at Tulane University told the reporter that the root of the problems in the city's school district was not the superintendent or the school board but deep poverty: "It's a school district without much of a middle class at all."[3]

Hurricane Katrina hit Louisiana on August 29, 2005, leaving more than one hundred public schools in New Orleans damaged or destroyed. In the aftermath, Friedman was not the only one with ideas for rebuilding the city's school system. Within weeks, even as much of the city remained uninhabitable, prominent national school reformers began debating the issue. Chester Finn Jr., president of the conservative-leaning Thomas B. Fordham Foundation in Washington, said it would be "really stupid" to "recreate a failed school system." Paul T. Hill, director of the Center on Reinventing Public Education at the University of Washington in Seattle, suggested the city create a "collection" of public schools for families. A headline in *Education Week* in September said, "New Orleans Eyed as Clean Educational Slate."[4]

About a month after Katrina, Hurricane Rita struck the Gulf Coast, damaging more schools, public and private, and displacing even more residents. Thousands of families fled to nearby states and enrolled their students in public, charter, and private schools. In response to the ongoing crisis, President Bush proposed a massive federal aid package, including about $488 million for families to pay tuition at private schools, or what some critics dubbed "hurricane vouchers." US Secretary of Education Margaret Spellings emphasized that the money was a one-year response to a crisis, but Democratic lawmakers accused the administration of taking advantage of the disaster. Senator Ted Kennedy of Massachusetts warned, "This is not the time for a partisan political debate on vouchers."[5]

The situation on the ground was dire, however. More than three hundred thousand students in the region were displaced, having fled to nine states. Texas alone enrolled about forty-five thousand new students. In New Orleans, where the public schools remained closed for months after the storm, the archdiocese had opened some of its schools, and principals were encouraged to enroll public school students, even if they couldn't pay tuition. The superintendent of the archdiocese told the *Wall Street Journal* that he would let voucher opponents explain why the government wouldn't pay for displaced students to attend schools that were open.[6]

In November, after intense criticism, Kennedy changed his mind. He cosponsored a bill to provide one-year federal vouchers for displaced students. He insisted the plan wasn't a voucher program, however, and he persuaded other Democrats to vote for it because the money would be funneled through school districts. Even with his support, the measure had to be tacked on to a budget bill to pass in the Senate. On December 30, 2005, President Bush signed the appropriations bill, which included the Hurricane Education Recovery Act.[7] It provided financial assistance to students and to public and private schools for the 2005–2006 school year.

Louisiana's Democratic leadership did see the crisis in New Orleans as an opportunity to address long-standing issues in the city's public schools, but it seemed unlikely vouchers would be the preferred solution. With widespread damage to school buildings, schools would need to be repaired and rebuilt before they could even be used. Democratic governor Kathleen Babineaux Blanco called on Americans to support a "historic effort to build a world-class, quality system of public education in New Orleans." State officials, including Cecil Picard, superintendent of education, and Leslie Jacobs, an influential member of the board of education, didn't want to rebuild the public school system as it had existed before Katrina. Jacobs said state officials were operating under "two guiding principles": the state didn't want to run the schools, but nor did it want the Orleans Parish School Board to run them. Jacobs said they wanted to avoid the "same tradition of failure."[8]

If state officials didn't want to run the schools, and they didn't want the school board to run them, who would? The answer soon began to take shape. Three months after the hurricane and on the eve of a special legislative session, Blanco announced that she wanted the state to "step in and assume responsibility for that city's failing schools, using, among other things, the charter school model as one of the tools in our recovery efforts." Picard, too, said publicly that he didn't believe the school board could run the system, and New Orleans mayor Ray Nagin indicated he would support skirting the school board's authority and opening charter schools. The school district's interim superintendent urged state officials to "slow things down a bit," while acknowledging that "they probably feel they don't have any other choice."

With the public schools still closed and thousands of residents away from the city, state leaders moved in November to take over most of the city's schools. The state already had the power to place struggling schools into a state-run Recovery School District. But legislators agreed to change the terms in a way that applied only to the Orleans Parish School Board, giving the RSD control of more than a hundred schools in New Orleans. (The school board retained some high-performing schools.) In the immediate aftermath of the crisis, the school board placed its teachers on paid leave. With the state takeover, the board said it couldn't afford to continue paying their benefits. More than seven thousand school employees, who were predominantly Black, lost their jobs. The mass layoff was so poorly executed that some notices were sent to old addresses, including houses destroyed by the storm. Teachers who wanted to appeal were instructed to go to a building that no longer existed. It, too, had been wrecked by Katrina.[9]

Before Katrina, Louisiana wasn't known for school choice. It offered no school vouchers, no tax-credit scholarships, and fewer than twenty charter schools. However, Louisiana had been among the wave of states passing charter school laws in the early to mid-1990s, in part as a reaction to failed efforts by Republican lawmakers to start a school voucher program. Similar to the situation in California in 1992, some state legislators saw charter schools as a more politically acceptable reform alternative. The original law, which was amended in 1997, was among the country's most conservative. After being amended, the state limited the number of charter schools that could open to forty-two.[10] As part of the state's takeover of New Orleans schools after Katrina, Blanco signed executive orders to suspend parts of the state's charter law, which required buy-in from staff and parents before a public school converted to charter status.

Within months of Katrina's landfall, the state forcibly cleaned the slate in New Orleans. In early December, the *Times-Picayune* ran a headline that read, "Orleans Schools Takeover Is Official." At a bill-signing ceremony, Blanco suggested that people who had fled the hurricane wouldn't return unless the city's school system was remade better than before. "We see an opportunity here to just do something that is incredible," she said. A month later, Picard said the state would talk to the people of New Orleans about what they "want their school system to look like." But the decision seemed to have been made already: Picard's statement came as part of a larger announcement that the Louisiana Department of Education was recruiting "high quality providers to run Orleans schools."[11]

><

UNLIKE LOUISIANA, FLORIDA had become a laboratory for school choice under the leadership of Governor Jeb Bush, now in his second term. He had championed the creation of three private school choice options: vouchers for students at low-performing public schools, vouchers for students with disabilities, and tax-credit scholarships for low-income students. About twenty-five thousand students were using the options to attend private schools. But the programs had been plagued by fraud, with private school operators claiming students they didn't enroll and spending tax dollars on items like cars and comedy show tickets. In at least one case, a school claimed to be a charter school while also accepting vouchers. In Polk County, where seven employees at a private Christian school were arrested for misusing state dollars, the county's local prosecutor said he was surprised by how little over-sight there was for the programs. He said he was "very, very concerned that the scenario we are discovering here is being repeated in other parts of the state." After Florida's department of education suggested that the arrests were "accountability in action," the state attorney said the state should be trying to prevent fraud, not waiting for the crimi-nal justice system to catch it after tax dollars had already been wasted. "That misses the point entirely," he said.[12]

One of the state's major newspapers, the *Palm Beach Post*, ran a se-ries of stories and editorials in 2003 and 2004 detailing abuses of the new programs. The headlines were embarrassing for state officials:

Private School Cashed In Vouchers for Public Students
Official: State Voucher School Records Altered
Voucher Crowd Silences a Whistleblower
Terror-Tied School Gets State Perk
380 Students Getting Vouchers for Home-Schooling
State Ok'd Unlicensed Voucher Recipient
Abuse of State Vouchers Reaches Criminal Stage[13]

One of the articles detailed how the cofounder of an Islamic acad-emy was arrested for supporting a terrorist organization while his school was taking roughly $350,000 from the state's tax-credit scholarship pro-gram. Other newspapers also reported on abuses in the system. After Republican lawmakers failed to address the issue in the 2004 legislative session, the *St. Petersburg Times* ran an editorial titled "F for Oversight": "The theft and fraud connected to Florida's school voucher programs have produced at least five criminal and administrative investigations to date. But don't bother asking lawmakers to answer for the mess. They left the Capitol last week without doing a thing."[14]

By 2005, after years of prominent newspaper coverage and even some calls for more regulation from the private school operators themselves, Bush said he would support tighter rules for the state's school choice programs. State Representative Ralph Arza, a Republican, said, "We need to learn from the past and make sure any time we are instituting any sort of a voucher that we take every sort of precaution to make sure our state dollars are protected."[15] Some of the proposed regulations were as basic as ensuring that a student using a voucher actually attended a school.

At the same time, Bush continued pushing to expand Florida's school choice programs. He proposed a "reading voucher" for students who failed the state's reading test three years in a row. The program would open voucher eligibility to more than 170,000 students statewide. In pitching the idea, he described vouchers as "American as apple pie" and suggested the concept was no longer so divisive. He said, "This was really controversial in 1999. It was a big darn deal. I don't think it's as controversial now."[16]

Despite Republican control of the legislature, neither proposal survived the 2005 session. Some Republican lawmakers said they were concerned about expanding school voucher programs during ongoing litigation involving the state's opportunity scholarships; lower courts had ruled that the program violated the state constitution's prohibition against providing aid to religious institutions. The Florida Supreme Court would rule next. A Republican senator introduced a bill to tighten regulations—it would prohibit schools from discriminating on the basis of religion, measure academic progress with a standardized test, and require an auditor to visit private schools—but it failed when a series of amendments were added on the last day of the session. Some lawmakers also were uncomfortable requiring background checks for employees of private schools. State Senator Jim King, who had sponsored the bill, said, "No one can deny the fact that this is necessary. We need to know whether or not those facilities out there exist, whether the kids we're paying for are actually going to school and whether they're learning anything."[17]

In the end, Republican lawmakers raised the cap on the tax-credit scholarships, allowing for an estimated nine thousand more scholarships.[18] But they didn't pursue any additional oversight for the program.

IN JANUARY 2006, the Florida Supreme Court struck down the state's opportunity scholarships, a devastating blow to Bush's legacy in his last year as governor and a ruling with national legal ramifications. The 5–2 ruling in *Bush vs. Holmes* was a surprise in some respects. The justices didn't consider whether the voucher program violated the state constitution's prohibition against aid to religious schools, sidestepping church-state issues. Instead, the majority found that school vouchers ran afoul of a 1998 amendment to the state constitution which called for a "uniform, efficient, safe, secure, and high-quality system of free public schools." In an opinion for the majority, Chief Justice Barbara Pariente wrote that the choice program diverted public dollars into "separate private systems parallel to and in competition with the free public schools." She wrote that the amendment was clear: it didn't create a "floor" for what the state could provide, it "specifies that the manner of fulfilling this obligation is by providing a uniform, high quality system of free public education, and does not authorize additional equivalent alternatives."[19]

In a dissenting opinion, Justice Kenneth Bell argued there was no record to support the idea that the amendment was meant to be exclusionary. "In its third sentence, it clearly mandates that the State make adequate provision for a system of free public schools. But, contrary to the majority's conclusion, it does not preclude the Legislature from using its general legislative powers to provide a private school scholarship to a finite number of parents who have a child in one of Florida's relatively few 'failing' public schools."

The ruling affected only Florida's smallest choice option—fewer than eight hundred students statewide used opportunity scholarships—but it had legal implications for other state education programs. Could the state's vouchers for students with disabilities be considered part of a "uniform" system of public education? No. Could tax-credit scholarships? No. Even Florida's 330 charter schools could conceivably be challenged for not being "uniform" under the majority's interpretation of the state constitution. Howard Simon, executive director of the American Civil Liberties Union in Florida, said it would be "naive" to think the ruling "doesn't speak to all state educational programs in which government funds are being diverted from public schools to private schools." Clark Neily, a lawyer for the Institute for Justice, said basing the ruling on the uniformity clause "opened a can of worms."[20]

To affect other programs, however, a court challenge would have to be brought first, and opponents weren't sure they wanted to file suit against the state's program for students with disabilities because of the potential for such an attack to turn into a public relations nightmare. For his part, Bush said he was "disappointed" and promised to pursue either a legislative fix in the upcoming session or an amendment to the state constitution.

For opponents of school vouchers, *Bush vs. Holmes* was a triumph. Coupled with the Colorado decision two years earlier, it demonstrated that a state-based war of attrition could work. What difference did *Zelman* make if voucher opponents could get programs struck down based on state constitutional grounds? When *Bush vs. Holmes* was originally filed in 1999 it was based on both state and federal arguments; after *Zelman* came down in 2002, Robert Chanin, the lawyer for the National Education Association, removed the establishment clause from the mix. Instead he and other lawyers argued that vouchers violated two clauses in the state constitution—no state aid and uniformity—

and they won the case based on one of the two. More than a dozen states had similar clauses in their constitutions, opening the door to focusing the voucher fight in the state courts. Chanin called the ruling in *Bush vs. Holmes* "an unqualified delight." Commentary in the *Harvard Law Review*, however, referred to "the court's adventurous reading and strained application of the Florida Constitution."[21]

Some voucher proponents saw political bias in the decision. Four of the five justices in the majority had been appointed by Democratic governor Lawton Chiles, Bush's predecessor. (The fifth was appointed jointly during the transition after the 1998 election.) The two dissenting justices were Bush appointees. State Representative Dennis Baxley, a Republican, said, "I'm certain that a lot of people looking at this ruling are going to feel that it's evidence of a bias against this governor by this court." Republican House Majority Leader Andy Gardiner called the ruling "judicial activism at its worst."[22]

Four months later, however, Republicans in the Senate voted down a ballot proposal to ask voters to preserve school vouchers in the state constitution. Four Republicans, including the majority leader, voted against the measure; it failed by one vote. One of the Republicans who voted it down said the measure was too broad; State Senator Evelyn Lynn called it an attack on public education that opened the door to vouchers for "any kind of reason."[23] It was a stunning defeat for Bush— and perhaps a sign that even some Republicans in a state known for education reform weren't yet ready to embrace universal school vouchers.

>←

As GOVERNOR BUSH had learned in Florida, creating a school voucher program was just the start of the political and court fights. Most proposals nationwide had failed. Legal battles were all but guaranteed. Even small programs, once enacted, faced shifting political winds and fierce opposition for years afterward. On the fiftieth anniversary of Milton Friedman's seminal essay, the country had programs in just three major

cities—Milwaukee, Cleveland, and Washington, DC—and two states,
Florida and Ohio. (Maine and Vermont also had long-standing programs to allow students in rural areas without public schools to attend
private school.) In Ohio in 2003, Republican lawmakers had passed a
voucher program for students with autism and then, two years later, a
statewide voucher program tied to public school accountability measures. Efforts to expand Milwaukee's program again failed several times
before Democratic governor Jim Doyle agreed in 2006—in exchange
for additional regulations.[24] Charter schools had proven far more popular than vouchers, with about one million students enrolled in more
than three thousand charter schools. Even with that explosive growth,
the majority of students in America were educated in traditional public
schools.

Education reformers suggested a number of reasons for the slow
growth of school voucher programs, despite the blessing of the US
Supreme Court. Hill, director of the Center on Reinventing Public
Education, said Americans weren't ready for a free-market approach
to education, preferring some level of government accountability. Andrew Rotherham, of the Progressive Policy Institute, said Americans
loved their public schools—and despite efforts to draw Black voters
in with school choice, many older Black Americans recalled the time
when vouchers had been used in southern states to avoid integration of
the public school system. Referring to Virginia in particular, Rotherham said, "If you're an African American of a certain age and you hear
'voucher' it does not connote choice and equity. It connotes images of
a pretty horrible period."[25]

At an event to mark the fiftieth anniversary of his influential essay,
Friedman said he had given a lot of thought to the way vouchers had
been used in the South in the 1950s and 1960s. He remained committed to his belief that vouchers were the solution to the problems
in American education, one that would bring students together, not
keep them apart. "If you had a real voucher program it would more

or less solve the problem of discrimination," he said. What he would change about school vouchers, he said, was the amount of the government subsidy: he would give less. Government, after all, could never be as efficient as business.[26]

Friedman died a little more than a year later, on November 16, 2006, at the age of ninety-four. He had lived long enough to see the concept explored in his 1955 essay become on-the-ground policy upheld by the US Supreme Court. In an obituary for the Nobel Prize–winning economist, the *New York Times* called him the "guiding light to American conservatives." The newspaper wrote that Friedman once had been accused of "going overboard" in some of his antistatism views, and he had responded, "In every generation, there's got to be somebody who goes the whole way, and that's why I believe as I do."[27] He died certain the education revolution he envisioned was just ahead.

22

"The Model Is Working"

Two years after Hurricane Katrina devastated New Orleans, the city's school system was largely dysfunctional. State leaders' vision for reimagining education in the Crescent City had run into the slow pace of the federal recovery effort. One of the biggest challenges school officials faced was finding habitable buildings in which schools could open. More than a hundred school buildings had been damaged or destroyed by the storm. In the Lower Ninth Ward, which endured catastrophic flooding, more than a dozen survivors of the hurricane had climbed onto the roof of Martin Luther King Jr. school and library to escape the rising floodwaters. For more than a year, the building remained unusable. The principal submitted an application to reopen as a charter school, and King reopened temporarily on the second floor of another damaged elementary school. The neighborhood's only public high school remained a time capsule of the storm's damage. A story in *Education Week* titled "Up from the Ruins" described the scene at Alfred Lawless High School in the fall of 2007: "Cracked mud coats the gym floor. A hole the size of a pickup truck gapes open on the school's south side, revealing clumps of dangling, rotten insulation. Mildewed athletic shoes are strewn among shoulder-high weeds and piles of brick rubble. And on a moldy interior wall, a bulletin board displays faded photos of smiling graduates in gowns and mortarboards."[1]

Even before Katrina, the school buildings in New Orleans had been "woefully inadequate," said Paul Pastorek, state superintendent of education.[2] Neglect had been evident in gymnasiums that couldn't be used for gym class or basketball practice, in track fields covered with overgrown weeds, in bathrooms suffering disrepair, and in orchestra pits littered with garbage. In 2003, a headline in the local newspaper, the *Times-Picayune*, read "New Superintendent Tours Needy Schools." Pastorek called for a six-month hard press to repair schools. Where schools couldn't be readily or easily fixed, modular buildings were installed. In some cases, negotiations with the Federal Emergency Management Agency over what could be replaced slowed the recovery efforts, leaving some schools, such as Alfred Lawless High School, stuck in limbo. The *Times-Picayune* reported that only one-tenth of the $241 million allocated by the federal government for rebuilding schools had been spent by the Recovery School District in 2007.[3]

With some students returning to the city, supplies were needed, classrooms were needed, entire schools were needed. And with the city's original teaching force scattered and laid off, teachers were needed. The situation was overwhelming. The first superintendent of the Recovery School District cited the stress of the job when she resigned in the spring of 2007. Immediate needs, such as feeding students and opening schools, had made it difficult to focus on instruction.[4]

The challenges in New Orleans didn't deter state leaders from their vision of transforming the city's school district. Leslie Jacobs, one of the main architects of the plan, said it was an "opportunity to hit a restart button." The new superintendent of the RSD echoed that sentiment when he took the job. Paul Vallas, who previously had served as schools chief in Philadelphia and Chicago, said he was attracted to the job in New Orleans by the "opportunity to create a new school system." Newspapers across the country used similar language in the months after Katrina. The *Star Tribune* in Minneapolis called Katrina a "chance to start fresh." A headline in the *Wall Street Journal* proclaimed, "Charting a New Course; After Katrina, New Orleans's Troubled Educational System Banks on Charter Schools." And the *Los Angeles Times* called the storm an "ironic gift."[5]

For some of the families returning to New Orleans, who had lost their homes and were trying to resettle in precarious conditions, the storm probably didn't feel like much of a gift. The new school system was a disorganized hodgepodge—*Education Week* described New Orleans as having "three systems of public schools" in the first eighteen months after Katrina—and was confusing for parents and guardians.[6] Start dates differed between schools, as did application requirements. One parent said his child was wait-listed at their former school for the 2006–2007 school year because he missed an enrollment deadline. To find an open seat, he had to go to a charter school across the river. The NAACP Legal Defense Fund sent a letter to state officials in January 2007 to complain that "at least 300 students" had been denied admission to any school in New Orleans, an infringement on their right to a free public education. Two lawsuits were subsequently filed, and the RSD had to quickly open two elementary schools in February to clear the "waiting list." By the spring, fifty-six schools had opened—most of them charters—and about twenty-eight thousand students were enrolled. Five schools were run by the Orleans Parish School Board, twenty by the Recovery School District, and thirty-one by charter operators, which numbered twenty-three. Half the residents in New Orleans who were surveyed in the spring of 2007 thought the public school system had gotten worse since Katrina.[7]

Despite the on-the-ground chaos, Jacobs bristled at the idea that New Orleans was an experiment. "I get really tired of that term 'experiment,' because experiment implies that you're just fooling around with something," she said. "We're building an entirely new school system, not experimenting."[8]

In truth, New Orleans was a large-scale experiment—the first of its kind—and, whatever the outcome, it would be viewed as a judgment on charter schools. By the summer of 2007, some critics were ready to write it off. A headline in the *American Prospect* read, "NOLA's Failed Education Experiment."[9]

THE EFFORT TO rebuild New Orleans's school system with charter schools was made possible, in part, by how rapidly the sector had grown since the country's first charter school had opened in Minnesota in 1992. From one school in a recreation center in St. Paul had sprung thousands. Successful charter schools transformed into national brand-name charter networks. Charter school founders created training programs for teachers and principals. Umbrella groups, such as the National Association of Charter School Authorizers, formed to provide guidance and support. Big-city mayors, such as New York City's Michael Bloomberg, made charter schools a key part of their plans for education reform: Bloomberg said he had tried to make New York the most "charter-friendly city in all of America," wooing charter operators with low rent and shared spaces in public school buildings.[10] And two presidents, Bill Clinton and George W. Bush, had encouraged the growth of charter schools nationwide, giving the reform continued bipartisan credibility and about fifteen years of support from the federal government.

The key to the sector's rapid growth, however, could be traced back to the embrace of charter schools by wealthy philanthropists, such as Bill Gates, Eli Broad, and Sam Walton, who used their foundations to push education initiatives, including merit pay for teachers, smaller high schools, common state standards, and school choice policies. After dumping more than $1 billion into creating smaller schools, the Bill and Melinda Gates Foundation turned to testing and accountability reforms in 2006. That year, the foundation also donated $30 million to help establish "high-quality, results-oriented" charter schools in New York City, Washington, DC, Oakland, Los Angeles, and Chicago. The Eli and Edythe Broad Foundation, founded in 1999, threw its weight behind charter schools, merit pay, and creating talent "pipelines" for district leaders. NewSchools Venture Fund, a venture philanthropy firm founded in 1998, focused on charter start-ups and charter management organizations, which run charter networks. And the Walton Family Foundation, founded in 1987, emphasized public and private school choice initiatives, putting about $117 million into both causes in 2007 alone.[11] Philanthropy didn't just pay for the expansion of charter schools; it also paid to promote the idea through conferences, books, research, and even movies.

One of the most successful charter "brands" was the Knowledge Is Power Program, or KIPP—a charter network that wouldn't have been able to expand nationally without philanthropic support. With money from the Doris and Donald Fisher Fund, David Levin and Mike Feinberg turned two small charter schools into a national system. They created a leadership program to train educators to run KIPP schools, opening more than fifty schools in sixteen states and serving more than twelve thousand students. They spoke at the Republican Party's national convention, were highlighted on *60 Minutes*, and were featured on *Oprah*. Minnesota's Republican governor even mentioned KIPP in his 2006 State of the State address, saying the state should "pursue other new and innovative approaches that produce results, such as the Knowledge Is Power Program."[12]

When Hurricane Katrina devastated New Orleans, many of the same people—charter operators and big-name philanthropists—responded, particularly as it became clear in the aftermath that Louisiana's state leaders viewed charter schools as a critical part of the rebuilding effort. The Broad Foundation, the Fisher Fund, and the Gates Foundation made a joint $17.5 million donation to three groups working in New Orleans's schools in late 2007, in what *USA Today* called the largest-ever donation made to the city's schools. The state also tapped the National Association of Charter School Authorizers, a nonprofit organization, to review and approve applications for new charter schools. And a new organization, New Schools for New Orleans, formed, which helped recruit teachers and charter operators to the city.[13]

Charter organizations leaned on their interwoven network to respond to the crisis. In the immediate aftermath of the storm, KIPP learned that many of its New Orleans students had taken shelter in the Houston Astrodome, more than three hundred miles from the students' home city. Feinberg, who lived in Houston, wandered around the Astrodome looking for students and their families. With New Orleans still largely underwater, he called the superintendent of the Houston school district to see if KIPP could open its New Orleans school there. He quickly lined up teachers through Teach for America, which puts new college graduates in teaching jobs in low-income communities. Within days, it was arranged: the school would open in Houston to serve displaced students. It would be called KIPP New Orleans West.[14]

✦

"I WANT EXPERIMENTATION, but I also want accountability," Democratic presidential nominee Barack Obama said on the campaign trail in the fall of 2008 at a public high school in Dayton, Ohio. Similar to President Clinton in 1992, Obama outlined an education platform that put him at odds with the national teachers' unions on some core issues, which allowed him to push back against opponents' claims that he was beholden to labor. Alongside calls for greater investments in early childhood education and a tuition credit to make college more affordable, Obama also talked about merit pay for teachers and replacing teachers who weren't "up to the job." He promised to dramatically expand federal funding for charter schools. And he said charter schools that weren't working would be "shut down."[15]

The debate over school choice took on a familiar tenor. Obama supported charter schools and opposed school vouchers.[16] Republican presidential nominee John McCain favored both charters and vouchers, and he criticized Obama for opposing vouchers while sending his daughters to private school. McCain also sent his children to private school, but he said the difference was that he supported creating more choices for low-income families through school vouchers. If the attack on the Obamas felt familiar it was because the same accusation had been wielded against the Clintons years before.

As an education issue, however, school choice was somewhat overshadowed in the 2008 election as Obama and McCain dueled over No Child Left Behind, President Bush's signature education law. NCLB had exposed achievement gaps among racial and socioeconomic groups, but its critics said it had resulted in an overemphasis on test preparation in the public schools and narrowed the curriculum as teachers and principals focused on the subjects that would be tested. Obama promised to "fix" the law and said it had "done more to stigmatize and demoralize our students and teachers in struggling schools than it has to marshal the talent and the determination and the resources to turn them around." McCain countered that NCLB allowed the country to "finally see what is happening to students who were previously invisible."[17]

At the third and final presidential debate, held in October at Hofstra University in New York, Obama and McCain sparred briefly over school choice. In ninety minutes that focused on domestic policy, the moderator, Bob Schieffer of CBS News, asked about education once, in the final question of the evening. He said the United States spent more per capita than other countries on education but often with worse results. "What do you intend to do about it?"

In his answer, McCain called education the "civil rights issue of the twenty-first century" and posed a question: "But what is the advantage in a low-income area of sending a child to a failed school and that being your only choice?" He continued:

So choice and competition amongst schools is one of the key elements that's already been proven in places like New Orleans and New York City and other places, where we have charter schools, where we take good teachers and we reward them and promote them. And we find bad teachers another line of work. And we have to be able to give parents the same choice, frankly, that Senator Obama and Mrs. Obama had and Cindy and I had to send our kids to the school—their kids to the school of their choice.

Choice. Competition. Civil rights. McCain hit all the Republican high notes. In his response, Obama said he and McCain agreed on two things: charter schools and removing bad teachers. "Where we disagree is on the idea that we can somehow give out vouchers—give vouchers as a way of securing the problems in our education system," he said.

McCain said vouchers "where they are requested and where they are agreed to, are a good and workable system. And it's been proven." Obama countered that the "data doesn't show that it actually solves the problem."[18]

The *Washington Post* called education "largely a footnote" in the presidential election, and it was, but the moment was telling.[19] Both candidates were generally in favor of choice and accountability—the parallel tracks of education reform for nearly two decades—but the line between Republican and Democrat remained firmly drawn over public dollars flowing to private institutions. When Obama won the White House the next month, it seemed clear that federal education policy would continue to focus on charter schools and accountability measures that targeted teachers and public school performance.

><

CHARTER SCHOOLS WERE originally billed as educational laboratories, a means to test innovative practices to share with traditional public schools. That mostly hadn't occurred in any comprehensive way, and a number of charters weren't very different from regular public schools. But in some cities with a growing number of charter schools, school districts did adopt some of the practices of successful charters and create new programs to compete for students. In Miami-Dade, Superintendent Rudy Crew launched a school improvement zone, often called "The Zone," in 2005 to target thirty-nine low-performing schools with additional resources. The Zone, which was modeled after a similar program he had developed in New York City in the late 1990s, employed some of the same practices as the "no excuses" charter schools, with a longer school day and year. Teachers were paid an extra 20 percent for working additional hours. In 2008, Harvard University named the project one of the top fifty innovations in government. Other school districts across the country, including Detroit, Pinellas County (in Florida), and San Diego, developed similar zones. Michael Casserly, executive director of the Council of the Great City Schools, said the setup gave schools the ability to "short-circuit normal bureaucratic channels and get what they need more quickly." Casserly wasn't specifically addressing charter schools, but his description could just as easily have applied to them. (Interestingly, Miami-Dade County Public Schools later found that The Zone didn't improve student achievement—the longer hours seemed to have exhausted students and teachers alike.)[20]

In the Denver Public Schools, Superintendent Michael Bennet unveiled a sweeping plan to address declining enrollment and budget constraints. The district had room for about a hundred thousand students yet only enrolled about sixty-one thousand. Bennet wanted to close underenrolled, low-performing schools and reinvest some of the savings back into the schools that would absorb the displaced students. He also wanted to open new, more attractive options. In 2008, he put out a request for proposals for "innovative new schools." The same year, Democratic governor Bill Ritter signed the Innovation Schools Act, which allowed schools and districts to apply for waivers from certain state laws, district regulations, and collective bargaining agreements. The idea was to give them greater control over budgets, hiring, teacher pay, and the length of the school day and year.[21] All those features were strikingly similar to the charter school model.

SIX MONTHS AFTER his inauguration in 2009, President Obama officially announced that his administration would hold a national education competition: school districts and states would compete for grants totaling $4.35 billion, an initiative billed as Race to the Top. There was a catch: to get approved, applicants had to pursue education reforms favored by the administration, including merit pay for teachers, data tracking, and common standardized tests. "We're looking to drive reform, reward excellence, and dramatically improve our nation's schools," said US Secretary of Education Arne Duncan. The initial announcement didn't explicitly mention charter schools, but Duncan made it clear that states without charters would find it difficult to compete for the much-needed stimulus dollars. Obama, too, had noted the administration's interest in charter schools as a method of innovation in a speech at the Hispanic Chamber of Commerce a few months earlier.[22]

The July announcement was somewhat awkwardly timed. A month earlier, a comprehensive research study released by Stanford University found that more than a third of charter schools performed worse than traditional public schools. The study, from Stanford's Center for Research on Education Outcomes, or CREDO, looked at more than twenty-four hundred charter schools in fifteen states and the District of Columbia. Only 17 percent of charter schools had seen academic growth that significantly exceeded that of regular public schools.[23]

Duncan did some damage control at the annual gathering of the National Alliance for Public Charter Schools in Washington, DC, where he warned in his speech that the "charter movement is putting itself at risk by allowing too many second-rate and third-rate schools to exist." He referred to the CREDO study as a "wake-up call." But Duncan also praised charter schools as "one of the most profound changes in American education, bringing tremendous new options to underserved communities." His staff gave the speech to the *New York Times* in advance, and the paper ran a story in the front section of the newspaper before the event: "Education Chief to Warn Advocates That Inferior Charter Schools Harm the Effort."[24]

The CREDO study analyzed the results by state since charter laws varied so much across the country. That breakdown gave pundits plenty to dissect. It found that charter schools in Chicago, Denver, Arkansas, Missouri, and Louisiana performed better than traditional public schools. Charter schools in Arizona, Florida, Minnesota, and Ohio did worse than their public counterparts, while those in California, Washington, DC, and Georgia were roughly the same as the district-run schools.

In some states that didn't have charter schools, such as Washington and West Virginia, critics pointed to the CREDO study as a reason to hold firm against efforts to create them. But some state officials feared that not having charter schools would hurt their chances to get money from Race to the Top. Several months after the announcement, Duncan suggested that states without charter schools could still be considered if they proposed something similar, such as innovation districts. West Virginia had legislation for an "Innovation Zone," but Washington did not.[25] Duncan said that would hurt Washington's chances. Other states quickly made changes to enhance their Race to the Top applications. Duncan called on states to lift their charter caps if they limited the number of charters that could open. Tennessee and Illinois didn't eliminate their caps, but they did increase the number of charters allowed.

In Louisiana, where New Orleans was pioneering a new charter-centric school system, state officials trumpeted the results of the CREDO study. The news came just as state lawmakers were considering lifting the state's cap on charter schools. Paul Pastorek, state superintendent of education, said it was "reassuring to confirm that Louisiana has implemented processes and standards that have resulted in fostering high-quality charter school programs."[26] Not long after the study's release, Louisiana lifted its charter cap.

Most of the state's charter schools were located in New Orleans. Test scores in the city had improved by the 2008–2009 school year, but some community leaders were unhappy that locals still had so little voice in the dramatic educational changes occurring post-Katrina. Race played an undeniable role in the tension. The majority of the district's students were Black, yet control of the city's schools was largely in the hands of white outsiders. The Orleans Parish School Board also had a white, reform-minded majority after the 2008 election. The teachers who were let go after the hurricane were predominantly Black—a significant part of the city's Black middle class—and they were largely replaced by white teachers, many of whom were young and inexperienced recruits from Teach for America or teachNOLA. As Douglas N. Harris, an economics professor, wrote, "The reforms were created and managed by white leaders. Three out of four teachers fired were black, compared with fewer than half of those subsequently hired. The charter authorization process, deliberately or otherwise, favored outside white groups over local community groups."[27]

The *Times-Picayune* wrote in the spring of 2009 about critics who rode on a bus to Baton Rouge to express their frustration directly to the state board of education about what the newspaper termed the "ever-expanding, state-controlled charter school movement in New Orleans." Critics also cast doubt on the reason for the improving test score results. Some said test scores had begun rising before the storm. Others said it was impossible to compare pre-Katrina and post-Katrina scores because some children had fled the city and never returned. School spending also increased significantly, with greater investment in the new charter-centric system.[28] If the traditional public schools had seen a similar influx of money before Katrina, student performance might have improved then, too.

State officials were confident the dramatic changes they had instituted were behind the improvements. Five years after Hurricane Katrina, Leslie Jacobs wrote an op-ed in the *Wall Street Journal*: "But from the flood waters, the most market-driven public school system in the country has emerged. Education reformers across America should take notice: The model is working."[29]

23

"It Was Never Supposed to Get This Big"

A FTER THREE DECADES IN THE WISCONSIN LEGISLATURE, Polly Williams left office in 2010. She didn't settle quietly into retirement. That just wasn't her style. When Republican governor Scott Walker took office the following year and pushed to lift the income restrictions on Milwaukee's school voucher program, Williams made her opposition known. She supported school vouchers for the poor, not for families who could afford private school. Many of the Republicans who had championed the original legislation, including former governor Tommy Thompson, had assured her—and the public—that they didn't want universal vouchers. Now, about twenty years later, the new Republican governor was gunning for it. Williams wanted her former constituents to understand what was at stake. She and the president of the school board organized a meeting at a church in Milwaukee in the spring of 2011, an event advertised as a chance to "discuss the expansion of the voucher program to wealthy parents sending their kids to elite private academies."[1] It wasn't a subtle message.

Williams wasn't the only voucher supporter to oppose Walker's plans. Howard Fuller, who had replaced Williams as the public face of the movement, came out strongly against it, writing in an op-ed in the *Milwaukee Journal Sentinel* that "the governor's plan would dramatically change the program's social justice mission and destroy its trailblazing legacy" as a program for low-income children. Fuller pleaded with Republican lawmakers not to prove Williams, and others, right about conservatives' long-term intentions.

> From the beginning, some critics of the parental choice movement have claimed that Republican lawmakers and other conservative individuals who have strongly supported the program over the years were only using poor children to establish the program. The real agenda, these critics have charged, has been to hijack the program and offer universal vouchers to even the wealthiest citizens.... Unfortunately, the governor's proposal fits the pattern that these critics have asserted for years. It is a gift to the opponents of the program.[2]

Walker scaled back his initial proposal that year, but he won several major victories. Lawmakers expanded Milwaukee's program, making some middle-class students eligible and eliminating the enrollment cap, and they created a new voucher for students in Racine, a city about thirty miles south of Milwaukee. At a public meeting in 2011, Williams lamented how much Milwaukee's program had grown. An earlier expansion in 2005 had allowed up to 22,500 students to attend private schools, which was then about a quarter of the school district's total enrollment. Now there was no limit at all. "It was never supposed to get this big," she maintained.[3]

Two years later, Walker came back with another proposal to expand school vouchers outside Milwaukee and Racine. He had survived a historic election recall in 2012, the first governor in US history to do so, after picking a headline-grabbing fight with the state's labor unions by restricting their right to collective bargaining. In 2013, he proposed tying school vouchers to the state's new "report card" for public schools, which would make students in nine school districts eligible. This time he included income limits. The proposal still sparked a swift backlash, with opposition from some Republicans, and it set off a public war of words, rallies, and efforts to sway public opinion. Once again, Williams came out forcefully against the expansion. She accused Republicans of undermining the original legislation and told a reporter at the *Milwaukee Journal Sentinel*, "They have hijacked the program."[4]

Her public opposition, which followed years of calling for greater accountability for vouchers, prompted a furious response from one of her former allies, George Mitchell, a longtime choice advocate. Mitchell, who is white, told a newspaper columnist that Williams was racist and had been "irrelevant" for years. Then he made a rather stunning comment: "Polly was useful to the school choice movement because of her race and her party affiliation." When the columnist asked Mitchell who used Williams, he responded, "Who didn't use her?"[5]

Williams dismissed the idea that Republicans had used her, but the ugly exchange made it clear that supporters who favored limited programs for low-income children were no longer at the forefront of the school choice movement. Fuller, too, had had a falling out with some conservative allies a few years earlier, after he had pushed for more regulations for the program. "For us, it was never a free-market issue. It was a social-justice issue," he said later.[6]

What Walker ultimately achieved in 2013—a statewide school voucher program for low-income and some middle-class students outside Milwaukee and Racine—was a considerable departure from the "experiment" Williams had championed in 1990. What she'd feared had come to pass.

✦

AFTER PRESIDENT OBAMA'S election in 2008, it seemed as if the push for school vouchers and other private school choice options had broken down. The Obama administration wanted charter schools. The Great Recession meant money was tight in state budgets. Democrats controlled the governorship in twenty-six states, including key states in the Midwest like Wisconsin and Ohio, and more than half the seats in state legislatures. School vouchers remained a reform idea Democrats wouldn't touch, and a growing body of research indicated private school choice wasn't the panacea some supporters expected. The *Wall Street Journal* declared the movement for school vouchers "under assault" in 2009. Frederick M. Hess, director of educational policy studies at the conservative-leaning American Enterprise Institute, wrote in the fall of 2010 in *National Affairs* that these "would seem to be dark days for the school choice movement." He pointed to several "champions of choice" who had grown disillusioned. One of them was Diane Ravitch, an education historian, who wrote a best-selling book retracting her support of school choice. Hess noted that Ravitch had written in her blog, "I just wish that choice proponents would stop promising charters and vouchers will bring us closer to that date when 100 percent of all children reach proficiency. If evidence mattered, they would tone down their rhetoric." Likewise, Paul Peterson, a Harvard professor and voucher proponent, said the results in Milwaukee were not "as startlingly positive as advocates originally hoped" and "the jury on charter schools is still out."[7]

Then the 2010 midterm elections swept through statehouses across the country like a tsunami, turning them red. Republicans got a boost from the emergence of the Tea Party, part of a conservative backlash fueled by anti-tax sentiments and racism after the election of the country's first Black president. The Republican Party also deliberately targeted statehouses in the elections, an effort unmatched by Democrats. Afterward, Republicans controlled two-thirds of the legislative chambers nationwide. The *Washington Post* wrote, "On Election Day 2010, the Democrats suffered massive losses at every level. They lost 63 seats in the House and control of the chamber. They lost six Senate seats. They suffered a net loss of six governorships. With special elections and party switches, Democrats lost 720 legislative seats; 26 legislatures were under full GOP control."[8]

Republican lawmakers suddenly had an opportunity to pass private school choice legislation, and they took advantage of it. It didn't matter what the research showed. The concept of school choice had become ingrained in the party's platform, and the overarching rationale for it had in some ways changed—or perhaps reverted to some of the earliest arguments for it. Choice, the ability of a parent to select their child's school and have that choice subsidized with tax dollars, was its own value apart from what it did or didn't do for the greater public school system. As Bernard Iddings Bell, an Episcopal priest, had argued decades before, "If only public schools are state-supported, if to send children to a school not state-run is possible only at a cost beyond the means of ordinary parents, then the usual parent is in effect coerced to accept the public school even against his conscience. Where then is the liberty guaranteed by the Constitution?"[9] In effect, school choice equaled greater parental freedom.

A flurry of legislation followed the midterm elections. New school voucher programs were created in Wisconsin, Indiana, and Ohio in 2011. The same year, Oklahoma enacted a tax-credit scholarship program, and Arizona created the first education savings accounts, which gave parents money in a limited account to pay for private school tuition, tutoring, online classes, or even to contribute to a college fund. Robert Enlow, president and CEO of the Friedman Foundation, wrote a piece for *Education Week* titled "Is 2011 Milton Friedman's Year of School Choice?"[10]

It didn't stop there. In 2012, Mississippi passed a voucher program for students with dyslexia, while New Hampshire, Virginia, and Pennsylvania created new tax-credit scholarship programs. In 2013, North

Carolina passed a school voucher program, and Wisconsin, Ohio, and Mississippi expanded theirs or added new ones. Alabama enacted a re-fundable tax-credit program.[11]

Republicans deepened their hold on power with the 2014 mid-term elections following President Obama's reelection in 2012. The *Christian Science Monitor* wrote, "The statehouse map of America is 'redder' (more Republican) than it has been in nearly 100 years."[12] New school choice programs were created over the next two years in Kansas, Wisconsin, Mississippi, Nevada, Montana, Arkansas, South Dakota, and Maryland. Charter schools continued their expansion at the same time, with new laws passed in Washington, Alabama, and Maine. It became easier to talk about which states didn't have charter school laws than about which did.

By 2016, more than sixty private school choice programs had been created in twenty-eight states and the District of Columbia.[13] It was a stunning expansion after years of frustrated efforts and failed attempts. Milton Friedman's prediction from two decades earlier had come true: school choice had swept "like a wildfire" through the country.

IN THE MIDDLE of the firestorm, Polly Williams died. She was seventy-seven years old and had been the longest-serving woman in Wisconsin's legislature when she retired. Before her death, Howard Fuller described her as a "consistent, forceful, unapologetic voice for the African American community." Without her, he said, "we would not have a school choice movement in this country." After she died, he described her simply as a "friend and a warrior." US Representative Gwen Moore, a Democrat who served with Williams in the state as-sembly, called her a legend who was "fearless in her convictions." Kevin Chavous, who had supported vouchers in Washington, DC, as a city council member, said Williams "laid the groundwork for a national movement." She had been dubbed the "mother of school choice" and even "education's Rosa Parks."[14]

Williams confounded her critics and allies alike, but she was only difficult to understand when viewed through the prism of partisan politics. Her guiding principle had been to do what she felt was right for her constituents in Milwaukee, who were predominantly Black. Williams had been willing to work with Republicans or Democrats to advance her causes. She was equally willing to fight them. To explain her unlikely and long-lasting political career, Williams said politicians had either money or people, and she had people. She was savvy but not circumspect. She spoke her mind. She acknowledged that her "pro-Black views" made some white people uncomfortable, but she wanted Black Americans to have more control over the public institutions that shaped their lives. She had once told the *Chicago Tribune*, "I vote my conscience, and my color."[15]

Education was her passion. Before she turned to school vouchers, Williams pushed to end busing for desegregation, to redirect additional resources into Milwaukee's predominantly Black schools, and to hire more Black teachers and classroom aides. She championed a proposal to carve out a predominantly Black school district from Milwaukee Public Schools. She also created the African American Education Council, an organization to give Black parents more say in reform efforts undertaken in the school district. She made her concerns about the direction of the school choice movement known, but she had no regrets about her role. In an interview, she said, "When they ask me, knowing what I know now, would I still do it? I say yes. Even though I may not agree with a parent's decision, they still have the right to make it."[16]

Several years before Williams died, a columnist for the *Milwaukee Journal Sentinel* described how the Midwestern city's school system had changed since 1990. Milwaukee Public Schools still had the highest enrollment in the city, with about eighty-seven thousand students, though that number had been on the decline for a decade. More than twenty thousand students attended 127 private schools with vouchers. More than eight thousand attended charter schools authorized by three entities: the school district, the city, and a major university. And nearly seven thousand were enrolled in suburban public schools, through either a long-standing voluntary integration program or the state's open-enrollment plan. Alan J. Borsuk wrote, "Almost a third of all Milwaukee students getting publicly funded educations are doing so outside the boundaries of what their parents—and for sure, their grandparents—defined as the public education system. In few, if any, places in America has the definition of public education been given so many different meanings."[17]

This was, in many ways, the legacy of Polly Williams. Without her, the country's first modern school voucher program would not exist. Without it, charter schools would not have taken off across the country as a more politically palatable alternative. It also was the shared legacy of other choice advocates like Milton Friedman, Virgil Blum, Christopher Jencks, and Ted Kolderie. Each imagined how America could educate children outside the traditional public school system, and those ideas eventually coalesced in real policies. Friedman wanted universal school vouchers with little regulation. Blum, who advocated for vouchers for religious schools, was open to accountability measures that would make private schools function more like public ones. Jencks envisioned highly regulated vouchers as a tool for low-income families, similar to how Williams came to view them. That version of vouchers took off in the 1990s before Friedman's original market-driven concept came to dominate. And Kolderie opposed private school choice but imagined the development of an entirely separate "second sector" of public education, with the "charter sector" acting as a vehicle to improve the overall system.[18] Their motivations were different, sometimes remarkably so, but the result was the same: the line drawn between public and private education in America for more than a hundred years had blurred, with millions of tax dollars flowing each year to educate students outside the traditional public school system.

⇥⇤

ADVOCATES FOR TRADITIONAL public education had grown increasingly concerned about those blurred lines, particularly in major cities where charter schools were growing in number. By 2015, charter schools accounted for 15 to 20 percent of public schools in Baltimore, Philadelphia, and Los Angeles. In Washington, DC, that figure was about 44 percent, though both traditional public schools and charter schools were growing.[19] Some advocates didn't view charter schools as public schools, and they raised questions about fraud, financial mismanagement, aggressive recruitment practices, and allegations that difficult-to-educate students were pushed out of them. One of the most well-publicized incidents occurred at Success Academy, a charter network in New York City, when parents sued after learning that their children were named on a principal's "Got-to-Go" list of challenging students. The network's founder called the list an anomaly that was not indicative of regular practices.[20]

Grassroots organizations formed nationwide to protest choice policies. The Philadelphia Coalition Advocating for Public Schools protested in 2014 outside city hall to draw attention to charters' recruitment practices. The group accused charter schools of creating a "climate of winners and losers in communities," and said, "We need to reaffirm the common, public purpose of our compulsory schools, and ensure that traditional and charter school sectors are working together to enhance, and not undermine, each other." In Chicago, parents and community activists fought back after years of school closures and charter conversions, which primarily affected Black neighborhoods. Parents and alumni feared they were losing an important part of their history. In 2015 a small group led a thirty-four-day hunger strike to stop the closure of a public high school in a historically Black neighborhood, the culmination of a multiyear effort. Sociologist Eve L. Ewing wrote about how the new charter schools erased Black history in the city: "Mary C. Terrell Elementary—named for a black suffragist who was a charter member of the NAACP—became ACE Technical Charter School in 2001. Two years later, Sojourner Truth Elementary School became the Chicago International Charter School. Ralph J. Bunche Elementary School, honoring the first African American to win a Nobel Prize, is now Providence Englewood Charter School." A similar dynamic occurred in New Orleans as that city's public schools were converted to charter schools after Hurricane Katrina. Some alumni campaigned to get historic school names restored. One high school in New Orleans, Alfred Lawless High, changed its name back to the original more than a decade and a half later. A petition calling for the name to be restored to the school described Lawless as a "local civil rights hero" and noted that he had served as principal of Fisk Colored School, "the first public school in New Orleans to provide modern instructional equipment and adult education classes to African Americans." The alumni wrote, "He deserves his part in our history. . . . We deserve our memories for future generations." More than a thousand people signed the petition.[21]

Ewing wrote, "A fight for a school is never just about a school. A school means the potential for stability in an unstable world, the potential for agency in the face of powerlessness, the enactment of one's own dreams and visions for one's own children. Because whether you're in Detroit or Austin or Louisiana or Chicago, you want to feel that your school is *your* school."

⇥⇤

NEARLY TWENTY-FIVE YEARS after the country's first charter school opened, the debate over the schools was as heated as it had ever been, if not more so. Studies on charter schools did little to quell the debate, as supporters and opponents latched on to results that confirmed their views. In 2013, Stanford University's Center for Research on Education Outcomes released another report about charter schools, this one with more positive results than its first comprehensive review in 2009. The study, which included twenty-five states, the District of Columbia, and New York City, found that students in charter schools performed better in reading than their public school counterparts, while they did about the same in math.[22]

Two years later, CREDO published another large-scale study focused on urban charter schools. The center's director said the research showed that many urban charters were "providing superior academic learning for their students, in many cases quite dramatically better." The study noted again that results varied widely by metropolitan area and state: "The charter sector is regularly treated as a monolithic set of schools, but recent research has made clear that across the U.S. there are in fact distinct charter markets with dramatically different student profiles, governance and oversight structures, and academic quality." Charter schools in Boston, for instance, were found to be higher performing, while those in Las Vegas were not. Other researchers pointed out that the effect sizes—essentially the differences of magnitude between the groups studied—were so small as to be relatively meaningless. In a review for the National Education Policy Center, Andrew Maul, an assistant professor at the University of California, Santa Barbara, wrote, "To call such an effect 'substantial' strains credulity."[23]

In the summer of 2016, ahead of the presidential election, the NAACP passed a resolution calling for a moratorium on charter school expansion. Delegates who voted for it cited a variety of issues, from increasing racial segregation to harsh discipline policies to financial mismanagement to tension caused by co-locating charter schools in traditional public school campuses. The Journey for Justice Alliance, a social justice group that supports public education, released a statement commending the NAACP for "joining the cacophony of voices from urban communities across the United States demanding the end of unwarranted expansion of charter schools." Matthew Chingos, an education researcher, told a reporter at the *Wall Street Journal* that part of the debate over charter schools stemmed from the larger question about what charter growth meant for the country's traditional school system. "The tension is, 'What's the end game here?' Is this a model to replace the traditional public school model?"[24]

><

IN 2016, THE fault lines of the school choice movement were exacerbated by the election of Republican president Donald J. Trump. For secretary of education, he nominated Betsy DeVos, a longtime school choice supporter, a billionaire, and the former chairperson of the Republican Party in Michigan. Not since President Reagan and his education secretary, Bill Bennett, had the White House seen such strong advocates of market-driven reform. Supporters of public education were horrified. The Leadership Conference on Civil and Human Rights, a wide-ranging coalition of national nonprofit organizations, said DeVos would "undermine bedrock American principles of equal opportunity, nondiscrimination and public education itself." Randi Weingarten, president of the American Federation of Teachers, called DeVos "the most ideological, anti-public education nominee put forward since President Carter created a cabinet-level Department of Education," and said Trump's selection of her "makes it loud and clear that his education policy will focus on privatizing, defunding and destroying public education in America."[25]

Choice supporters were somewhat split on the nomination, as DeVos was known to support both private choice options and charter schools. The president of the conservative Heritage Foundation, Jim DeMint, said of the selection, "The school choice movement will have a champion in the Education Department." Howard Fuller disliked Trump's racist rhetoric but said he supported DeVos. Anthony Williams, former mayor of Washington, DC, endorsed her as a "proven reformer" who supported the effort to get vouchers in the district. Eli

Broad, a philanthropist who had thrown his financial weight behind charter schools, wrote a letter to the Senate in which he called DeVos "unprepared and unqualified." If senators didn't vote against her nomination, "much of the good work that has been accomplished to improve public education for all of America's children could be undone." The Massachusetts Charter Public School Association expressed reservations about DeVos's role in "creating" a charter sector in Michigan that "has been widely criticized for lax oversight and poor academic performance, and appears to be dominated by for-profit interests."[26]

DeVos's nomination was approved after a strong push to derail it by Democrats, teachers' unions, and advocates for public education. Senate Minority Leader Chuck Schumer, a Democrat from New York, said DeVos "could not answer the most fundamental questions about public education."[27] Her fumbles during her confirmation hearing were pilloried on *Saturday Night Live*. Vice President Mike Pence broke a 50–50 tie in the Senate, the first time in US history a tie-breaking vote had been required for a cabinet nomination. Two Republicans voted against her.

DeVos seemed to take it in stride. Speaking at the Conservative Political Action Conference several weeks later, she acknowledged some of the less than flattering news coverage—"The media has had its fun with me, and that's OK"—but she came out hard against the "education establishment" and "the system." She declared, "We have a unique window of opportunity to make school choice a reality for millions of families."[28] Similar to the Reagan years, when the administration advocated abolishing the US Department of Education, it was a somewhat awkward juxtaposition: the country's highest-ranking education official didn't seem to like America's public schools.

DeVos's appointment and Trump's racial politics were so divisive that some of the underlying tensions within the school choice movement threatened to derail any progress that might have been made with a staunch choice supporter as education secretary. DeVos remained an object of ridicule. After she gave a widely criticized interview in 2018 with *60 Minutes*, a columnist for the *Washington Post* ruthlessly mocked her, writing, "Whenever DeVos speaks, it feels as though the sum total of human knowledge is somehow diminished."[29]

Democratic politicians distanced themselves from school choice. One of the most conspicuous examples was Senator Cory Booker of New Jersey. Booker had championed charter schools as mayor of Newark, expressed support for vouchers, and served with DeVos on the boards of voucher advocacy groups. But he voted against her nomination and then walked a careful line on his previous support for school choice. He said he opposed vouchers and suggested charter schools in Newark had been a response to a dramatic situation in which he was "desperate" for any help for students. This from someone who had famously worked with a Republican governor to promote charters as a tool of reform and had convinced a young Mark Zuckerberg to donate $100 million to the cause, saying he wanted to free the children of his city from their "imprisonment" in public schools, or what he called "institutions of failure."[30]

Major newspapers and think tanks noted that where charter schools were concerned, any association with DeVos was toxic. The headline of an op-ed in the *New York Times* read, "Betsy DeVos Loves Charter Schools. That's Bad for Charter Schools." At the Brookings Institution, an article was titled "Do the Current Democratic Politics Spell Doom for Charter Schools?"[31]

ON A BACK-TO-SCHOOL Tour in the fall of 2019, DeVos forecast what the future would hold for education in America—and she thanked the late Polly Williams for her role in shaping that future. The trip began in Milwaukee, or what education department officials dubbed the "Birthplace of Education Freedom," at St. Marcus Lutheran School, one of the city's highest-performing voucher schools.

In many ways, the visit was a microcosm of America's debate over school choice. St. Marcus, a faith-based school, enrolled predominantly Black, low-income students who thrived in its structured environment. Many of the nearby public schools posted devastatingly low test scores in comparison to St. Marcus—a fact the public knew because the state started publicly releasing voucher schools' results on state standardized tests in 2010. The school's leader, Henry Tyson, described the school's attitude as "no excuses has become radical expectations." Most of the students paid tuition with vouchers, and the school had expanded from a low of fifty-four students in the 1980s, when white families were fleeing the city, to more than nine hundred. To operate, the school still had to raise outside funds apart from what it received from the voucher program. Tyson said the school showed what is possible when "young people are given access to great schools." St. Marcus also was unapologetically Christian. At the event with DeVos, Tyson talked about the school's "core values of Christ first, Biblical discipleship, sacrificial love and radical expectations."[32]

On the day of DeVos's visit in the fall of 2019, Black parents dropped off their children at the school while protesters, most of whom were white, waved signs that read, "Save Our Public Schools" and "Public Dollars for Public Schools." Ron Kelly, a parent, didn't approach the protesters, but he wished he could tell them something: "You're debating someone else's child."[33]

There's no question that school vouchers and charter schools have transformed the educational landscape in Milwaukee, resulting in three primary tiers: traditional public schools, private schools, and charter schools. Enrollment in the district has declined; some schools are underenrolled, and parents have complained about the lack of supplies, cuts to art and music programs, and, at some schools, swelling class sizes. A slate of public school advocates joined the school board in 2019, including Marva Herndon, a retired computer programmer, who had raised concerns about "fly-by-night" voucher schools for years. After noticing that some charter and voucher schools were opening in "dilapidated buildings, factories and garages," she successfully advocated in 2012 for a city ordinance requiring that new elementary schools have access to a playground. Choice supporters like Howard Fuller viewed the change on the school board with a shrug. After all, the board's power in the current system was far more limited.[34]

At St. Marcus Lutheran, DeVos credited Williams as the "mother of our movement" and told the story of how school vouchers had come to Milwaukee nearly thirty years before:

> Polly worked with anyone and everyone to help students—and pushed back against anyone who didn't. She and civil rights icon Howard Fuller fought their own political party, the NAACP, and the unions. And they won when Governor Tommy Thompson, who was from a different political party, established the Milwaukee Parental Choice Program. . . . You wouldn't be here—and I wouldn't be here—if not for the courage of Polly, Howard, and the parents who joined them in the fight. So I've come to Milwaukee—the birthplace of education freedom—to stand on the shoulders of giants and say that: now is the time to ignite a new birth of freedom for all of America's students.

She described her vision for American education:

> If the government-assigned school isn't working for your child, you can take him or her anywhere else. And if your school is working for your child, you can stay put. Another parent's freedom to make a choice doesn't mean you have to make the same choice. If you want to homeschool your children for part of the week and send them to a classical academy the rest of the week, you can do that. If one type of learning or instruction is best for your son and another is better

for your daughter, you have the flexibility to make those choices. If a school closer to your work is a better fit for your family, that's your choice. You should be free to make the decisions that work best for your children and for your family. . . . This isn't about picking a school building. That's thinking too small.[35]

The future of American education was not to be found in a system of common schools for everyone, but in everyone making à la carte educational choices for themselves.

Acknowledgments

I STARTED RESEARCHING THIS BOOK IN THE FALL OF 2017 AFTER about a decade of covering education in Florida, a state that had long been a laboratory for school choice. One of the questions I wanted to explore was what the options were for disadvantaged students who were assigned to low-performing, underresourced, segregated public schools. I had interviewed parents who were desperate to get out of such schools, who had moved their children from a public school to a charter school to a private school with the help of a voucher. Sometimes they found a better school, and sometimes they didn't. I took my questions to Columbia University as a Spencer education fellow for the 2017–2018 school year, where I initially planned to write more about school segregation. Professor Sam Freedman, who served as my mentor that year, encouraged me to look at the broader history of school vouchers. I will never forget sitting with him on a bench outside the Graduate School of Journalism and hearing him say, "You're familiar with Milton Friedman?" Little did I know where the question would take me. Thank you, Sam, for that push and many others.

My first two years of research and writing on this project would not have been possible without financial support from the Spencer Foundation, New America, and the Russell Sage Foundation. Those grants allowed me to take time off from my regular job, paid for research trips and records, and covered childcare for my children. They also gave me access to critical research databases and library assistance. Gershom Gorenberg, a historian and journalist, allowed me to sit in his class, the Journalist as Historian, at Columbia, which is where I learned how to approach historical research. Gorenberg also talked to me about the politics of language and its application to school choice. By coincidence, Christopher Jencks and his wife, Jane Mansbridge, were scholars at Russell Sage during my time there. I am grateful to Jencks for his time and for his suggestion that I consider how research studies affected key events. None of the staff members at these organizations tried to influence my work, nor did they read the book before publication.

I am incredibly grateful to the historians I consulted about the early tuition grant period. Thomas O'Brien, Jim Carl, and James H. Hershman Jr. were so generous with their time and thoughts about the project. Hershman, in particular, sent me articles and primary source documents, even work of his own that hadn't been published yet. He also agreed to review some parts of the draft for historical accuracy. Carl's work was a key source for me on Virgil Blum and Cleveland's voucher program.

I am indebted to other historians, researchers, and writers whose work I cited in the book, particularly Bill Dahlk, Patrick J. McGuinn, Gregory B. Bodwell, and Jack Dougherty. I appreciated and relied on Ursula Hackett and Desmond King's effort to pin down the number of tuition grants given to students in the South in the 1950s and 1960s in their piece "The Reinvention of Vouchers for a Color-Blind Era: A Racial Orders Account." Phil Magness sent me G. Warren Nutter and James M. Buchanan's *Report on the Virginia Plan for Universal Education*, which provided some numbers and context. I also relied on memoirs written by some of the key players in this history, including Howard Fuller, Virginia Walden Ford, Mikel Holt, Tommy Thompson, Rudy Perpich, David Brennan, Milton and Rose Friedman, and Ember Reichgott Junge.

I am grateful to the archivists I worked with at Marquette University, the Wisconsin Historical Society, the University of Wisconsin–Milwaukee, Ohio University Libraries, the Minnesota Historical Society, and the Schomburg Center for Research in Black Culture at the New York Public Library. In particular I want to thank Bill Fliss at Marquette, who guided me through one of my first visits to an archive, told me about his own research on Virgil Blum, and opened the archive on a Saturday morning for me. I look forward to reading his forthcoming work on Blum.

Many people talked to me during the five years I spent researching and writing this book. I want to thank some of them, including John Coons, Milo Cutter, Robert Enlow, Tom Gonzalez, Marva Herndon, Bert Grover, Douglas Harris, Paul Peterson, Henry Tyson, John Witte, and Patrick Wolf. Thank you to the families at St. Marcus Lutheran School in Milwaukee, Wisconsin, who agreed to be interviewed about their experiences for both an article and the book. Thank you to the teachers and students at City Academy in St. Paul, Minnesota, for allowing me to spend time with you. Both Milo Cutter and Tom Gonzalez were generous with their time and made sure I got lunch. I am especially grateful to Howard Fuller, who met with me several times, set up a tour of Dr. Howard Fuller Collegiate Academy in Milwaukee, Wisconsin, and allowed me to watch him teach a seminar there. He also dug up old documents for me. Ted Kolderie emailed with me, talked on the phone, invited me into his home, and didn't blink when I took photos of the items displayed on his wall. Joe Nathan talked to me several times, invited me to breakfast, and connected me with others whose knowledge of the development of charter schools was essential to my research. I am grateful to Clint Bolick for sharing his knowledge of the law, insight about the history of school choice, and memories of the courtroom battles. His book, *Voucher Wars: Waging the Legal Battle over School Choice*, was one of the first I read. Robert Chanin also was generous with his time and memories.

I read everything I could get my hands on, diving into newspaper archives, policy journals, and academic studies. I am grateful to the journalists across the country who covered these issues in real time, including Erin Richards, Sarah Carr, Mark Walsh, Jeff Solochek, Patrick Wall, Kat McGrory, Kim Miller, S. V. Date, Alan J. Borsuk, Greg Toppo, Spencer S. Hsu, Dana Goldstein, Erica Green, and Craig Harris, among others. Erin Richards sent me a care package of Milwaukee books from her desk as she changed jobs. I gained a deeper understanding of the issues by reading books by Diane Ravitch, Jeffrey Henig, John Witte, Jay Mathews, Richard D. Kahlenberg, Thomas Toch, and Steven M. Teles. Robin Harris had interviewed her cousin, Polly Williams, and her work deepened my knowledge of Williams. It also answered a key question I had about how Williams felt about the long-term trajectory of school choice.

My wonderful agent, Jessica Papin, helped shape my proposal, which was originally about school vouchers, and guided me through the daunting prospect of selling the book. She was a consistently reassuring voice when the coronavirus pandemic upended my research trips, closed archives, and left me without childcare for more than a year. Connor Guy, then at Basic Books, believed in the original idea and sold me on writing a larger history of school choice. After Connor left, I was lucky to work with editor Kyle Gipson at Basic Books. He understood what I was trying to do, pushed me to make stronger connections and arguments, and improved my work. He did not let me skip transitions, much as I wanted to at times, and his editing notes were both encouraging and insightful. I am grateful to everyone at Basic Books who worked on this project and pushed me gently away from some of my wonkier tendencies. Kelley Blewster's eagle eye caught typos and missing citations and improved many sentences.

The good people at Chalkbeat knew I was in the middle of a grueling book project and hired me anyway in June 2020. My colleagues were unfailingly kind and supportive during the pandemic's many disruptions. They surrounded me with love and comfort when I lost a pregnancy. Emiliana Sandoval is the world's best boss. She, Jennifer Bramble, and Nicole Avery Nichols didn't flinch when I asked for book leave to finish the manuscript. JB, in particular, made me feel incredibly supported and valued. Matt Barnum, one of my favorite reporters, answered my questions about education research, listened to me ramble about the book over coffee, and dug up many studies for me. Sarah Darville, Amy Zimmer, Carrie Melago, and Gabrielle Birkner were all gracious when I forced them to listen to my progress updates.

When I needed help with research and untangling complicated court cases, Peter Franceschina went above and beyond the call of friendship. He built me timelines of relevant cases, dug up historical documents and sources, and explained legal terms. He also read the entire manuscript and gave me numerous edits. Gabriel Baumgaertner was a scrupulous fact-checker who backed up my research with his own, adding sources and suggesting I look at this or that document. Kat McGrory made time in her extremely busy life, between chasing a toddler and winning the Pulitzer Prize, to read the manuscript and make edits, big and small. Her feedback improved the book and made me feel much better in general. I am so thankful for her support and friendship.

When I was tired, drinking too much coffee, eating too many cookies, and despairing that this would ever get done, many friends offered encouragement. I'd like to thank Lisa Gartner, Cynthia Roldán, Daphne Duret, Adam Playford, Louise Radnofsky, Taryn Balcom, and Melissa Hoyos for their friendship.

My parents, Daniel and Darla Fitzpatrick, have been a constant source of love and support during my life. After my family and I spent three months trapped in a New York City apartment at the start of the coronavirus pandemic, my parents welcomed us into their home— even though we arrived with three kids, a cat, and a gerbil. We stayed for nearly a year, and my mom homeschooled our two older children. She and my dad pitched in for nap time and walks with our toddler. Their support made it possible for my husband and me to work without childcare and for me to continue making progress on the book. My mom also read the manuscript and gave me her notes. The rest of my family offered encouragement throughout the project. I want to thank Breanne, Burke, Jeremy, Lexi, Cruz, and Sierra.

There were times during this project when I was able to spend time with my children, including caring for our infant son when he had major surgery and months of therapy. I am so glad I could take that time with them, exploring New York City's many playgrounds and museums, going to the Bronx Zoo, ordering too much takeout, and playing board games. There were also months and months when I was consumed by writing and research and I shut myself in my bedroom to work. They rarely complained, and my daughter occasionally asked me to edit her own stories. I love you, Liv, Alexander, and Franklin.

My husband, Michael LaForgia, is an incredible partner and father. He is one of the best journalists I know—and the most hardworking. It is not easy to find balance in a household with two journalists and three children, but he tries every day to make it work. I worked weekends on this project for years, and Michael took the kids out for many, many adventures so I could have some quiet time to conduct interviews and write. I love you more.

Notes

INTRODUCTION: A NEW DEFINITION OF PUBLIC EDUCATION

1. Kevin Mahnken, "Rash of New Polls Raises Red Flags for Democrats on Education," The 74, July 20, 2022.

2. Speer's Stuff, "AZ Gov Doug Ducey Speaking at Phoenix Christian School Prior to Signing Universal ESA into State Law," video, YouTube, August 16, 2022; "DeSantis Redefines Public Education," *Tampa Bay Times*, February 18, 2019.

3. Lloyd P. Jorgenson, *The State and the Non-Public School, 1825–1925* (Columbia: University of Missouri Press, 1987), 7.

4. Grant Addison, "What 'Education Freedom' Means," *Washington Examiner*, August 11, 2022. See also Daniel D. McGarry and Leo Ward, eds., *Educational Freedom: And the Case for Government Aid to Students in Independent Schools* (Milwaukee: Bruce Publishing Company, 1966); and Corey DeAngelis, "Fund Students Instead of Systems," Cato Institute, August 10, 2020.

5. Betsy DeVos, *Hostages No More: The Fight for Education Freedom and the Future of the American Child* (New York: Center Street, 2022), 57–58.

6. Jeffrey R. Henig, *Rethinking School Choice: Limits of the Market Metaphor* (Princeton, NJ: Princeton University Press, 1994), 94; John F. Witte, *The Market Approach to Education: An Analysis of America's First Voucher*

Program (Princeton, NJ: Princeton University Press, 2000), 163; James J. Kilpatrick, "In Defense of Tuition Grants," *Newsday*, January 31, 1968.

7. Zelman vs. Simmons-Harris, 536 US 639 (2002).

8. Andrew Rotherham, "The Other Supreme Court Case Last Week: Three Ways *Makin* Could Be Complicated for School Choice and Charter Schools," *Eduwonk*, June 27, 2022; Carson vs. Makin, 596 US ___ (2022).

9. Diane Ravitch, "Charter Schools Damage Public Education," *Washington Post*, June 22, 2018.

10. Carl E. Kaestle, *Pillars of the Republic: Common Schools and American Society, 1780–1860* (New York: Hill and Wang, 1983), 8–9, 62–63, 64; Benjamin Rush, "A plan for the establishment of public schools and the diffusion of knowledge in Pennsylvania; to which are added thoughts upon the mode of education, proper in a republic. Addressed to the legislature and citizens of the state" (Philadelphia: Thomas Dobson, 1786); Thomas Paine, *The Rights of Man*, 1791.

11. Kaestle, *Pillars of the Republic*, 92.

12. Robert N. Gross, *Public vs. Private: The Early History of School Choice in America* (New York: Oxford University Press, 2018), 1–4, 43. For histories of early American education, also see Kaestle, *Pillars of the Republic*; Tracy L. Steffes, *School, Society, and State: A New Education to Govern Modern America, 1890–1940* (Chicago: University of Chicago Press, 2012); Jorgenson, *The State and the Non-Public School*.

13. Mike McShane, "School Choice Keeps Winning," *Forbes*, July 12, 2021.

14. Erica L. Green and Eliza Shapiro, "Minority Voters Chafe as Candidates Abandon Charter Schools," *New York Times*, November 26, 2019.

15. Dana Goldstein, "West Virginia Teachers Walk Out (Again) and Score a Win in Hours," *New York Times*, February 19, 2019.

16. Aaron Smith and Christian Barnard, "How to Garner Rural Republican Support of School Choice," *Education Next*, August 17, 2022; Fauzeya Rahman, "Public School Advocates Say No Voucher Bills Have Passed in Texas Legislature," *PolitiFact*, March 16, 2017; Patrick Svitek, "Pushing for 'School Choice,' U.S. Sen. Ted Cruz Splits with Gov. Greg Abbott in His Endorsements for Texas House Runoffs," *Texas Tribune*, April 19, 2022.

17. Jeb Bush, "Jeb Bush on Florida School Choice, Vouchers, and Education Reform," Gradebook with Jeffrey S. Solochek, *Tampa Bay Times*, February 28, 2019.

18. Kevin Carey, "No More School Districts!," *Democracy: A Journal of Ideas* no. 55 (Winter 2021); Henry M. Levin, "The Public-Private Nexus

in Education," *American Behavioral Scientist* 43, no. 1 (September 1999): 124–137.

19. Milton Friedman and Rose Friedman, *Free to Choose: A Personal Statement: The Classic Inquiry into the Relationship Between Freedom and Economics* (New York: Harcourt, 1980), 161–162.

20. Patrick J. Wolf, Jonathan N. Mills, Yujie Sude, Heidi H. Erickson, and Matthew L. Lee, *How Has the Louisiana Scholarship Program Affected Students? A Comprehensive Summary of Effects After Four Years. Updated* (School Choice Demonstration Project, 2019); R. J. Waddington and Mark Berends, "Impact of the Indiana Choice Scholarship Program: Achievement Effects for Students in Upper Elementary and Middle School," *Journal of Policy Analysis and Management* 37, no. 4 (October 2018): 783–808; David Figlio and Krzysztof Karbownik, *Evaluation of Ohio's EdChoice Scholarship Program: Selection, Competition, and Performance Effects* (Thomas B. Fordham Institute, 2016); Mark Dynarski, Ning Rui, Ann Webber, and Babette Gutmann, *Evaluation of the DC Opportunity Scholarship Program: Impacts Two Years After Students Applied* (National Center for Education Evaluation and Regional Assistance, 2018).

21. Philip Gleason, Melissa Clark, Christina Clark Tuttle, and Emily Dwoyer, *The Evaluation of Charter School Impacts: Final Report* (National Center for Education Evaluation and Regional Assistance, 2010); Julian R. Betts and Y. E. Tang, *The Effect of Charter Schools on Student Achievement: A Meta-Analysis of the Literature* (Center on Reinventing Public Education, 2011).

22. Caroline M. Hoxby, Sonali Murarka, and Jenny Kang, *How New York City's Charter Schools Affect Achievement*, 2nd report in series (New York City Charter Schools Evaluation Project, September 2009); Joshua D. Angrist, Sarah R. Cohodes, Susan M. Dynarski, Jon B. Fullerton, Thomas J. Kane, Parag A. Pathak, and Christopher R. Walters, *Student Achievement in Massachusetts' Charter Schools* (Center for Education Policy Research, January 2011); CREDO, *Charter School Performance in Los Angeles* (Stanford, CA: Center for Research on Education Outcomes, 2014); Douglas N. Harris, "What Effect Did the Post-Katrina School Reforms Have on Student Outcomes," *Education Next*, October 26, 2015.

23. Chester E. Finn Jr., Bruno V. Manno, and Brandon L. Wright, *Charter Schools at the Crossroads: Predicaments, Paradoxes, Possibilities* (Cambridge, MA: Harvard Education Press, 2016), 111–112.

24. Matthew M. Chingos, Daniel Kuehn, Tomas Monarrez, Patrick J. Wolf, John F. Witte, and Brian Kisida, *The Effects of Means-Tested Private*

School Choice Programs on College Enrollment and Graduation (Urban Institute, 2019).

25. David N. Figlio, Cassandra M. D. Hart, and Krzysztof Karbownik, "Effects of Scaling Up Private School Choice Programs on Public School Students" (working paper, National Bureau of Economic Research, 2020); Huriya Jabbar, Carlton J. Fong, Emily Germain, Dongmei Li, Joanna Sanchez, Wei-Ling Sun, and Michelle Devall, "The Competitive Effects of School Choice on Student Achievement: A Systematic Review," *Educational Policy* 36, no. 2 (2022): 247–281.

26. Feng Chen and Douglas N. Harris, *The Combined Effects of Charter Schools on Student Outcomes: A National Analysis of School Districts* (REACH, December 2021).

27. Christopher Rufo, "Laying Siege to the Institutions," speech at Hillsdale College, video, YouTube, April 5, 2022; Benjamin Wallace-Wells, "How a Conservative Activist Invented the Conflict over Critical Race Theory," *New Yorker*, June 18, 2021; Jay Greene and James Paul, "Time for the School Choice Movement to Embrace the Culture War," Heritage Foundation, February 9, 2022.

28. Brown vs. Board of Education of Topeka, 347 US 483 (1954).

CHAPTER 1: PRIVATE IN NAME ONLY

1. "Notice Served Upon Negroes in Georgia," *Times and Democrat*, October 3, 1950; Thomas V. O'Brien, "The Dog That Didn't Bark: *Aaron v. Cook* and the NAACP Strategy in Georgia Before *Brown*," *Journal of Negro History* 84, no. 1 (Winter 1999): 79–88.

2. Thomas V. O'Brien, *The Politics of Race and Schooling: Public Education in Georgia, 1900–1961* (Lanham, MD: Lexington Books, 2000), 67–70; "Sweatt Says He'll Enroll in September," *Fort Worth Star Telegram*, June 6, 1950; "Talmadge Defiant; Others Hail Court," *New York Times*, June 6, 1950.

3. Jennifer E. Spreng, "Scenes from the Southside: A Desegregation Drama in Five Acts," *University of Arkansas at Little Rock Law Review* 19, no. 3 (1997): 333.

4. Brian J. Daugherity and Brian Grogan, eds., *A Little Child Shall Lead Them* (Charlottesville: University of Virginia Press, 2019), 34, 35, 45; Davis vs. County School Board of Prince Edward County, 149 F. Supp. 431 (E.D. Va. 1957).

5. "Race Amendment Pushed in Georgia," *New York Times*, February 1, 1951. Also: "Georgia Planning to Set Up Schools as Private," *Philadelphia Tribune*, February 10, 1951; O'Brien, *Politics of Race and Schooling*, 84–85.

6. Henry Lesesne, "South Carolina Girding: Attack on School Segregation Biggest Issue Since Secession, *New York Herald Tribune*, June 17, 1951.

7. Rebecca Brückmann, "'Work ... Done Mostly by Men': Cornelia Dabney Tucker and Female Grassroots Activism in Massive Resistance in South Carolina, 1950–1963," *South Carolina Historical Magazine*, April 2016.

8. Lester A. Huston, "Supreme Court Asked to End School Segregation in Nation," *New York Times*, December 10, 1952; Leon Friedman, ed., *Brown v. Board: The Landmark Oral Argument Before the Supreme Court* (New Press: New York, 2004), 99.

9. O'Brien, *Politics of Race and Schooling*, 91.

10. "40% of Public School Pupils in U.S. Are in Areas Where Laws Require Segregation ... ," *New York Times*, May 18, 1954.

11. Brown vs. Board of Education of Topeka, 347 US 483 (1954).

12. Matthew D. Lassiter and Andrew B. Lewis, eds., *The Moderates' Dilemma: Massive Resistance to School Desegregation in Virginia* (Charlottesville: University of Virginia Press, 1998), 55–56.

13. O'Brien, *Politics of Race and Schooling*, 106–109.

14. Milton Friedman, "The Role of Government in Education," in *Economics and the Public Interest*, ed. Robert A. Solo (New Brunswick, NJ: Rutgers University Press, 1955), 123–144.

15. John Stuart Mill, *On Liberty*, chapter 1 (1859); Lanny Ebenstein, *Milton Friedman: A Biography* (New York: Palgrave MacMillan, 2007), 8, 10, 13–15.

16. Ebenstein, *Milton Friedman*, 18.

17. Ebenstein, *Milton Friedman*, 55; John Maynard Keynes, *The End of Laissez-Faire*, 1926, 46–47.

18. Friedman, "The Role of Government in Education."

19. Earl Black and Merle Black, *The Rise of Southern Republicans* (Cambridge, MA: Belknap Press of Harvard University Press, 2002), 2; William P. Hustwit, *James J. Kilpatrick: Salesman for Segregation* (Chapel Hill: University of North Carolina Press, 2013), 9.

20. Letters between Robert A. Solo and Milton Friedman, October 5, 12, 15, 1954, box 33, Milton Friedman Papers, Hoover Institution, Stanford University, Stanford, CA.

21. Ebenstein, *Milton Friedman*, 22.

22. "Private School Plan Declared 'Unworkable,'" *Virginian Pilot*, July 29, 1958. See also Hall vs. St. Helena Parish School Board, 197 F. Supp. 649 (E.D. La. 1961); US District Court for the Eastern District of Louisiana, 197 F. Support. 649 (E.D. La. 1961). See also Walter F. Murphy, "Private Education with Public Funds?," *Journal of Politics* 20, no. 4 (November 1958), 635, 637. See also Charles Boger and Elizabeth Jean Bower, "The Emerging Law of Race and Student Assignment Plans," *North Carolina Law Review* (Winter 2001): 3.

23. Brown vs. Board of Education of Topeka (2), 349 US 294 (1955); Briggs vs. Elliott, 132 F. Supp. 776 (E.D. S.C. 1955).

24. "Segregation Test Looms in Alabama," *Christian Science Monitor*, August 29, 1956; letter from Emerson Schmidt to Garland Gray, January 16, 1956, Friedman Papers.

25. Hustwit, *James J. Kilpatrick*, 10.

26. Benjamin Muse, *Virginia's Massive Resistance* (Bloomington: Indiana University Press, 1961), 21.

27. "Byrd Summons South to 'Massive Resistance,'" *Washington Post and Times Herald*, February 26, 1956; "96 Dixie Congressmen Pledge Fight on Integration," *Baltimore Sun*, March 12, 1956.

28. Johanna Miller Lewis, "Implementing Brown in Arkansas," in *With All Deliberate Speed: Implementing Brown v. Board of Education*, ed. Brian J. Daugherity and Charles C. Bolton (Fayetteville: University of Arkansas Press, 2008), 3, 5–7; US Commission on Civil Rights, *Report of the US Commission on Civil Rights, 1959* (US Government Printing Office, 1961).

29. Jim Carl, *Freedom of Choice: Vouchers in American Education* (Santa Barbara, CA: Praeger, 2011), 28–29; *The Pearsall Plan to Save Our Schools*, brochure, 1956, Internet Archive, accessed November 15, 2022, https://ia800402 .us.archive.org/26/items/pearsallplantosa00nort/pearsallplantosa00nort.pdf; Woodrow Price, "Tar Heel Leaders Discuss Impact of Pearsall Plan," *News and Observer*, September 18, 1956.

30. "Court Voids Virginia Plan to Keep Pupil Segregation," *New York Times*, January 12, 1957.

31. John Connors and George Gill, "Private Schools Plan Set in Prince Edward," *Richmond News Leader*, July 15, 1957; Lassiter and Lewis, *The Moderates' Dilemma*, 75; "Virginia Schools for Whites Ready: Prince Edward County Has Organized System to Thwart Integration," *New York Times*, July 21, 1957.

32. Anthony Lewis, "Suits Prod South to Desegregate," *New York Times*, May 31, 1956.

33. Michael O'Donnell, "Commander vs. Chief," *The Atlantic*, April 2018.

34. David Wallace, "Orval Faubus: The Central Figure at Little Rock Central High School," *Arkansas Historical Quarterly* 39, no. 4 (Winter 1980): 314–329.

35. "Negroes Slip by Angry Mob, Enter School; Whites Leave," United Press International, September 23, 1957; Lewis, "Implementing Brown in Arkansas," in *With All Deliberate Speed*, 12–13; Clay Gowren, "U.S. Troops in Little Rock," *Chicago Daily Tribune*, September 25, 1957.

36. "Eisenhower Address on Little Rock Crisis," *New York Times*, September 25, 1957.

CHAPTER 2: "NEW WEAPONS AND NEW TACTICS"

1. Bryce Miller, "Faubus Races Supreme Court," *Daily Defender*, August 27, 1958.

2. Cooper vs. Aaron, 358 US 1 (1958); "Supreme Court Refuses Delay in Integration at Little Rock; Faubus Orders Schools Closed," *Hartford Courant*, September 13, 1958.

3. John D. Morris, "Virginia Governor Assumes Control of Closed School," *New York Times*, September 13, 1958; "Almond Is Ready to Close Schools," *New York Times*, August 22, 1958.

4. Robert E. Baker, "Boothe Makes Eloquent Proposal Against Keeping Schools Closed," *Washington Post and Times Herald*, March 1, 1958; "'Massive Resistance' Reaches Point of No Return," *Afro-American*, September 20, 1958.

5. Virgil C. Blum, *Freedom of Choice in Education* (New York: Macmillan, 1958), 1–22.

6. "Priest Predicts Future Benefits for Schools," *Pittsburgh Catholic*, October 31, 1957.

7. Robert P. Lockwood, "Anti-Catholicism and the History of Catholic School Funding," Catholic League, February 2000, www.catholicleague.org /anti-catholicism-and-the-history-of-catholic-school-funding/; Steven K. Green, *The Bible, the School, and the Constitution: The Clash That Shaped Modern Church-State Doctrine* (Oxford, UK: Oxford University Press, 2012), 12, 29, 86.

8. Harold A. Buetow, *Of Singular Benefit: The Story of Catholic Education in the United States* (New York: Macmillan, 1970), 178; "A Preacher Replies,"

Pittsburgh Dispatch, August 26, 1889; Robert N. Gross, *Public vs. Private: The Early History of School Choice in America* (Oxford, UK: Oxford University Press, 2018), 3, 32, 38.

9. Pierce vs. Society of Sisters, 268 US 510 (1925).

10. Virgil C. Blum, "Educational Benefits Without Enforced Conformity," *Homiletic and Pastoral Review* 58, no. 1 (October 1957), writings and manuscripts, UNIV, C-1.14, series 2-VCB, subseries 3, box 1, Blum Papers, Marquette University, Milwaukee, WI.

11. Everson vs. Board of Education of the Township of Ewing, 330 US 1 (1947).

12. Virgil C. Blum, "The Right to Choose Your Own School," *Catholic World*, October 1959, writings and manuscripts, UNIV C-1.14, series 2-VCB, subseries 3, box 1, Blum Papers; Virgil C. Blum, "Notes for Speech at the Knights of Columbus 50 Year Jubilee Event," St. Francis Church, Council Bluffs, Iowa, 1955, writings and manuscripts, UNIV C-1.14, series 2-VCB, subseries 3, box 3, Blum Papers.

13. Blum, *Freedom of Choice in Education*, 1.

14. David Lawrence, "Plan for Education Grants Seen Integration Solution," *New York Herald Tribune*, October 22, 1957.

15. Blum, "Notes for Speech."

16. Joseph J. Thorndike, "'The Sometimes Sordid Level of Race and Segregation:' James J. Kilpatrick and the Virginia Campaign against Brown," in *The Moderates' Dilemma: Massive Resistance to School Desegregation in Virginia*, Matthew D. Lassiter and Andrew B. Lewis, eds. (Charlottesville: University Press of Virginia, 1998), 63.

17. William P. Hustwit, *James J. Kilpatrick: Salesman for Segregation* (Chapel Hill: University of North Carolina Press, 2013), 66–75.

18. John D. Morris, "Almond Orders Charlottesville to Shut 2 Schools," *New York Times*, September 19, 1958; James H. Hershman Jr., email to author, October 24, 2022.

19. Al Kuettner, "Va., Ark., Rush Substitutes for Closed School Doors," United Press International, September 22, 1958; "2 Schools Enroll 637 in Little Rock," *New York Times*, October 21, 1958.

20. Charles L. Whipple, "Virginia Children Hungry for School," *Boston Sunday Globe*, October 12, 1958.

21. Hershman, email to author, October 24, 2022; "5,000 Virginia Teachers: . . . No Time for Closed Schools," *New Journal and Guide*, November

8, 1958; Al Kuettner, "Change of Heart by Many White Southerners," *New Journal and Guide*, December 27, 1958.

22. James vs. Almond, 170 F. Supp. 331 (E.D. Va. 1959); Harrison vs. Day, 200 Va. 439 (1959).

23. "Unfavorable Reaction," *New Journal and Guide*, January 24, 1959.

24. Leonard Buder, "Virginia Widens Its Integration: Mixed Classes Begin Quietly at Warren County High and in Charlottesville," *New York Times*, September 9, 1959; see also Robert E. Baker and Mechlin Moore, "Only Negroes Enroll at Front Royal," *Washington Post and Times Herald*, February 19, 1959; Hustwit, *James J. Kilpatrick*, 85.

25. Cooper vs. Aaron, 358 US 1 (1958).

26. US Commission on Civil Rights, *Report of the US Commission on Civil Rights, 1959* (US Government Printing Office, 1961), 240–242.

27. "Davis vs. County School Board of Prince Edward County, Virginia: Supplemental Memorandum for Appellees on Further Reargument," Supreme Court records on Davis vs. County School Board of Prince Edward County, 149 F. Supp. 431 (E.D. Va. 1957), 4–6.

28. Sara Kathryn Eskridge, "Virginia's Pupil Placement Board and the Massive Resistance Movement, 1956–1966," (master's thesis, Virginia Commonwealth University, 2006), 59–60.

29. Letter from Ralph T. Catterall to Leon Dure, January 9, 1959, Leon Dure Papers, Special Collections, Alderman Library, University of Virginia, Charlottesville, VA. Courtesy of James H. Hershman Jr.

30. Charles H. Ford and Jeffrey L. Littlejohn, "Reconstructing the Old Dominion," *Virginia Magazine of History and Biography* 121, no. 2 (2013): 157; James H. Hershman Jr., "Massive Resistance Meets Its Match: The Emergence of a Pro-Public School Majority," in *The Moderates' Dilemma: Massive Resistance to School Desegregation in Virginia*, ed. Matthew D. Lassiter and Andrew B. Lewis (Charlottesville: University of Virginia Press, 1998), 126–128.

31. Hershman, "Massive Resistance Meets Its Match."

32. "Civic Groups Back Recall," *Courier News*, May 22, 1959; Claude Sitton, "School Election Test for Faubus," *New York Times*, May 24, 1959.

33. "Faubus Says Election No Victory," *Daily Defender*, May 28, 1959; "Ex–Little Rock Schools Chief Hails Election," *Chicago Daily Tribune*, May 30, 1959; "Only Slight Stir 2nd Day of L.R. Integration," *Hope Star*, August 13, 1959.

CHAPTER 3: THE TEST CASE FOR SCHOOL VOUCHERS

1. US Commission on Civil Rights, *Education: 1961 Commission on Civil Rights Report, Book 2* (Washington, DC: US Government Printing Office, 1961), 2, 42, 55, 73, 177.

2. "Georgia Drops Massive Segregation," *Christian Science Monitor*, February 1, 1961; James E. Clayton, "Solid South's Segregation Armor Begins to Crack," *Washington Post and Times Herald*, January 29, 1961.

3. "Leon Dure Finds the Whole South Turning to Freedom of Choice as Schools Solution," *Daily Progress*, March 29, 1961.

4. Leon Dure, "The New Southern Response: Anatomy of Two New Freedoms," *Georgia Review* 15, no. 4 (Winter 1961): 401–402.

5. James H. Hershman Jr., "'The Wayward Liberal' and Virginia's Massive Resistance: Donald Richberg, Libertarian Economics, and Militant Segregation" (working article, July 9, 2020), 6.

6. Dure, "The New Southern Response," 402; "State Tuition Aid Urged by Faubus," *New York Times*, February 10, 1959.

7. Ursula Hackett and Desmond King, "The Reinvention of Vouchers for a Color-Blind Era: A Racial Orders Account," *Studies in American Political Development*, 33 (October 2019): 240. See also Dure, "The New Southern Response," 404.

8. "Almond Backs Tuition Grants," *Washington Post and Times Herald*, February 18, 1961.

9. Dure, "The New Southern Response."

10. Stuart H. Loory, "$400,000 Virginia 'Monument to White Supremacy,'" *New York Herald Tribune*, August 22, 1961.

11. "Va. Whites Beg Negroes to Establish Pte. Schools," *New Pittsburgh Courier*, July 2, 1960. See also Brian E. Lee, "A Matter of National Concern: The Kennedy Administration's Campaign to Restore Public Education to Prince Edward County, Virginia" (PhD diss., University of North Carolina at Greensboro, 2015), 60–62.

12. William P. Hustwit, *James J. Kilpatrick: Salesman for Segregation* (Chapel Hill: University of North Carolina Press, 2013), 107.

13. Jennifer E. Spreng, "Scenes from the Southside: A Desegregation Drama in Five Acts," *University of Arkansas at Little Rock Law Review* 19, no. 3 (1997): 350.

14. Elsie Carper, "New Edward School Battle Opens in Court," *Washington Post and Times Herald*, May 9, 1961.

15. Allen vs. County School Board of Prince Edward County, 198 F. Supp. 497 (1961).

16. "In Prince Edward County: 1,109 Parents OK Desegregation Plan," *Afro-American*, December 2, 1961.

17. Brian J. Daugherity and Brian Grogan, eds., *A Little Child Shall Lead Them* (Charlottesville: University of Virginia Press, 2019), 114.

18. Dure, "The New Southern Response," 403.

19. Jim Carl, *Freedom of Choice: Vouchers in American Education* (Santa Barbara, CA: Praeger, 2011), 51; letter from Milton Friedman to Virgil Blum, December 19, 1968, personal correspondence, UNIV C-1.14, series 2-VCB, subseries 2, box 6, folder E to M, Blum Papers, Marquette University, Milwaukee, WI.

20. Letter from Leon Dure to Virgil Blum, December 21, 1961, personal correspondence, UNIV C-1.14, series 2-VCB, subseries 2, folder D to F, Blum Papers.

21. Carl, *Freedom of Choice*, 92–97.

22. "Leon Dure Finds the Whole South"; Hershman, "'The Wayward Liberal' and Virginia's Massive Resistance," 22.

23. Milton Friedman, *Capitalism and Freedom: A Leading Economist's View of the Proper Role of Competitive Capitalism* (Chicago: University of Chicago Press, 1962), 117–118.

24. "S.C. Tuition Aid Urged," *Washington Post*, January 30, 1963; "President Warns of Revolution," *The Sun*, June 12, 1963; "Tuition Grants Voted by Alabama Senate," *Washington Post and Times Herald*, August 8, 1965.

25. Carl, *Freedom of Choice*, 48; Elsie Carper, "Virginia Tuition Grants Go Astray," *Washington Post and Times Herald*, January 2, 1960.

26. Thomas Jefferson Center for Studies in Political Economy, University of Virginia, "Report on the Virginia Plan for Universal Education" (Occasional Paper No. 2, March 1965), 40, courtesy Phillip W. Magness; F. L. Shuttlesworth, "A Southerner Speaks," *Pittsburgh Courier*, September 23, 1961; Hardy Cross Dillard, "Freedom of Choice and Democratic Values," *Virginia Quarterly Review* 38, no. 3 (Summer 1962): 410–435.

27. Griffin vs. School Board, 377 US 218 (1964).

28. Lee, "A Matter of National Concern," 398–399.

29. "Prince Edward County Tuition Grants Voted," *Los Angeles Times*, July 2, 1964.

30. Spreng, "Scenes from the Southside"; "'Treasury Raid' to Be Resisted in Balky Prince Edward County," *New Journal and Guide*, August 15, 1964.

31. Griffin vs. State Board of Education, 239 F. Supp. 560 (E.D. Va. 1965).

CHAPTER 4: THE "NEW LEFT" AND THE "OLD RIGHT" CONCUR

1. Christopher Jencks, "Is the Public School Obsolete?," *Public Interest* 2 (Winter 1966): 145; Christopher Jencks, "Who Should Control Education?," *Dissent* 13, no. 2 (March 1, 1966): 18–27.

2. Milton Friedman, "A Free Market in Education," *Public Interest* 3 (Spring 1966): 107.

3. Henry M. Levin, "The Failure of the Public Schools and the Free Market Remedy," *Urban Review* 2 (1968): 32–37.

4. Charles C. Bolton, "The Last Holdout," in *With All Deliberate Speed: Implementing Brown v. Board of Education*, ed. Brian J. Daugherity and Charles C. Bolton (Fayetteville: University of Arkansas Press, 2008), 132–135; Gene Roberts, "Integration Meets Token Resistance," *New York Times*, September 8, 1965; "Armed Guards Placed Around Dynamited Ala. High School," *Afro-American*, March 5, 1966; US Civil Rights Commission, *Survey of School Desegregation in the Southern and Border States, 1965–1966* (Washington, DC: US Government Printing Office, 1966), 1.

5. "S.C. Tuition Grants Junked by Top Court," *New Journal and Guide*, December 14, 1968; Ursula Hackett and Desmond King, "The Reinvention of Vouchers for a Color-Blind Era: A Racial Orders Account," *Studies in American Political Development* 33 (October 2019): 234–257.

6. Adam Clymer, "Alabama Is Sued on Tuition Funds," *The Sun*, August 31, 1966; Jim Leeson, "Private Schools Continue to Increase in the South," *Southern Education Report*, November 1966, 24.

7. David Nevin and Robert E. Bills, *The Schools That Fear Built: Segregationist Academies in the South* (Washington, DC: Acropolis Books, 1976), 14; Leeson, "Private Schools," 23, 25; "State Helps Segregation in Alabama," *Hartford Courant*, August 19, 1966.

8. Neil Maxwell, "More Southern Whites Open Private Schools That Exclude Negroes," *Wall Street Journal*, August 29, 1966; "Selma Starts Private School 'Whites Only,'" *Austin Statesman*, July 27, 1965; "State Helps Segregation in Alabama," *Hartford Courant*, August 19, 1966.

9. Erica Frankenberg and Kendra Taylor, "ESEA and the Civil Rights Act: An Interbranch Approach to Furthering Desegregation," *RSF: The Russell Sage Foundation Journal of the Social Sciences* 1, no. 3 (2015): 32–49;

Ben A. Franklin, "Schools in South Integrate to Bar Loss of U.S. Aid," *New York Times*, March 7, 1965.

10. Katie Nodjimbadem, "The Racial Segregation of American Cities Was Anything but Accidental," *Smithsonian Magazine*, May 30, 2017; "More than 10,000 March in Protest on School Pairing," *New York Times*, March 13, 1964.

11. Matthew F. Delmont, *Why Busing Failed: Race, Media, and the National Resistance to School Desegregation* (Oakland: University of California Press, 2016), 4, 49–51; Leeson, "Private Schools," 24; Coffey vs. State Educational Finance Commission, 296 F. Supp. 1389 (Dist. Court, SD Mississippi 1969).

12. "Alabama Schools Told to End Bias: U.S. Court Orders Start on State-wide Desegregation," *New York Times*, March 23, 1967; "Federal Judges Knock Down Mississippi's Tuition Grants," *Afro-American*, February 8, 1969; "S.C. Tuition Grants Junked by Top Court"; "La. Tuition Grants Out, U.S. Court Judges Rule," *New Journal and Guide*, September 2, 1967; Helen Dewar, "Tuition Grants Are Outlawed," *Washington Post and Times Herald*, February 12, 1969.

13. Poindexter vs. Louisiana Fin. Assistance Commission, 239 F. Supp. 560 (1967). See also Poindexter vs. Louisiana Financial Assistance Commission, 296 F. Supp. 686 (E.D. La. 1968).

14. Green vs. County Sch. Bd. of New Kent County, 391 US 430 (1968); Griffin vs. State Board of Education, 296 F. Supp. 1178 (1969); "Va. Won't Appeal Tuition Grant Rule," *Washington Post and Times Herald*, February 21, 1969.

15. James J. Kilpatrick, "High Court Remains United On Schools," *Hartford Courant*, June 4, 1968; James J. Kilpatrick, "In Defense of Tuition Grants," *Newsday*, January 31, 1968.

16. James H. Hershman Jr., "Leon S. Dure (1907–1993)," *Encyclopedia Virginia*, accessed October 29, 2022, https://encyclopediavirginia.org /entries/dure-leon-s-1907-1993/#heading1.

17. Kenneth B. Clark, "Alternative Public School Systems," *Harvard Educational Review* 38, no. 1 (Winter 1968): 100–113.

18. Christopher Jencks, "Private Schools for Black Children," *New York Times*, November 3, 1968; Clark, "Alternative Public School Systems."

19. Theodore Sizer and Phillip Whitten, "A Proposal for a Poor Children's Bill of Rights," *Psychology Today*, August 1968.

20. Board of Education vs. Allen, 392 US 236 (1968).

21. Letter from Virgil Blum to Edward J. Hartmann, July 26, 1965, personal correspondence, UNIV C-1.14, series 2-VCB, subseries 2, box 5, folder 1960 to 1967, Blum Papers, Marquette University, Milwaukee, WI;

letter from Blum to Norbert Dall, January 23, 1969, personal correspondence, UNIV C-1.14, series 2-VCB, subseries 2, box 5, folder 1968 to 1969, Blum Papers.

22. Letter from Blum to Thomas Kenney, February 25, 1968, personal correspondence, UNIV C-1.14, series 2-VCB, subseries 2, box 5, folder 1968 to 1969, Blum Papers; Erik J. Chaput, "Diversity and Independence in the Educational Marketplace: The Rhode Island CEF and the 1968 Tuition-Grant Debate," *Catholic Historical Review* 95, no. 1 (January 2009): 73–74.

23. "'Parochaid' Bills Foster Race, Creed Segregation?," *Michigan Chronicle*, March 23, 1968.

24. "Drive to Save Catholic Schools Gains Support," United Press International, July 12, 1969; Tim Metz, "Drives in Many States Seek More Tax Funds for Private Education," *Wall Street Journal*, March 26, 1969; Chaput, "Diversity and Independence in the Educational Marketplace," 63; "'Parochaid' Disputed," *Christian Science Monitor*, December 12, 1969.

25. Chaput, "Diversity and Independence in the Educational Marketplace," 62, 72.

26. Tim Metz, "Drives in Many States Seek More Tax Funds for Private Education," *Wall Street Journal*, March 26, 1969.

CHAPTER 5: A (FAILED) FEDERAL EXPERIMENT

1. Center for the Study of Public Policy, *Education Vouchers: A Report on Financing Elementary Education by Grants to Parents* (US Office of Economic Opportunity, December 1970), vii, viii, 8.

2. "The 'Chit' Plan: Way to Go in Education?," *Los Angeles Times*, April 25, 1971.

3. Lemon vs. Kurtzman, 403 US 602 (1971); Committee for Public Education vs. Nyquist, 413 US 756 (1973).

4. "Parochial System Hurt by a Ruling," *New York Times*, April 4, 1971; "Parochaid Loses Again," *Chicago Tribune*, October 16, 1972; Glen Elsasser, "Parochaid Ruled Illegal by High Court," *Chicago Tribune*, June 26, 1973.

5. Virgil C. Blum, "Is the Supreme Court Anti-Catholic?," *Homiletic and Pastoral Review* 74, no. 8 (May 1974), writings and manuscripts, UNIV C-1.14, series 2-VCB, subseries 3, box 1, Blum Papers, Marquette University, Milwaukee, WI.

6. Evan Jenkins, "A School Voucher Experiment Rates an 'A' in Coast District: Some Fear Ill Effects," *New York Times*, May 29, 1973.

7. Jim Carl, *Freedom of Choice: Vouchers in American Education* (Santa Barbara, CA: Praeger, 2011), 67–73.

8. "Interview with Milton Friedman," *Playboy*, February 1, 1973.

9. Milton Friedman, "The Voucher Idea: Selling Schooling like Groceries," *New York Times Magazine*, September 23, 1973.

10. Carl, *Freedom of Choice*, 72–74.

11. William F. Buckley Jr., "Government's Plan for Schools," *Newsday*, May 24, 1973; James J. Kilpatrick, "In New Hampshire, a Financial Experiment to Allow Educational Choice," *Los Angeles Times*, May 30, 1973; Russell Kirk, "2 Plans to Diversify Schooling," *The Sun*, June 13, 1973.

12. Robert Reinhold, "School Vouchers: Quick Defeats Raise Question on Test Validity," *New York Times*, June 4, 1975.

13. Carl, *Freedom of Choice*, 72–73, 81–82.

14. "Test of Voucher System Flops," *Hartford Courant*, September 26, 1976.

15. Jack McCurdy, "Voucher Experiment Is Mostly Ballyhoo," *Los Angeles Times*, January 7, 1979.

16. Richard J. Cattani, "Parochiaid: A Push That Just Won't Quit," *Christian Science Monitor*, October 18, 1977.

17. E. Babette Edwards to the New York State Board of Regents, September 10, 1975, SC MG 809, folder 3, box 24, Babette Edwards Education Reform in Harlem Collection, Schomburg Center for Research in Black Culture, New York Public Library; "Boycotting Parents Want Funds Used for Private Schools," *New York Times*, January 22, 1976; Milton Friedman, Milton Friedman Speaks: "Putting Learning Back in the Classroom," September 15, 1977, video, Collected Works of Milton Friedman, Hoover Institution Library and Archives, Stanford University, Stanford, CA.

18. Brittney Lewer, "Pursuing 'Real Power to Parents': Babette Edwards' Activism from Community Control to Charter Schools," in *Educating Harlem: A Century of Schooling and Resistance in a Black Community*, Ansley T. Erickson and Ernest Morrell, eds. (New York: Columbia University Press, 2019), 282–285.

19. Daniel Patrick Moynihan, "Government and the Ruin of Private Education," *Harper's*, April 1978.

20. Oscar Jimenez-Castellanos and Lawrence O. Picus, "Serrano v. Priest 50th Anniversary: Origins, Impact and Future," *BYU Education and Law Journal* (2022): 1–13; Rachel F. Moran, "School Finance Reform and Professor Stephen D. Sugarman's Lasting Legacy," *California Law Review* 109, no. 2 (2021): 355.

21. Jack McCurdy, "Public School Leaders Assail Voucher Proposal," *Los Angeles Times*, October 11, 1979; Laurie Becklund, "School-Voucher Aid Campaign Dropped," *Los Angeles Times*, December 26, 1979.

22. "Radical Change in the Schools: Two Views on the Voucher Plan," *New York Times*, December 30, 1979.

CHAPTER 6: A NEW TYPE OF PUBLIC SCHOOL

1. Richard D. Kahlenberg, *Tough Liberal: Albert Shanker and the Battles over Schools, Unions, Race, and Democracy* (New York: Columbia University Press, 2007), 16, 18, 238; "Radical Change in the Schools: Two Views on Voucher Plan: John E. Coons, Albert Shanker," *New York Times*, December 30, 1979.

2. "More Cuts Slated for Education," *Chicago Tribune*, September 20, 1981; Charles R. Babeock, "Deeper Education Cuts Planned," *Boston Globe*, December 8, 1981; "Reagan Wants Tuition Tax Credits—Later," *Boston Globe*, June 3, 1981; "Reagan Seeks to Delay Action on Tuition Tax Credits," *New York Times*, June 4, 1981.

3. "Bias Issue Delays Tuition Tax Credits," *Chicago Tribune*, August 12, 1982; James J. Kilpatrick, "A Lost Cause: Tuition Tax Credits," *Hartford Courant*, May 8, 1982; "Tuition Tax Credits in Trouble," *Washington Post*, August 27, 1982.

4. Associated Press, "Teachers March Against Reagan; NEA Vows to Defeat Tuition Tax Credit," *Boston Globe*, July 7, 1982; "School Tax Credit Isn't Seen Reaching House This Session," *Wall Street Journal*, September 17, 1982.

5. David P. Gardner, et al., National Commission on Excellence in Education, *A Nation at Risk: The Imperative for Educational Reform* (Washington DC: Government Printing Office, April 1983), 5; Patrick J. McGuinn, *No Child Left Behind and the Transformation of Federal Education Policy, 1965–2005* (Lawrence: University Press of Kansas, 2006), 43.

6. McGuinn, *No Child Left Behind*, 43; Edward B. Fiske, "Top Objectives Elude Reagan as Education Policy Evolves," *New York Times*, December 27, 1983; Mary Franklin, "Reagan's Voucher Proposal Blasted as Harmful to Poor," *Afro-American*, April 16, 1983.

7. Robert Shogan, "Reagan Seizes Initiative in Debate on Education," *Los Angeles Times*, July 4, 1983.

8. Mueller vs. Allen, 463 US 388 (1983).

9. Cheryl W. Heilman, "*Booker vs. Special School District No. 1*: A History of School Desegregation in Minneapolis, Minnesota," *Minnesota Journal of Law and Inequality* 12, no. 1 (1994): 127–175.

10. Ted Kolderie, *Thinking Out the How*, rev. ed. (St. Paul, MN: Center for Policy Design Press, 2021), 172–173; Ted Kolderie, interview with the author, February 18, 2021.

11. "Minnesota to Pay for Students' Head Start in College Classes," *Los Angeles Times*, August 4, 1985.

12. Gregor W. Pinney, "Perpich Abandons Open Enrollment Plan," *Minneapolis Star Tribune*, May 21, 1986.

13. Robert Marquand, "School Vouchers for the Poor: Reagan Plan to Give Aid Directly to Parents Stirs Debate," *Christian Science Monitor*, November 13, 1985; National Governors Association, *Time for Results: The Governors' 1991 Report on Education* (1986).

14. Thomas Toch, "Free-Market Approach to Public Schools Gains Backers," *The Sun*, December 13, 1987.

15. Kahlenberg, *Tough Liberal*, 5, 275–277.

16. Albert Shanker, "National Press Club Speech, Washington, D.C., March 31, 1988" (digital copy), Shanker Papers, Walter P. Reuther Library, Archives of Labor and Urban Affairs, Wayne State University, Detroit, MI.

17. Ray Budde, "The Evolution of the Charter Concept," *Phi Delta Kappan* 78, no. 1 (1996): 72; Ray Budde, *Education by Charter: Restructuring School Districts Key to Long-Term Continuing Improvement in American Education* (Andover, MA: Regional Laboratory for Educational Improvement of the Northeast and Islands, 1988); Richard D. Kahlenberg and Halley Potter, "A Smarter Charter," *Poverty and Race* 23, no. 6 (November/December 2014); Rachel Cohen, "The Untold History of Charter Schools," *Democracy: A Journal of Ideas* (April 27, 2017).

18. Shanker, "National Press Club Speech"; "Shanker Asks Greater Autonomy for Teachers and School Officials," *New York Times*, April 1, 1988.

19. Kahlenberg, *Tough Liberal*, 1–7.

20. Budde, "Evolution of the Charter Concept"; Richard Kahlenberg and Halley Potter, "Restoring Shanker's Vision for Charter Schools," *American Educator*, Winter 2014–2015.

21. "Itasca Seminar: Balancing Educational Excellence and Equity in the Public Schools," Minnesota Public Radio Archive, audio file, December 12, 1988.

22. Teaching Committee, *Citizens League Report: Cooperatively Managed Schools: Teachers as Partners* (August 5, 1987), accessed November 16, 2022, https://citizensleague.org/wp-content/uploads/2017/07/PolicyReport EducationAug-1987.pdf.

23. Kolderie, interview with the author; Joe Nathan, interview with the author, July 27, 2020; Ember Reichgott Junge, *Zero Chance of Passage: The Pioneering Charter School Story* (Edina, MN: Beaver's Pond Press, 2012), 33–36, 40–45.

24. School Structure Committee, *Citizens League Report: Chartered Schools = Choices for Educators + Quality for All Students* (November 17, 1988), i, ii, 14–16.

CHAPTER 7: "IF WE DO THIS, I WANT TO WIN"

1. Bill Dahlk, *Against the Wind: African Americans and the Schools in Milwaukee, 1963–2002* (Milwaukee, WI: Marquette University Press, 2010), 412; David E. Umhoefer, "Williams Backed on Busing Stance," *Milwaukee Journal*, May 7, 1985.

2. Howard Fuller and Michael Smith, "A Manifesto for New Directions in the Education of Black Children in the City of Milwaukee" (1987), 4, courtesy Howard Fuller.

3. Tommy G. Thompson, *Power to the People: An American State at Work* (New York: Harper Collins, 1996), 90–91. Some members of the group couldn't recall this meeting in later years. See Daniel Bice and Richard P. Jones, "Thompson's Claims Called into Question," *Milwaukee Journal Sentinel*, August 10, 1996.

4. Rogers Worthington, "Milwaukee Proposal Splits City, Educators' School Plan Called 'Urban Apartheid,'" *Chicago Tribune*, November 22, 1987.

5. Derrick Bell, "Control Not Color: The Real Issue in the Milwaukee Manifesto," *Milwaukee Journal*, September 30, 1987, box 5, folder 4, Barbara L. Ulichny Papers, Archives Division of the State Historical Society of Wisconsin, Madison.

6. Dahlk, *Against the Wind*, 405.

7. "Bronzeville," *Encyclopedia of Milwaukee*, accessed October 26, 2022, https://emke.uwm.edu/entry/bronzeville/. See also Jessie Paulson, Meghan Wierschke, and Gabe Jun Ha Kim, "Milwaukee's History of Segregation and Development: A Biography of Four Neighborhoods" (Geography Undergraduate Symposium, University of Wisconsin–Madison, fall 2016); John

Schmid, "Heavy Job Losses Since the 1970s Hit Milwaukee's Black Community the Hardest. Here's Why," *Milwaukee Journal Sentinel*, August 28, 2019.

8. Howard Fuller, interview with the author, August 25, 2020.

9. Howard Fuller with Lisa Frazier Page, *No Struggle No Progress: A Warrior's Life from Black Power to Education Reform* (Milwaukee, WI: Marquette University Press, 2014), 14–19; Dahlk, *Against the Wind*, 33.

10. Debra Viadero, "Wis. Governor Seeks Voucher-Style Plan," *Education Week*, February 3, 1988.

11. Thompson, *Power to the People*, 97; Mikel Holt, *Not Yet "Free at Last": The Unfinished Business of the Civil Rights Movement, Our Battle for School Choice* (Oakland, CA: Institute for Contemporary Studies, 2000), 57; Viadero, "Wis. Governor Seeks."

12. Barbara Johnson Wood, "The Legislative Development and Enactment of the Milwaukee Parental Choice Program: A Case Study of a Change in the Politics of Education" (PhD diss., University of Wisconsin–Madison, 1999), 325; Amy Stuart Wells, *Time to Choose: America at the Crossroads of School Choice Policy* (New York: Hill and Wang, 1993), 89.

13. Jim Carl, *Freedom of Choice: Vouchers in American Education* (Santa Barbara, CA: Praeger, 2011), 124–125.

14. Carl, *Freedom of Choice*, 121.

15. Holt, *Not Yet*, 57–59.

16. Carl, *Freedom of Choice*, 107–110; John F. Witte, *The Market Approach to Education: An Analysis of America's First Voucher Program* (Princeton, NJ: Princeton University Press, 2000), 90, 116; Holt, *Not Yet*, 59.

17. Deborah L. Cohen, "Milwaukee Proposal on Private Schools Stirs Debate," *Education Week*, May 17, 1989; "Milwaukee Choice," 1990, Milwaukee Manuscript Collection, box 3, Choice Proposal folder 3, Mary Bills Papers, University of Wisconsin–Milwaukee.

18. Carl, *Freedom of Choice*, 123–128.

19. Holt, *Not Yet*, 57–59, 63–64.

CHAPTER 8: "LET EDUCATION BE THE FOCUS"

1. Mikel Holt, *Not Yet "Free at Last": The Unfinished Business of the Civil Rights Movement, Our Battle for School Choice* (Oakland, CA: Institute for Contemporary Studies, 2000), 66–67; Jim Carl, *Freedom of Choice: Vouchers in American Education* (Santa Barbara, CA: Praeger, 2011), 118, 133.

2. Tommy G. Thompson, *Power to the People: An American State at Work* (New York: HarperCollins, 1996), 92; Patrick J. McGuinn, *No Child Left Behind and the Transformation of Federal Education Policy, 1965–2005* (Lawrence: University Press of Kansas, 2006), 51, 58; Carl, *Freedom of Choice*, 87.

3. Barbara Johnson Wood, "The Legislative Development and Enactment of the Milwaukee Parental Choice Program: A Case Study of a Change in the Politics of Education" (PhD diss., University of Wisconsin–Madison, 1999), 438–439.

4. Bill Dahlk, *Against the Wind: African Americans and the Schools in Milwaukee, 1963–2002* (Milwaukee, WI: Marquette University Press, 2010), 34–35.

5. Dahlk, *Against the Wind*, 37; Jack Dougherty, *More than One Struggle: The Evolution of Black School Reform in Milwaukee* (Chapel Hill: University of North Carolina Press, 2004), 94–95.

6. Dahlk, *Against the Wind*, 42.

7. William Dahlk, "Milwaukee Public Schools," *Encyclopedia of Milwaukee*, accessed October 16, 2022, https://emke.uwm.edu/entry/milwaukee-public-schools/; Dougherty, *More than One Struggle*, 153; Dahlk, *Against the Wind*, 304.

8. Robert A. Frahm, "Milwaukee Integration Plan Praised, Panned," *Hartford Courant*, May 1, 1988; John F. Witte, *The Market Approach to Education: An Analysis of America's First Voucher Program* (Princeton, NJ: Princeton University Press, 2000), 79–81; Milliken vs. Bradley, 418 US 717 (1974).

9. Dougherty, *More than One Struggle*, 159–161.

10. Carl, *Freedom of Choice*, 101–102, 107–108; Dahlk, *Against the Wind*, 424–425. See also John F. Witte and Daniel J. Walsh, *Staff Report to the Study Commission on the Quality of Education in the Metropolitan Milwaukee Public Schools*, Report 3, 4, 6, 7 (1985).

11. Dahlk, *Against the Wind*, 425–427.

12. Robin Harris, "For Maverick Polly Williams, the Mother of School Choice, the Point Was Always to Empower Parents and Improve Education for Black Children," The 74, January 28, 2020.

13. Holt, *Not Yet*, 65, 66.

14. Carl, *Freedom of Choice*, 122.

15. Holt, *Not Yet*, 67–72; Wood, "The Legislative Development and Enactment," 445; "Lawmakers Bombarded with Support for Choice Proposal," *Milwaukee Community Journal*, February 28, 1990.

16. Holt, *Not Yet*, 74, 976.

17. Wood, "Legislative Development and Enactment," 488, 489, 491; Holt, *Not Yet*, 76–77.

18. 1989 Wisconsin Act 336 (Vetoed in Part), accessed October 16, 2022, https://docs.legis.wisconsin.gov/1989/related/acts/336.pdf.

19. Rogers Worthington, "For Inner-City Kids, Private Schools Beckon," *Chicago Tribune*, April 1, 1990; Clint Bolick, interview with the author, July 29, 2022. See also Alan Bonsteel and Carlos A. Bonilla, *A Choice for Our Children in America's Schools: Curing the Crisis in America's Schools* (San Francisco, CA: Institute for Contemporary Studies, 1997), 191–193. In it, Milton Friedman credits Wilbur Cohen, former secretary of the US Department of Health, Education, and Welfare, for coining this phrase, and he explains why he came to agree with Cohen.

CHAPTER 9: "THE UNHOLY ALLIANCE"

1. "Plan Will Send Kids to Private Schools," *Washington Times*, March 27, 1990.

2. "Shoeshine Businessman Standing Tall in Victory," *New York Times*, April 19, 1989.

3. Clint Bolick, *Voucher Wars: Waging the Legal Battle over School Choice* (Washington, DC: Cato Institute, 2003), 12, 17, 18–20. Also see Polly Williams, "School Choice: A Vehicle for Achieving Educational Excellence in the African-American Community," transcript of speech delivered at the Heritage Foundation, October 9, 1992.

4. "The Polly Williams Backlash," *Wall Street Journal*, June 14, 1990; Elaine Ciulla Kamarck, "Poor People Hoping for Help, Try Looking to Your Right," *Newsday*, April 30, 1990.

5. Clint Bolick, "State Constitutions as a Bulwark for Freedom," *Oklahoma City University Law Review* 37, no. 1 (Spring 2012): 1–15.

6. Eric Harrison, "Milwaukee School Choice Proposal Ignites Bitter Racial, Political Battles," *Los Angeles Times*, August 3, 1990; George A. Clowes, "The Model for the Nation: An Exclusive Interview with Annette Polly Williams," Heartland Institute, August 30, 2002.

7. Rogers Worthington, "Tax Funding for Private Schools Faces Court Test," *Chicago Tribune*, July 23, 1990.

8. Virgil Blum, "'Choice' Education Programs Suppress Rights of Parents," *Arlington Catholic Herald*, March 9, 1989.

9. "Priest Nearing Finish Line with Fund-Raiser," *Milwaukee Journal*, March 31, 1990.

10. "Virgil Blum Dies; Started Catholic League," *Milwaukee Journal*, April 6, 1990.

11. Bolick, *Voucher Wars*, 27; "Blocking the Schoolhouse Door," *Wall Street Journal*, June 27, 1990.

12. Bolick, *Voucher Wars*, 18–19, 24.

13. John E. Chubb and Terry M. Moe, *Politics, Markets, and America's Schools* (Washington, DC: Brookings Institution, 1990), ix, 23, 207, 217, 219, 227.

14. "Attorney Claims School Choice Program Could Increase Segregation," *Los Angeles Times*, July 29, 1990.

15. Bolick, *Voucher Wars*, 29.

16. "Attorney Claims School Choice."

17. David Nicholson, "Schools in Transition," *Washington Post*, August 5, 1990.

CHAPTER 10: TWO DUELING EDUCATION IDEAS

1. Ted Kolderie, "The States Will Have to Withdraw the Exclusive: Public Services Redesign Project—July 1990," Education Evolving, accessed November 5, 2022, www.educationevolving.org/pdf/StatesWillHavetoWithdraw theExclusive.pdf.

2. "Milwaukee Students Start School Under Voucher Program," *St. Petersburg Times*, September 5, 1990.

3. Frank A. Aukofer, "Williams on Ascent with Ideas for Schools," *Milwaukee Journal*, May 13, 1990; Elaine Ciulla Kamarck, "Poor People Hoping for Help, Try Looking to Your Right," *Newsday*, April 30, 1990; "How 'Conservative' Won Vouchers," *Crain's Chicago Business*, April 16, 1990; "The Polly Williams Backlash," *Wall Street Journal*, June 14, 1990; Center for Education Reform, "School Choice in WI—National Opposition, Support for Milwaukee's Voucher Program," *60 Minutes*, video, YouTube, October 1991.

4. John F. Witte, *The Market Approach to Education: An Analysis of America's First Voucher Program* (Princeton, NJ: Princeton University Press, 2000), 44–46; "A Dialogue with Polly Williams," *Emerge* 2, no. 1 (October 1990): 19.

5. Davis vs. Grover, 464 NW 2d 220 (Wis. Court of Appeals, 1990).

6. Millicent Lawton, "Private School Opts Out of Milwaukee Choice Program," *Education Week*, January 16, 1991; Clint Bolick, *Voucher Wars:*

Waging the Legal Battle over School Choice (Washington, DC: Cato Institute, 2003), 32.

7. School Structure Committee, *Citizens League Report: Chartered Schools = Choices for Educators + Quality for All Students* (November 17, 1988), i, ii.

8. Unless otherwise attributed, the narrative of events and the quotes in the rest of the chapter come from Ember Reichgott Junge, *Zero Chance of Passage: The Pioneering Charter School Story* (Edina, MN: Beaver's Pond Press, 2012), 85, 126, 149, 324–325.

9. Dennis J. McGrath, "'Chartered Schools' Getting More Support," *Minneapolis Star Tribune*, March 2, 1991.

10. Mary Jane Smetanka, "Liberated Learning: Minnesota Is First to Give Teachers, Parents the Right to Open Schools," *Minneapolis Star Tribune*, May 26, 1991.

CHAPTER 11: SCHOOL CHOICE, PUBLIC OR PRIVATE?

1. Sue Urahn and Dan Stewart, *Minnesota Charter Schools: A Research Report* (Minnesota House of Representatives, December 1994).

2. Milo Cutter, interview with the author, November 2021.

3. Tom Gonzalez, interview with the author, July 2021.

4. Laurel Sharper Walters, "Bush, Clinton Education Plans Look Similar—on the Surface," *Christian Science Monitor*, August 25, 1992.

5. Patrick J. McGuinn, *No Child Left Behind and the Transformation of Federal Education Policy, 1965–2005* (Lawrence: University Press of Kansas, 2006), 64–67; Walters, "Bush, Clinton Education Plans Look Similar."

6. Davis vs. Grover, 480 NW 2d 460 (Wis. Supreme Court, 1992); Mark Walsh, "Wisconsin Court Upholds State's Test of Vouchers," *Education Week*, March 11, 1992.

7. George H. W. Bush, "Remarks Announcing Proposed Legislation to Establish a 'GI Bill' for Children," June 25, 1992, Public Papers of the Presidents of the United States (1992, Book I), www.govinfo.gov/content/pkg/PPP -1992-book1/pdf/PPP-1992-book1-doc-pg1012.pdf; letter from Bill Clinton to Polly Williams, October 18, 1990, Center for Education Reform, accessed November 16, 2022, https://edreform.com/wp-content/uploads/2013 /01/Bill_Clinton_on_School_Choice_1990.pdf; Bill Clinton, keynote address, Democratic Leadership Council, Cleveland, video, C-SPAN, May 6, 1991.

8. Ember Reichgott Junge, *Zero Chance of Passage: The Pioneering Charter School Story* (Edina, MN: Beaver's Pond Press, 2012), 186; Ted Kolderie,

Beyond Choice to New Public Schools: Withdrawing the Exclusive Franchise in Public Education (Progressive Policy Institute, November 1990).

9. Gwen Ifill, "The 1992 Campaign: The Challenger, Clinton Offers National Education Plan," *New York Times*, May 15, 1992; Julie A. Miller, "With a Track Record on Education, Campaigner Clinton Speaks with Authority," *Education Week*, February 5, 1992; McGuinn, *No Child Left Behind*, 81.

10. Gary K. Hart and Sue Burr, "The Story of California's Charter School Legislation," *Phi Delta Kappan* 78, no. 1 (September 1996): 37; National Charter Schools Institute, "California's Charter Schools Story: A Conversation with Ember Reichgott Junge, Sue Burr, Eric Premack, and Gary Hart," video, April 11, 2019, https://charterlibrary.org/library /californias-charter-schools-story/.

11. Gary K. Hart's office, "Education Chairs Introduce 'Charter Schools' Bills," press release, February 11, 1992, https://nationalcharterschools.org/wp -content/uploads/2020/04/Hart-1992-CA-EducationChairsIntroduce CharterSchoolsBills.pdf.

12. Lynn Olson, "Calif. Is Second State to Allow Charter Schools: Law Partly Aimed at Heading Off Vouchers," *Education Week*, September 30, 1992.

13. Dan Morain, "Teachers Union Shows Clout in Fight Against Prop 174," *Los Angeles Times*, October 25, 1993.

14. Lynn Olson, "Opponents of Proposition 174 Hold Giant Fund-Raising Advantage," *Education Week*, October 20, 1993; Morain, "Teachers Union Shows Clout"; Dennis Michael Doyle, "Choice, Politics, and Public Schools: A Case Study of the California Proposition 174 Voucher Campaigns" (PhD diss., Claremont Graduate University and San Diego State University, 1994), 103.

15. "School Choice on Trial," *Washington Post*, June 24, 1992.

16. Clint Bolick, *Voucher Wars: Waging the Legal Battle over School Choice* (Washington, DC: Cato Institute, 2003), 59; Clint Bolick, "Puerto Rico: Leading the Way in School Choice: The Americas," *Wall Street Journal*, January 14, 1994.

17. Ted Kolderie, *Thinking Out the How*, rev. ed. (St. Paul, MN: Center for Policy Design Press, 2021), 184.

CHAPTER 12: "SLIPPERY SLOPE"

1. John F. Witte, *The Market Approach to Education: An Analysis of America's First Voucher Program* (Princeton, NJ: Prince University Press,

2000), 163; Tommy Thompson, State of the State address, transcript, January 25, 1995, Tommy Thompson file, 1995 folder, series 1, box 5, PAVE Records, Marquette University, Milwaukee, WI; John Stuart Mill, *On Liberty*, chapter 5 (1859), 191.

2. Witte, *Market Approach to Education*, 45.

3. Matt Pommer, "Governor Defends Choice Program," *Capital Times*, January 20, 1995, Milwaukee manuscripts, box 13, School Choice Counter Proposals, folder 4, Tony Baez Papers, Marquette University, Milwaukee, WI; Richard P. Jones, "Coalition Attacks Idea of Extending Choice Program to Religious Schools," *Milwaukee Journal*, February 17, 1995; Steve Schultze, "Thompson May Expand School Choice," *Milwaukee Journal*, March 14, 1995; "Wisconsin Governor Backs Wider School Choice," *Chicago Tribune*, January 17, 1995.

4. Witte, *Market Approach to Education*, 166; Eldon Knoche, "Expansion of Choice Supported," *Milwaukee Sentinel*, February 18, 1995.

5. Witte, *Market Approach to Education*, 168; memo from Dan McKinley, February 21, 1995, Memoranda/Correspondence 1991–2007, series 1, box 3, PAVE Records.

6. Knoche, "Expansion of Choice Supported."

7. "Choice Researcher Urges Keeping Religious Schools out of the Program," *Milwaukee Journal*, February 3, 1995.

8. "School Choice in the United States, State by State Analysis, 1993," Center for Education Reform, accessed November 5, 2022, https://edreform.com/edreform-university/resource/school-choice-in-the-united-states-1993/.

9. Milton Friedman, "Public Schools: Make Them Private," *Washington Post*, February 19, 1995.

10. "School at the Vanguard of Change," *Los Angeles Times*, January 18, 1993.

11. Albert Shanker, "Where We Stand, Goals Not Gimmicks," *New York Times*, November 7, 1993.

12. Mary Jane Smetanka, "Innovative Charter Schools Are Running into Opposition," *Minneapolis Star Tribune*, March 16, 1992; "For VA. Education, a Minnesota Model," *Washington Post*, December 5, 1994.

13. Howard Fuller with Lisa Frazier Page, *No Struggle No Progress: A Warrior's Life from Black Power to Educational Reform* (Milwaukee, WI: Marquette University Press, 2014), 230–237; "Now, Can School Board Govern?," *Milwaukee Journal Sentinel*, April 23, 1995.

CHAPTER 13: "A CLEAR AND CALCULATED UNDERMINING OF PUBLIC EDUCATION"

1. Edward Walsh, "Holding Hard to the Middle: Managerial Style Plays to Voters' Mood," *Washington Post*, July 21, 1994.

2. Jim Carl, *Freedom of Choice: Vouchers in American Education* (Santa Barbara, CA: Praeger, 2011), 164–165, 170; Ronald Kozar and James Damask, *Giving Choice a Chance: Cleveland and the Future of School Reform* (Dayton, OH: Buckeye Institute for Public Policy Solutions, 1998), 12; Gregory B. Bodwell, "Grassroots, Inc.: A Sociopolitical History of the Cleveland School Voucher Battle, 1992–2002" (PhD diss., Case Western Reserve University, 2006), 40.

3. Kozar and Damask, *Giving Choice a Chance*, 10; Sandy Theis, "State Readies for School Voucher Fight," *Dayton Daily News*, December 11, 1994; Mary Yost, "Using Taxes for Private Schooling Is Proposed," *Columbus Dispatch*, June 26, 1992.

4. Jonathan Riskind, "Giving Students Choice of Schools Extolled," *Columbus Dispatch*, December 17, 1992; Carl, *Freedom of Choice*, 170.

5. Bodwell, "Grassroots, Inc.," 50.

6. Riskind, "Giving Students Choice"; Bodwell, "Grassroots, Inc.," 48; Theis, "State Readies."

7. Letter from George Voinovich to David Brennan, May 31, 1994, Voinovich, George V., 1936–et al., "Correspondence Between Governor Voinovich, David Brennan, Richard Stoff, Fred Brothers, April 26–May 31, 1994, re: School Choice Task Force," Voinovich Collections, Ohio University, digitized collections, accessed February 22, 2018. (This item no longer appears in the digital collection.)

8. Glenn Gamboa, Bob Paynter, and Andrew Zajac, "David Brennan: Big Man in Akron," *Akron Beacon Journal*, October 15, 2018.

9. David L. Brennan, *Victory for Kids: The Cleveland School Voucher Case* (Beverly Hills, CA: New Millennium Press, 2002), 69.

10. Brennan, *Victory for Kids*, 73; Alan Johnson, "Democrats Expect It to Be Rough Election Year," *Columbus Dispatch*, March 13, 1994; Lee Leonard, "Ohio House Control at Stake in Election," *Columbus Dispatch*, October 30, 1994; Lee Leonard, "Ohio House: GOP May Take the Reins," *Columbus Dispatch*, September 11, 1994.

11. "Voinovich, GOP Crush Opposition," *Dayton Daily News*, November 9, 1994.

12. "Voinovich's Vouchers Shouldn't Be for Those Who Have School Choice," *Dayton Daily News*, December 20, 1994.

13. "Voinovich, GOP Crush Opposition."

14. Walsh, "Holding Hard to the Middle"; Ohio Gubernatorial Debate, October 22, 1990, video, C-SPAN, accessed November 5, 2022, www.c-span.org/video/?14637-1/ohio-gubernatorial-debate; Tim Miller, "Voinovich Wants to Be 'Education Governor,'" *Dayton Daily News*, January 29, 1995.

15. Carl, *Freedom of Choice*, 154.

16. Bodwell, "Grassroots, Inc.," 56–58.

17. Carl, *Freedom of Choice*, 145–149; Patrice M. Jones, Evelyn Theiss, Desiree F. Hicks, and Scott Stephens, "The Cleveland Schools Crisis," *Plain Dealer*, March 9, 1995.

18. Evelyn Theiss, "Parrish Calls on Union to Support Magnet Plan," *Plain Dealer*, April 23, 1993.

19. Carl, *Freedom of Choice*, 170.

20. McKenna, "Politics of School Vouchers"; Carl, *Freedom of Choice*, 158.

21. "Fannie Lewis," *Encyclopedia of Cleveland History*, Case Western Reserve University, accessed November 2, 2022, https://case.edu/ech/articles/l/lewis-fannie.

22. Bodwell, "Grassroots, Inc.," 51; Kathy Wray Coleman, "White Joins Lewis in Support of School Vouchers," *Call and Post*, November 17, 1994.

23. "State of the State: Education, Welfare Reforms Go Beyond Money," *Columbus Dispatch*, January 27, 1995; Jonathan Riskind, "Clevelanders Lobby for Voucher Plan," *Columbus Dispatch*, February 1, 1995; "Choice Breakthrough," *Wall Street Journal*, June 30, 1995; Scott Stephens, "Storming the Statehouse: Local Voucher Plan Supporters State Their Case in Columbus," *Plain Dealer*, February 1, 1995.

24. Thomas Suddes, "Voinovich's Voucher Plan May Be Limited to Cleveland," *Plain Dealer*, March 17, 1995; K. W. Coleman, "Hundreds Gather to Oppose Vouchers," *Call and Post*, April 6, 1995; "Choice Breakthrough"; Bodwell, "Grassroots, Inc.," 60.

25. "Ohio Voucher Plan Oversold as a Reform," *Dayton Daily News*, June 1, 1995.

CHAPTER 14: CONSTITUTIONAL INSURANCE

1. Clint Bolick, interview with the author, July 29, 2022. See also Clint Bolick, *Voucher Wars: Waging the Legal Battle over School Choice* (Washington, DC: Cato Institute, 2003), 68–70.

2. Letter from Thomas Jefferson to the Danbury Baptists, January 1, 1802, Library of Congress, accessed January 16, 2023, www.loc.gov/loc/lcib /9806/danpre.html.

3. Pierce vs. Society of Sisters, 268 US 510 (1925).

4. Everson vs. Board of Education, 330 US 1 (1947); Lemon vs. Kurtzman, 403 US 602 (1971).

5. Lemon vs. Kurtzman, 403 US 602 (1971); Committee for Public Education and Religious Liberty vs. Nyquist, 413 US 756 (1973).

6. Mueller vs. Allen, 463 US 388 (1983).

7. Witters vs. Washington Department of Services for the Blind, 474 US 481 (1986); Zobrest vs. Catalina Foothills School District, 509 US 1 (1993).

8. Rosenberger vs. Rector and Visitors of the University of Virginia, 515 US 819 (1995).

9. Nina J. Easton, *Gang of Five: Leaders at the Center of the Conservative Ascendancy* (New York: Touchstone, 2000), 196.

10. Michael Edwards and Mark Walsh, *More than a Lawyer: Robert Chanin, the National Education Association, and the Fight for Public Education, Employee Rights, and Social Justice* (Washington, DC: National Education Association, 2010), 4–7, 17–18; Bolick, interview with the author; Robert Chanin, interview with the author, August 28, 2022.

11. "Blackboard Jungle," *American Lawyer*, May 1, 2000; Mark Walsh, "Bolick v. Chanin," *Education Week*, April 1, 1998.

12. "Milwaukee's Pioneering Choice Program Nears Expansion," *Chicago Tribune*, July 16, 1995.

13. Steven Walters, "Governor Wants Choice Ruling: He Asks State Supreme Court to Take Case Now," *Milwaukee Journal Sentinel*, August 11, 1995. See also Richard P. Jones, "Court Temporarily Bars Religious School Choice: State Justices Halt Program Expansion Until Ruling on Legality," *Milwaukee Journal Sentinel*, August 26, 1995.

14. Peter Applebome, "Milwaukee Forces Debate on Vouchers: With Issue in Courts, Gifts Keep Needy Students in Church Schools," *New York Times*, September 1, 1995; Rene Sanchez, "Wisconsin High Court Suspends Vouchers for Religious Schools," *Washington Post*, August 26, 1995.

15. Applebome, "Milwaukee Forces Debate."

16. Jeanne Ponessa, "Lawsuit Seeks to Block Vouchers in Cleveland," *Education Week*, January 17, 1996; Gregory B. Bodwell, "Grassroots, Inc.: A Sociopolitical History of the Cleveland School Voucher Battle, 1992–2002" (PhD diss., Case Western Reserve University, 2006), 101.

17. Ponessa, "Lawsuit Seeks to Block."

18. Zelman vs. Simmons-Harris, 536 US 639 (2002). See also Bolick, *Voucher Wars*, 93.

19. Mark Walsh, "Religious School Vouchers Get Their Day in Court," *Education Week*, March 6, 1996.

20. Walsh, "Religious School Vouchers Get Their Day."

21. "Court Deadlocks on Vouchers," *Education Week*, May 1, 1996.

22. Bolick, *Voucher Wars*, 95; "Ohio Court Clears Voucher Pilot," *Education Week*, August 7, 1996.

23. Mark Walsh, "For First Time, Students Use Vouchers for Religious Schools," *Education Week*, September 4, 1996.

CHAPTER 15: THE UNHOLY ALLIANCE FRACTURES

1. John F. Witte, *The Market Approach to Education: An Analysis of America's First Voucher Program* (Princeton, NJ: Princeton University Press, 2000), 168.

2. "Rift Seen in Support of Choice," *Milwaukee Journal Sentinel*, September 10, 1995.

3. Witte, *Market Approach to Education*, 108; Robin Harris, "For Maverick Polly Williams, the Mother of School Choice, the Point Was Always to Empower Parents and Improve Education for Black Children," The 74, January 28, 2020.

4. Jay P. Greene, Paul E. Peterson, and Jiangtao Du, "The Effectiveness of School Choice in Milwaukee: A Secondary Analysis of Data from the Program's Evaluation," paper presented at the Annual Meeting of the American Political Science Association (San Francisco, CA: August 30, 1996); "School Vouchers Pass One Exam," *Chicago Tribune*, August 13, 1996.

5. Bob Davis, "Class Warfare: Dueling Professors Have Milwaukee Dazed over School Vouchers," *Wall Street Journal*, October 11, 1996; Paul E. Peterson and Jay P. Greene, "School Choice Data Rescued from Bad Science," *Wall Street Journal*, August 14, 1996.

6. "School Vouchers Pass One Exam."

7. Clint Bolick, *Voucher Wars: Waging the Legal Battle over School Choice* (Washington, DC: Cato Institute, 2003), 100.

8. Alex Molnar, Walter C. Farrell Jr., James H. Johnson, and Marty Sapp, "A Flawed Design," *New York Beacon*, October 9, 1996.

9. "Bob Dole 1996 on the Issues: Where Bob Dole Stands on K–12 Education," 4President.org, accessed October 18, 2022, www.4president.org /issues/dole1996/dole1996education.htm; text of Robert Dole's speech to the Republican National Convention, August 15, 1996, CNN, www.cnn .com/ALLPOLITICS/1996/conventions/san.diego/transcripts/0815/dole .fdch.shtml.

10. "Presidential Race: Dole Touts School Choice," *Dayton Daily News*, September 6, 1996; Stephen D. Sugarman and Frank R. Kemerer, *School Choice and Social Controversy: Politics, Policy, and Law* (Washington, DC: Brookings Institution Press, 1999), 23; William J. Clinton, "Remarks Accepting the Presidential Nomination at the Democratic National Convention in Chicago," American Presidency Project, August 29, 1996, www.presidency.ucsb.edu /documents/remarks-accepting-the-presidential-nomination-the-democratic -national-convention-chicago.

11. Sara Mosle, "The Answer Is National Standards," *New York Times*, October 27, 1996.

12. "Politics of School Vouchers," *Minneapolis Star Tribune*, October 14, 1996.

13. Rene Sanchez, "Cleveland Charts New Educational Course; State Vouchers for Poor Families Include Religious Schools as Options," *Washington Post*, September 10, 1996.

14. "Politics of School Vouchers."

15. Matt Pommer, "Rep. Hits Church School 'Choice,'" *Madison Capital Times*, May 26, 1997.

CHAPTER 16: BOLICK VS. CHANIN

1. Mark Walsh, "Judge Overturns Expanded Wis. Voucher Plan," *Education Week*, January 22, 1997; Chittenden Town School District vs. Department of Education, 169 Vt. 310, 738 A.2d 539 (Vt. 1999); Jackson vs. Benson, 570 NW 2d 407 (Wis. Court of Appeals 1997).

2. Clint Bolick, *Voucher Wars: Waging the Legal Battle over School Choice* (Washington, DC: Cato Institute, 2003), 104–105, 107.

3. John E. Chubb and Terry M. Moe, *Politics, Markets, and America's Schools* (Washington, DC: Brookings Institution, 1990), 207; John F. Witte, *The Market Approach to Education: An Analysis of America's First Voucher Program* (Princeton, NJ: Princeton University Press, 2000), 160; Michael

Mintrom, "The State-Local Nexus in Policy Innovation Diffusion: The Case of School Choice," *Publius* 27, no. 3 (Summer 1997): 41–59.

4. Tommy Thompson, State of the State address, transcript, January 25, 1995, Tommy Thompson file, 1995 folder, series 1, box 5, PAVE records, Marquette University, Milwaukee, WI; Jeffrey R. Henig, *Rethinking School Choice: Limits of the Market Metaphor* (Princeton, NJ: Princeton University Press, 1994), 94–95.

5. Kimberly J. McLarin, "Voucher Plan Is Unveiled for Schools in Jersey City," *New York Times*, October 6, 1994; Neil MacFarquhar, "Public, but Independent, Schools Are Inspiring Hope and Hostility," *New York Times*, December 27, 1996.

6. "Vouchers May Open Few Doors," *Washington Post*, September 20, 1997.

7. Scott Shepard, "House Narrowly Approves D.C. School Voucher Test," *Atlanta Journal*, October 10, 1997; Teresa Malcom, "Secretary Attacks Vouchers," *National Catholic Reporter* 33, no. 43 (October 10, 1997): 6.

8. "Poll: More Blacks Like School Vouchers," Associated Press, July 28, 1997.

9. Virginia Walden Ford, *School Choice: A Legacy to Keep* (New York: Beaufort Books, 2019), 45–48, 53–54.

10. Trent Franks, "Tuition Tax Credit Legislation Good for Kids, Country," *Arizona Republic*, February 16, 1999.

11. "Choice Wins in Arizona," *Wall Street Journal*, April 7, 1997.

12. Bolick, *Voucher Wars*, 76–77, 119.

13. Emily Parker, *Constitutional Obligations for Public Education: 50-State Review* (Education Commission of the States, March 2016).

14. Peter Schmidt, "Constitutionality of Mich. Charter Law Weighed," *Education Week*, November 2, 1994; "Home Schooling in Charter Schools: A Michigan Test Case Goes to Court," *Christian Science Monitor*, August 22, 1994.

15. "Judge Blocks Michigan's Charter School Plan," *Washington Post*, November 3, 1994.

16. Clint Bolick, interview with the author, July 29, 2022; Mark Walsh, "Bolick v. Chanin," *Education Week*, April 1, 1998.

17. Michael Edwards and Mark Walsh, *More than a Lawyer: Robert Chanin, the National Education Association, and the Fight for Public Education, Employee Rights and Social Justice* (Washington, DC: National Education Association, 2010), 265–266.

18. Bolick, *Voucher Wars*, 122; Robert Chanin, interview with the author, August 28, 2022.

CHAPTER 17: FLORIDA GETS IN THE VOUCHER GAME

1. "Will A-Plus Pass the Florida Test?," *Sarasota Herald Tribune*, February 28, 1999.

2. "Jeb Bush Is Feeling Charter School Heat," *Sun Sentinel*, December 21, 1997.

3. Jeb Bush, "Florida State of the State Address," video, C-SPAN, March 1999, www.c-span.org/video/?121210-1/florida-state-state-address.

4. "School Choice in Michigan: A Primer for Freedom in Education," Mackinac Center for Public Policy, July 1999, www.mackinac.org/archives /1999/s1999-06.pdf; "Jeb Bush Touts School Vouchers to Congress," *Palm Beach Post*, September 24, 1999.

5. Agostini vs. Felton, 521 US 203 (1997); Jackson vs. Benson, 218 Wis. 2d 835 (Wis. 1998); "Wisconsin Court Upholds Vouchers in Church Schools," *New York Times*, June 11, 1998; John F. Witte, *The Market Approach to Education: An Analysis of America's First Voucher Program* (Princeton, NJ: Princeton University Press, 2000), 185; Tony Mauro, "Court Allows School Vouchers, Lets Stand Ruling on Wis. Program," *USA Today*, November 10, 1998.

6. "School Vouchers Look like a Sure Thing," *Orlando Sentinel*, April 27, 1999.

7. "New York City Groups Join to Stop Vouchers," *People's Weekly World*, March 20, 1999; Dan Barry, "Raze School System, Giuliani Says," *New York Times*, April 23, 1999; Mark Oswald, "Special Report: School Vouchers," *Santa Fe New Mexican*, April 27, 1999.

8. Kathy Barks Hoffman, Associated Press, "Number of School Districts with Low Graduation Rates Shrinks," *Grand Rapids Press*, September 26, 1999.

9. Associated Press, "Governor Touts School Vouchers: NM Considers Plan, Despite Its Obstacles," *Denver Post*, March 7, 1999.

10. "Bush Proposes Plan to Improve Schools," *New York Times*, September 3, 1999.

11. "New Mexico Legislature Votes Down School Vouchers," *People's Weekly World*, June 19, 1999.

12. Rick Bragg, "Florida Will Award Vouchers for Pupils Whose Schools Fail," *New York Times*, April 28, 1999.

13. "Florida Pupils Teach Nation About Vouchers," *USA Today*, September 1, 1999.

14. Felicia Thomas-Lynn, "School Choice Pioneer Chafes at Her Status: Conservatives Have 'Hijacked' Movement She Sparked, Williams Says," *Milwaukee Journal Sentinel*, June 29, 1998; "Voucher Godmother Skeptical of Allies," *National Catholic Reporter*, March 26, 1999; Tamara Henry, "'Rosa Parks' of Choice Sits Out Voucher Fight," *USA Today*, January 5, 1999.

15. Howard Fuller with Lisa Frazier Page, *No Struggle No Progress: A Warrior's Life from Black Power to Education Reform* (Milwaukee, WI: Marquette University Press, 2014), 240, 245, 248.

16. Thomas-Lynn, "School Choice Pioneer Chafes."

17. "Vouchers Are Constitutional," *Detroit News*, June 15, 1999; "Ohio's Supreme Court Strikes Down Vouchers," *Orlando Sentinel*, May 28, 1999; Marcy Oster, "Ohio Supreme Court Rules Vouchers Unconstitutional: Opponents of Vouchers Score Technical Victory as Cleveland Pilot Program Struck Down," *Cleveland Jewish News*, June 4, 1999.

18. Pam Belluck, "Voucher System for Private Schools Blocked in Cleveland Day Before Classes Begin: Federal Judge Halts Program for Poor Students," *Milwaukee Journal Sentinel*, August 25, 1999.

19. "Judge Eases Ban," Associated Press, August 28, 1999.

20. Simmons-Harris vs. Zelman, 72 F. Supp. 2d 834 (N.D. Ohio 1999).

21. Jodi Wilgoren, "A Ruling Voids Use of Vouchers in Ohio Schools: Appeals Court Rules Against School Vouchers in Cleveland," *New York Times*, December 12, 2000.

22. Associated Press, "Supreme Court Declines to Rule on Separation of Church and State Cases: Court's Rejection of Three Appeals Will Fuel Debate on School Vouchers," *St. Louis Post-Dispatch*, October 13, 1999.

23. Wilgoren, "A Ruling Voids Use of Vouchers in Ohio Schools."

CHAPTER 18: A CHARTERED FUTURE?

1. Milo Cutter, interview with the author, November 2021.

2. US Department of Education, National Center for Education Statistics, "Common Core of Data (CCD): Public Elementary/Secondary School Universe Survey," 1999–2000 through 2014–2015; William J. Clinton, "Remarks at the City Academy in St. Paul, Minnesota," American Presidency Project, May 4, 2000, www.presidency.ucsb.edu/documents/remarks

-the-city-academy-st-paul-minnesota. In his remarks, Clinton said there were more than seventeen hundred charter schools; the NCES put that figure at just above fifteen hundred.

3. Debra Nussbaum, "Staking Claims to New Frontiers in Education: Plenty of Pioneers but Few Detailed Maps in Flourishing Charter School Movement," *New York Times*, February 27, 2000; Miriam Stawowy, "A Chartered Future?," *Daily Press*, August 7, 2000.

4. Anne E. Kornblut, "Bush Ties School Aid, Test Scores: Vouchers Downplayed," *Boston Globe*, January 24, 2001.

5. John Mintz, "George W. Bush: The Record in Texas," *Washington Post*, April 21, 2000.

6. Christopher T. Cross, *Political Education: National Policy Comes of Age* (New York: Teachers College Press, 2010), 129, 134; Kornblut, "Bush Ties School Aid."

7. Jesse H. Rhodes, *An Education in Politics: The Origins and Evolution of No Child Left Behind* (Ithaca, NY: Cornell University Press, 2012), 149, 150–151, 155–156.

8. Cross, *Political Education*, 138; Dana Milbank, "With Fanfare, Bush Signs Education Bill," *Washington Post*, January 9, 2002; Kate Zernike, "Mike Pence's Record on Education Is One of Turmoil and Mixed Results," *New York Times*, July 19, 2016.

9. Kate Zernike, "Lawmakers OK More Charter Schools," *Boston Globe*, July 2, 1997.

10. Jay Mathews, *Work Hard. Be Nice: How Two Inspired Teachers Created the Most Promising Schools in America* (Chapel Hill, NC: Algonquin Books, 2009); Sandy Banks, "Disney Awards Teacher with a Touch of Class," *Los Angeles Times*, December 6, 1992.

11. Samuel Casey Carter, *No Excuses: Lessons from 21 High-Performing, High-Poverty Schools* (Washington, DC: Heritage Foundation, 2001), 93; Abby Goodnough, "Structure and Basics Bring South Bronx School Acclaim," *New York Times*, October 20, 1999; Gail Russell Chaddock, "Success for Kids Accustomed to Failure," *Christian Science Monitor*, April 13, 1999.

12. Mathews, *Work Hard. Be Nice*, 11, 14, 31–42, 57–62, 89–90, 264–267.

13. Jessica L. Sandham, "Challenges to Charter Laws Mount," *Education Week*, May 2, 2001; Robert Worth, "In a Charter School Debate, Race Becomes an Issue," *New York Times*, October 15, 2000.

14. Amy Hetzner, "Focus on Student Results Urged for Charter Schools," *Milwaukee Journal Sentinel*, June 24, 2002; Sarah Tantillo, *Hit the Drum: An*

Insider's Account of How the Charter School Idea Became a National Movement (self-pub., 2019), 127.

15. Eve Pell, "The Charter School Magnate," *Salon*, May 24, 2000.

16. "Ohio Teachers Challenge Charter Funds," *Washington Times*, April 6, 2001.

17. Cara Stillings Candal, *The Fight for the Best Charter Public Schools in the Nation* (Boston: Pioneer Institute, 2018), 38.

18. Hetzner, "Focus on Student Results."

19. Hetzner, "Focus on Student Results."

20. "Extra Credit," *Wall Street Journal*, September 5, 2001.

21. Rachel Smolkin, "Tax Credits Next in School Choice Arsenal," *Pittsburgh Post-Gazette*, February 24, 2002.

CHAPTER 19: FINALLY, THE US SUPREME COURT

1. Karla Scoon Reid, "Supreme Court's Voucher Showdown Draws Hundreds to Witness History," *Education Week*, February 27, 2002.

2. Brief for the United States as amicus curiae, Zelman vs. Simmons-Harris, 536 US 639 (2002), 2.

3. Joe Williams, "It's Time for Schoolwork," *Milwaukee Journal Sentinel*, March 12, 1998.

4. Brief for the Ohio School Boards Association as amicus curiae, Zelman vs. Simmons-Harris, 2.

5. Brief for the Institute for Justice as amicus curiae, Zelman vs. Simmons-Harris.

6. Clint Bolick, *Voucher Wars: Waging the Legal Battle over School Choice* (Washington, DC: Cato Institute, 2003), 171–173; Howard Fuller, interview with the author, August 25, 2020; James Forman Jr., "The Rise and Fall of School Vouchers: A Story of Religion, Race, and Politics," *UCLA Law Review* 54, no. 3 (2007): 577; Charles Lane, "Court to Rule on Vouchers," *Washington Post*, September 26, 2001; David G. Savage, "Supreme Court Takes Voucher Case," *Los Angeles Times*, September 26, 2001; Gaylord Shaw, "High Court to Decide on Vouchers," *Newsday*, September 26, 2001.

7. Brief for respondents Doris Simmons-Harris et al., Zelman vs. Simmons-Harris.

8. Joan Biskupic, *Sandra Day O'Connor: How the First Woman on the Supreme Court Became Its Most Influential Justice* (New York: Ecco, 2005), 277–278, 288.

9. Jeffrey Rosen, "A Majority of One," *New York Times Magazine*, June 3, 2001.

10. Jesse H. Choper, "Federal Constitutional Issues," *School Choice and Social Controversy: Politics, Policy, and Law*, Stephen D. Sugarman and Frank R. Kemerer, eds. (Washington, DC: Brookings Institution Press, 1999), 237; Leonard W. Levy, *The Establishment Clause: Religion and the First Amendment* (Chapel Hill: University of North Carolina Press, 1994), 159.

11. Biskupic, *Sandra Day O'Connor*, 283.

12. Agostini vs. Felton, 521 US 203 (1997); Patrick M. Garry, "*Agostini v. Felton* and the Court's Modification of the *Lemon* Test," SSRN, 2007, https://ssrn.com/abstract=2286405 or http://dx.doi.org/10.2139/ssrn.2286405.

13. Sugarman and Kemerer, *School Choice and Social Controversy*, 240.

14. Linda Greenhouse, "Cleveland's School Vouchers Weighed by Supreme Court," *New York Times*, February 21, 2002.

15. Oral arguments, Zelman vs. Simmons-Harris, audio, Oyez Project, February 20, 2002, www.oyez.org/cases/2001/00-1751.

16. Bolick, *Voucher Wars*, 183.

CHAPTER 20: A DECISIVE STEP

1. Zelman vs. Simmons-Harris, 536 US 639 (2002).

2. "President Lauds Supreme Court School Choice Decision," press release, White House archives, July 1, 2002, https://georgewbush-whitehouse.archives.gov/news/releases/2002/07/20020701-7.html; Rod Paige, "A Win for America's Children," *Washington Post*, June 28, 2002; "Vouchers Have Overcome," *Wall Street Journal*, June 28, 2002.

3. Linda Greenhouse, "Win the Debate, Not Just the Case," *New York Times*, July 14, 2002.

4. Robert Chanin, interview with the author, August 28, 2022.

5. Greenhouse, "Win the Debate"; Mark Walsh, "Justices Settle Case, Nettle Policy Debate," *Education Week*, July 10, 2002.

6. Clint Bolick, *Voucher Wars: Waging the Legal Battle over School Choice* (Washington, DC: Cato Institute, 2003), 156; Mark Walsh, "Voucher Advocates Plan a Multi-State Legal Battle," *Education Week*, October 16, 2002; Brigid Schulte, "Voters Protective of Public Schools, Wary of Vouchers," *Washington Post*, June 28, 2002.

7. "Let These Pupils Go," *Wall Street Journal*, December 2, 2002.

8. Kevin Chavous, "Let the District Choose for Itself," *Washington Post*, July 7, 2002.

9. Virginia Walden Ford, *School Choice: A Legacy to Keep* (New York: Beaufort Books, 2019), 44–47, 103–104, 108–109.

10. Spencer S. Hsu, "Two Passionately Involved Parents, One Divisive Issue," *Washington Post*, September 14, 2003.

11. Parents United for the D.C. Public Schools Civic Leader Advisory Committee, *Separate and Unequal: The State of the District of Columbia Public Schools Fifty Years After* Brown *and* Bolling (March 2005); Justin Blum, "School Repairs Threatened, Group Says," *Washington Post*, July 24, 2003.

12. Wendy S. Grigg, Mary C. Daane, Ying Jin, and Jay R. Campbell, *The Nation's Report Card: Reading 2002* (Washington, DC: National Center for Education Statistics, 2003); Jennifer Laird, Stephen Lew, Matthew DeBell, and Chris Chapman, *Dropout Rates in the United States: 2002 and 2003* (Washington, DC: National Center for Education Statistics, 2006), 9; Parents United, *Separate and Unequal*; June Kronholz, "Capital Opportunity for School Vouchers," *Wall Street Journal*, September 25, 2003.

13. Courtland Milloy, "Williams Wants Write-Ins When People Can't Read," *Washington Post*, August 11, 2002.

14. Peggy Cooper Cafritz, "Making the Most of Vouchers," *Washington Post*, March 29, 2003; Craig Timberg and Justin Blum, "Mayor Endorses Vouchers in D.C.," *Washington Post*, May 2, 2003.

15. Spencer S. Hsu, "How Vouchers Came to D.C.: The Inside Story," *Education Next*, Fall 2004; Rob Hotakainen, "Coleman Backs D.C. Vouchers," *Minneapolis Star Tribune*, October 13, 2003; Dianne Feinstein, "Let D.C. Try Vouchers," *Washington Post*, July 22, 2003.

16. Bruce Alpert, "Group Explains Its Scolding of Landrieu: Her Rejection of Voucher Bill a 'Disappointment,'" *Times-Picayune*, September 3, 2003; "Mary's Choice," *Wall Street Journal*, September 5, 2003; Spencer S. Hsu, "D.C. Vouchers Clear Senate Panel," *Washington Post*, September 5, 2003.

17. Spencer S. Hsu and Justin Blum, "D.C. School Voucher Bill Passes in House by 1 Vote," *Washington Post*, September 10, 2003.

18. Spencer S. Hsu, "Senate Backs Off D.C. School Vouchers," *Washington Post*, October 1, 2003.

19. Public Law 108–199, 108th Congress, January 23, 2004.

20. Owens vs. Colorado Congress of Parents, Teachers and Students, 92 P.3d 933 (2004).

CHAPTER 21: "PARALLEL TO AND IN COMPETITION
WITH THE FREE PUBLIC SCHOOLS"

1. Milton Friedman, "The Promise of Vouchers," *Wall Street Journal*, December 5, 2005.

2. Walter C. Stern, *Race and Education in New Orleans: Creating the Segregated City, 1764–1960* (Baton Rouge: Louisiana State University, 2018), 44–46, 76, 81, 234.

3. Brian Thevenot, "N.O. Schools Chief Will Fire Janitorial Firm—Filthy Campuses, Rising Costs, Cited as Reasons to Cancel Contract," *Times-Picayune*, October 9, 2004; Adam Nossiter, "New Orleans Schools a National Horror Tale," Associated Press, April 19, 2005.

4. "New Orleans Eyed as Clean Educational Slate," *Education Week*, September 16, 2005.

5. Nick Anderson, "Bush Proposes Private School Relief Plan," *Washington Post*, September 17, 2005.

6. Robert Tomsho, "After Katrina, School Choice Gains New Fans," *Wall Street Journal*, November 16, 2005.

7. "Senate Votes $1.66 Billion for Storm-Displaced Pupils," *New York Times*, November 4, 2005.

8. "New Orleans Eyed"; Terry M. Moe, *The Politics of Institutional Reform: Katrina, Education, and the Second Face of Power* (Cambridge, UK: Cambridge University Press, 2019), 75–76.

9. Laura Maggi, "N.O. Takeover Idea Has Legs: House, Senate Panels Tackle Bills This Week," *Times-Picayune*, November 9, 2005; Danielle Dreilinger, "7,000 New Orleans Teachers, Laid Off After Katrina, Win Court Ruling," *Times-Picayune*, January 17, 2014.

10. Moe, *Politics*, 53–54.

11. Capital Bureau, "Orleans Schools Takeover Is Official, *Times-Picayune*, December 1, 2005; "Louisiana Seeks High Quality Providers to Run Orleans Schools," US Federal News Service, January 31, 2006.

12. Kimberly Miller and S. V. Date, "Seven Charged in Voucher Scam: False Claims by School Alleged," *Palm Beach Post*, June 30, 2004; S. V. Date, "Voucher Oversight Remains Minimal," *Palm Beach Post*, July 1, 2004.

13. S.V. Date, "Private School Cashed In Vouchers for Public Students," *Palm Beach Post*, March 19, 2004; S.V. Date, "Official: State Voucher School Records Altered," *Palm Beach Post*, July 10, 2003; "Voucher Crowd Silences a Whistle-Blower," *Palm Beach Post*, March 12, 2004; Kimberly

Miller, "Terror-Tied School Gets State Perk," *Palm Beach Post*, July 17, 2003; Kimberly Miller and S.V. Date, "380 Students Getting Vouchers for Home-Schooling," *Palm Beach Post*, November 6, 2003; Kimberly Miller and S.V. Date, "State Ok'd Unlicensed Voucher Recipient," *Palm Beach Post*, August 24, 2003; "Abuse of State Vouchers Reaches Criminal Stage," *Palm Beach Post*, February 8, 2004.

14. "F for Oversight," *St. Petersburg Times*, May 4, 2004.

15. Jeffrey S. Solochek, "Tightening Up on Vouchers," *St. Petersburg Times*, March 6, 2005.

16. Linda Kleindienst, "Governor Seeks Expansion of Voucher Program," *Sun Sentinel*, February 24, 2005.

17. Carrie Johnson and Joni James, "Increased Voucher Scrutiny Fizzes Out," *St. Petersburg Times*, May 9, 2005.

18. Joretta L. Sack, "Gov. Bush's Voucher, Class Size Proposals Fail in 2005 Session," *Education Week*, May 17, 2005.

19. Bush vs. Holmes, 919 So. 2d 392 (Fla. 2006).

20. Kimberly Miller, "Ruling Also Could Threaten McKay Scholarships," *Palm Beach Post*, January 6, 2006; Ron Matus and Melanie Ave, "Some Vouchers Out, but the Rest?," *St. Petersburg Times*, January 7, 2006.

21. Michael Edwards and Mark Walsh, *More than a Lawyer: Robert Chanin, the National Education Association, and the Fight for Public Education, Employee Rights and Social Justice* (Washington, DC: National Education Association, 2010), 276; "Bush v. Holmes Florida Supreme Court Declares State's School Voucher Program Unconstitutional," *Harvard Law Review* 120, no. 4 (February 1, 2007): 1097.

22. Leslie Postal and John Kennedy, "Florida's Top Court Bars Vouchers for F Schools," *Orlando Sentinel*, January 6, 2006; Jim Saunders and Linda Trimble, "Court Outlaws School Vouchers: Gov. Bush Calls Ruling a Sad Day," *Daytona Beach News-Journal*, January 6, 2006.

23. John Kennedy, "Senate Blocks Bush on Vouchers: Governor Loses Bid to Put Constitutional Amendment on Ballot," *Orlando Sentinel*, May 2, 2006; Jim Saunders, "School Voucher Measure Falters," *Daytona Beach News-Journal*, May 2, 2006.

24. 2005 Wisconsin Act 125.

25. Sam Dillon, "For Parents Seeking a Choice, Charter Schools Prove More Popular than Vouchers," *New York Times*, July 13, 2005; Greg Toppo, "Father of Vouchers Foresees 'Breakthrough': Milton Friedman Says Interest Growing Despite Low Numbers," *USA Today*, June 23, 2005.

26. Toppo, "Father of Vouchers."

27. "Milton Friedman, Free Markets Theorist, Dies at 94," *New York Times*, November 16, 2006.

CHAPTER 22: "THE MODEL IS WORKING"

1. Lesli A. Maxwell, "Up from the Ruins," *Education Week*, October 3, 2007.

2. The previous state superintendent of education, Cecil Picard, died in February 2007.

3. Aesha Rasheed, "New Superintendent Tours Needy Schools," *Times-Picayune*, February 19, 2003; Warner Coleman and Darran Simon, "Classroom Space Is in Crisis: Officials Scurrying to Find Room for Students," *Times-Picayune*, May 1, 2007.

4. "New Orleans Hires Veteran to Run City's Schools," *All Things Considered*, NPR, May 4, 2007.

5. Ann Carrns, "Charting a New Course; After Katrina, New Orleans's Troubled Educational System Banks on Charter Schools," *Wall Street Journal*, August 24, 2006; Adam Nossiter, "Prominent Education Reformer to Lead New Orleans Schools," *New York Times*, May 5, 2007; headlines from the *Star Tribune* on June 25, 2006, the *Wall Street Journal* on August 24, 2006, and the *Los Angeles Times* on June 4, 2006.

6. Lesli A. Maxwell, "Under Pressure, State Opens Two Schools in New Orleans," *Education Week*, February 13, 2007.

7. Carrns, "Charting a New Course"; letter from Damon Hewitt to Cecil J. Picard et al., NAACP Legal Defense Fund, January 30, 2007, www.naacpldf.org/wp-content/uploads/NewOrleansDOEDemandLetter.pdf; Maxwell, "Under Pressure"; Darran Simon, "Council Gets Input from Teachers, Students, Citizens," *Times-Picayune*, March 22, 2007; Terry M. Moe, *The Politics of Institutional Reform: Katrina, Education, and the Second Face of Power* (Cambridge, UK: Cambridge University Press, 2019), 85.

8. Michael Kunzelman, Associated Press, "Charter Schools Are Put to Test in Post-Katrina New Orleans," *Pittsburgh Post-Gazette*, April 22, 2007.

9. Ralph Adamo, "NOLA's Failed Education Experiment," *American Prospect*, August 15, 2007.

10. "18 New Charter Schools to Open in September, Bloomberg Announces," *New York Times*, August 18, 2008.

11. Bill and Melinda Gates Foundation, "Major New Investment Supports NewSchools Venture Fund's Efforts to Provide 200 High-Quality Charter Schools for 100,000 Low-Income Students," press release, October 2006; Megan Tompkins-Stange, *Policy Patrons: Philanthropy, Education Reform, and the Politics of Influence* (Cambridge, MA: Harvard Education Press, 2016), 20–22, 28–32, 56–58; "Walton Family Puts Stamp on Education Landscape," *Education Week*, February 22, 2019.

12. "Twin Cities Selected for New Knowledge Is Power Program Public School Expansion Site in 2008," US Federal News Service, November 28, 2006; Jay Mathews, *Work Hard. Be Nice: How Two Inspired Teachers Created the Most Promising Schools in America* (Chapel Hill, NC: Algonquin Books of Chapel Hill, 2009), 253–256; Mike Tolson, "KIPP's Experiment Moving to Grand Scale," *Houston Chronicle*, April 2, 2007.

13. Greg Toppo, "New Orleans Schools Get Record $17.5 Million Gift," *USA Today*, December 13, 2007; Moe, *Politics*, 82–83.

14. Sarah Tantillo, *Hit the Drum: An Insider's Account of How the Charter School Idea Became a National Movement* (self-pub., 2019), 161–162.

15. "Obama Outlined Education Plan at Stebbins HS," *Dayton Daily News*, September 9, 2008; "Obama Unveils Education Reform Plan," *St. Louis American*, September 10, 2008; Nedra Pickler, "Obama Vows to Double Funding for Charter Schools," *Chicago Citizen*, September 10, 2008.

16. Early in the campaign, Obama had indicated in an interview with the *Milwaukee Journal Sentinel's* editorial board that he would be open to school vouchers if there was evidence they worked, but his staff walked back his comments afterward. David J. Hoff and Alyson Klein, "Democrats' K–12 Views Differ, Subtly: Clinton Often Chides NCLB; Obama Open to Vouchers?," *Education Week*, February 27, 2008.

17. Barack Obama, "In Major Policy Speech, Obama Announces Plan to Provide All Americans with a World-Class Education," American Presidency Project, November 20, 2007, www.presidency.ucsb.edu/documents/press-release-major-policy-speech-obama-announces-plan-provide-all-americans-with-world; "Primary: John McCain," *Herald Bulletin*, May 3, 2008.

18. October 15, 2008 Debate Transcript, Commission on Presidential Debates, accessed November 5, 2022, www.debates.org/voter-education/debate-transcripts/october-15-2008-debate-transcript/.

19. Bill Turque, "Candidates Touch on DC Schools," *Washington Post*, October 16, 2008.

20. Donna Winchester and Ron Matus, "Struggling 'Zone' Sees Mixed Results," *Tampa Bay Times*, July 20, 2008; "Additional School Time Questioned," *Education Week*, May 19, 2009.

21. "Bennet Announces District's Reform Plan," US Federal News Service, October 2, 2007; Allison Sherry, "Key Question: Students Better Off? Bennet 'Absolutely Convinced' Plan Will Put Kids in Stronger Environments," *Denver Post*, October 2, 2007; "Gov. Ritter Signs Innovation Zones Bill into Law," US Federal News Service, including US States News, May 28, 2008.

22. "President Obama, U.S. Secretary of Education Duncan Announce National Competition to Advance School Reform," press release, US Department of Education, July 24, 2009, www2.ed.gov/news/pressreleases/2009/07/07242009.html; "Transcript: President Obama's Remarks to the Hispanic Chamber of Commerce," *New York Times*, March 10, 2009.

23. CREDO, *Multiple Choice: Charter School Performance in 16 States* (Stanford, CA: Center for Research on Education Outcomes, 2009).

24. Sam Dillon, "Education Chief to Warn Advocates That Inferior Charter Schools Harm the Effort," *New York Times*, June 22, 2009.

25. Harold Zack, "U.S. Official Says Charter Schools Not Sole Factor in Funding: Advocates Have Said Reluctance to Establish the Schools Will Cost W.Va. Federal Money," *Charleston Daily Mail*, November 13, 2009.

26. "National Study Finds Louisiana's Charter Schools Outperform Traditional Public Schools," US Federal News Service, June 19, 2009.

27. Douglas N. Harris, *Charter School City: What the End of Traditional Public Schools in New Orleans Means for American Education* (Chicago: University of Chicago Press, 2020), 233.

28. Sarah Carr, Darran Simon, and Brian Thevenot, "Higher LEAP Scores Add Fuel to Debate Over Charters—Scores on Rise Before Katrina, Critics Say," *Times-Picayune*, May 31, 2009.

29. Leslie Jacobs, "After the Deluge, a New Education System," *Wall Street Journal*, August 30, 2010.

CHAPTER 23: "IT WAS NEVER SUPPOSED TO GET THIS BIG"

1. Erin Richards, "Universal School Voucher Opponents to Rally Thursday," *Milwaukee Journal Sentinel*, May 5, 2011.

2. Howard Fuller, "Keep Intact the Mission of Choice Program," *Milwaukee Journal Sentinel*, April 23, 2011.

3. Erin Richards, "Milwaukee's Voucher Verdict: What 26 Years of Vouchers Can Teach the Private School-Choice Movement—If Only It Would Listen," *American Prospect*, January 12, 2017.

4. Matthew DeFour, "School of Thought: Supporters and Opponents Alike Are Mobilizing to Sway Public Opinion on a Crucial Item in Gov. Walker's Latest Budget: Private School Vouchers," *Wisconsin State Journal*, May 5, 2013; Patrick Marley, "Past School Voucher Advocate Rips Gov. Walker's Plan," *Milwaukee Journal Sentinel*, May 16, 2013.

5. Daniel Bice, "School Choice Advocate George Mitchell Blasts Ex-Lawmaker Annette Polly Williams: After She Criticizes Scott Walker's Expansion Plan, Mitchell Calls Her Racist and Irrelevant," *Milwaukee Journal Sentinel*, May 29, 2013.

6. Howard Fuller, interview with the author, January 2020.

7. Jeff Greenfield, "We're Still Feeling Aftershocks of the 2010 Midterm Elections," *Washington Post*, May 16, 2021; Frederick Hess, "Does School Choice Work?," *National Affairs*, Fall 2010, www.nationalaffairs.com /publications/detail/does-school-choice-work.

8. Greenfield, "We're Still Feeling Aftershocks."

9. Daniel D. McGarry and Leo Ward, *Educational Freedom: And the Case for Government Aid to Students in Independent Schools* (Milwaukee, WI: Bruce Publishing Company, 1966), 34.

10. Robert Enlow, "Is 2011 Milton Friedman's Year of School Choice?," *Education Week*, July 28, 2011.

11. "School Choice in America Dashboard," EdChoice, last modified March 1, 2021, www.edchoice.org/school-choice/school-choice-in -america.

12. Mark Trumbull, "State Legislatures Now Redder than They've Been in Nearly a Century," *Christian Science Monitor*, November 5, 2014.

13. Richards, "Milwaukee's Voucher Verdict."

14. Paul Gores and Jessica Garza, "Williams Won't Run for Reelection to Assembly," *Milwaukee Journal Sentinel*, May 22, 2010; Meg Jones, "Annette Polly Williams, Longest-Serving Woman in the Legislature, Dies," *Milwaukee Journal Sentinel*, November 9, 2014; American Federation for Children, "American Federation for Children Mourns the Loss of School Choice Pioneer Annette 'Polly' Williams," press release, November 10, 2014; Joe Williams, "Polly Williams, Education's Rosa Parks," *Wall Street Journal*, November 21, 2014; Eugene Kane, "Ruling Pleases the Mother of School Choice," *Milwaukee Journal Sentinel*, June 11, 1998.

15. Robin Harris, "For Maverick Polly Williams, the Mother of School Choice, the Point Was Always to Empower Parents and Improve Education for Black Children," The 74, January 28, 2020; Bice, "School Choice Advocate George Mitchell Blasts"; Ron Grossman, "Polly's Political Paradox: Wisconsin's Champion of School Choice Is No Liberal—But No Conservative Either," *Chicago Tribune*, August 20, 1993.

16. Harris, "For Maverick Polly Williams."

17. Alan J. Borsuk, "20,000 Students Now Use Vouchers," *Milwaukee Journal Sentinel*, November 9, 2008.

18. Ted Kolderie, "'Charter Schools' Is System Change," Education Evolving, June 2017.

19. Executive Office of the Mayor, "Enrollment Increases at DCPS and Public Charter Schools in 2015–16 School Year," press release, October 20, 2015, https://mayor.dc.gov/release/enrollment-increases-dcps-public-charter-schools-2015-16-school-year.

20. Kate Taylor, "Success Academy Principal Who Created 'Got to Go' List Takes Leave," *New York Times*, January 4, 2016.

21. Wilford Shamlin III, "Protesters Demand Charter School Accountability," *Philadelphia Tribune*, March 16, 2014; Eve L. Ewing, *Ghosts in the Schoolyard: Racism and School Closings on Chicago's South Side* (Chicago: University of Chicago Press, 2018), 45, 145–146; Katy Reckdahl, "After 17 Years, the Alfred Lawless Name Is Returning to This New Orleans High School," *Times-Picayune*, March 6, 2022; "Change Our School Name Back to Alfred Lawless High School in New Orleans, Louisiana," petition, Change.org, accessed October 23, 2022.

22. CREDO, *National Charter School Study* (Stanford, CA: Center for Research on Education Outcomes, 2013).

23. CREDO, *Urban Charter School Study Report on 41 Regions* (Stanford, CA: Center for Research on Education Outcomes, 2015); Andrew Maul, "NEPC Review: *Urban Charter School Study Report on 41 Regions 2015*," National Education Policy Center, April 27, 2015, https://nepc.info/node/7104.

24. Ryanne Persinger, "NAACP Seeks Moratorium on Charter Schools," *Philadelphia Tribune*, August 23, 2016; Jennifer Levitz, "Charter School Battle Heats Up: As These Privately Run, Publicly Funded Schools Expand, Traditional Ones Are Feeling Threatened," *Wall Street Journal*, October 11, 2015.

25. Valerie Strauss, "Opposition Grows to Senate Confirmation of Betsy DeVos, Trump's Education Nominee," *Washington Post*, January 10, 2017;

Peter Jamison, "Former D.C. Mayor Tony Williams Endorses Betsy DeVos," *Washington Post*, January 17, 2017.

26. Emma Brown, "Trump Picks Billionaire Betsy DeVos, School Voucher Advocate, as Education Secretary," *Washington Post*, November 23, 2016; Geoff Mulvihill, "Voucher Proposals Expose Rift in School Choice Movement," *St. Louis Dispatch*, May 14, 2017.

27. Todd Spangler, "DeVos to Lead Education Department: Michigan Activist Wins Confirmation as Pence Casts Historic, Tie-Breaking Vote," *Detroit Free Press*, February 8, 2017.

28. ABC News, "CPAC 2017: Betsy DeVos Speech (Full)," video, YouTube, February 23, 2017.

29. Dana Milbank, "The Unappreciated Genius of Betsy DeVos: Whenever DeVos Speaks, It Feels as Though the Sum Total of Human Knowledge Is Somehow Diminished," *Washington Post*, March 12, 2018.

30. Michael Kranish, "Cory Booker Once Allied Himself with Betsy DeVos on School Choice. Not Anymore," *Washington Post*, September 20, 2019; Laura McKenna, "Exclusive: Senator Cory Booker Speaks Out About Newark School Reform, Equity, and Mark Zuckerberg's Millions Ahead of a Possible Run for the Presidency," The 74, September 4, 2018; Patrick Wall, "In Newark, Cory Booker's Most Enduring Legacy May Be City's Spreading Charter Schools," Chalkbeat, February 8, 2019.

31. These headlines appeared in 2018 and 2019.

32. Henry Tyson, interview with the author, January 8, 2020; US Department of Education, "Secretary DeVos' Education Freedom Tour Full Kickoff Speech," video, YouTube, September 17, 2019.

33. Ron Kelly, interview with the author, January 2020.

34. Marva Herndon, interview with the author, January 2020; Howard Fuller, interview with the author, January 2020.

35. US Department of Education, "Secretary DeVos' Education Freedom Tour Full Kickoff Speech."

Index

CARA FITZPATRICK is an editor at Chalkbeat. She won the Pulitzer Prize for Local Reporting in 2016 for a series about school segregation. She was a New Arizona fellow in 2019 at New America and a Spencer fellow at Columbia University's Graduate School of Journalism in 2018. Fitzpatrick lives in New York City with her husband and children.